MODERN ARCHITECTURE

HENRY-RUSSELL HITCHCOCK JR.

MODERN ARCHITECTURE
ROMANTICISM AND REINTEGRATION

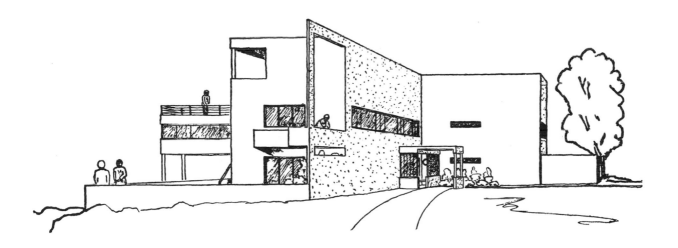

1970

HACKER ART BOOKS NEW YORK 1970

First Published by
Payson and Clarke, Ltd. 1929

Reprinted by
Hacker Art Books
New York 1970

Library of Congress Catalog Card Number 73-116356
SBN 0-87817-044-8

TO THE MEMORY OF
PETER VAN DER MEULEN SMITH

ACKNOWLEDGMENTS

FOR purchased photographs the photographers' names have in general been given beneath the illustrations. Thanks are due to the comte de Breda for the photograph of his château at Le-Plessis-Brion, to John A. Bryan for permission to use the photograph of the house in Saint Louis by Richardson, to Mr. and Mrs. F. E. Lowell for permission to use that of their own house provided by the architect, to the vicomte de Vaulchier for two photographs of houses by Le Corbusier, to André Lurçat for the photographs of the dairy by Buroff, to Mr. and Mrs. Fred S. Smith for their son's project and his photograph of the Medical Centre, and to Professor Adolph Goldschmidt of the University of Berlin for obtaining that of the Hofgärtnerei by Persius. Otherwise the photographs have been most kindly provided by the architects. Some of the material of Parts Two and Three has appeared in the last two years in the *Architectural Record, The Arts*, the *Hound and Horn, i10*, and the *Cahiers d'Art*. In the editions of the last have also appeared two monographs, of which the one on Oud is here re-used with little or no change. To the Editors of these periodicals are due the acknowledgment of indebtedness for permitting the incorporation, usually in much amplified form, of that material here; and thanks for their assistance in the matter of illustrations. George N. Kates, Professor Kingsley Porter of Harvard University and Mrs. Kingsley Porter have been of the greatest aid in the matter of arrangement of material and of style. Among critics of Modern architecture many architects have also assisted, and in addition, perhaps unwittingly, Lewis Mumford, Peter Meyer and Geoffrey Scott, with whom valuable discussion has been possible because their points of view were far from coincident and none of them were whole-heartedly in sympathy with the New Pioneers.

TABLE OF CONTENTS

PART THREE: THE NEW PIONEERS

LIST OF ILLUSTRATIONS

INTRODUCTION

INTRODUCTION

"NEW DIMENSIONS," "New Ways of Living, New Ways of Building," "Towards a New Architecture," "The New Style Victorious" . . . a dozen books have proclaimed in the last years a new architecture. "Modern Dutch Architecture," "Modern French Architecture," "Modern European Buildings" . . . at least as many more have displayed that as "International Architecture" it exists throughout the Western World. And from the mere titles of still other books one may surmise how it is dependent on new methods of construction and new problems that our age has to solve: "How America Builds," "Industrial and Commercial Architecture," "Form in Concrete," "The Steel Church," . . .

All these books in English, French, German and Dutch provide a wealth of documentation and illustration. Moreover, for those who wish to study contemporary production in further detail there exist the periodicals of Europe and America and an increasing flood of monographs on individual architects supplementing the more general publications of whose quantity and variety the lists above give a summary idea.*

The literature of the architecture of the present seems disproportionally profuse beside that of the architecture of the past. Thus the illusion is reinforced that the present is a period distinct from and opposed to the past. Historical criticism should however be able to show that as regards architecture the present is the last realized point in the dialectic of history, and

* The Bibliographical Note is at the end of the book. The references to foreign books in the first paragraph above are free renderings of the actual titles.

that even the most advanced contemporary forms constitute no rootless phenomenon but the last phase in a long line of development.

To trace in full this line of development would be to rewrite the history of architecture for at least the last five centuries. For the phases through which European architecture has passed since the culmination of the High Gothic in the thirteenth century are not to be considered as constituting successive independent styles comparable to those of the earlier past, the Greek or the Egyptian for example, but rather as subsidiary manners of one Modern style. Those architects and builders who have worked within this Modern style have had on the one hand more or less conscious intellectual interests in abstract form and have frequently preferred experiment to the continuance of inherited tradition. But on the other hand, their free tendencies have until the last few years been balanced by a sentimental desire to recall one or several styles of the far past and by an inertia which has caused a considerable retention of the features of style of the near past.

The changing nature of these copyings and retentions has given to the history of architecture in the last five hundred years its considerable complexity. Thus also the manifestations of the non-reminiscent side of the Modern style have been to some extent obscured. But under the surface of the pseudo-styles, Late Gothic, Renaissance and Baroque, the continuing search for new values and the recurrent attempts at freedom from inherited restraints may nevertheless be easily distinguished. There is moreover a greater common denominator of spirit between the first and the last of the pseudo-styles just mentioned than there is between even the first of them and the immediately preceding Mediæval style-phases. This is best illustrated by specific examples:

The Rococo decorations added in the reign of Louis XV to the Flamboyant apse of Saint Maclou in Rouen are not at all inharmonious in feeling (Figure 1); and the eighteenth century rearrangement of the choir of Saint Merri in Paris is better related to the rest of the church, also Flamboyant, than are the supposedly conscientious nineteenth century restorations in many important Mediæval churches. Yet the contrast between the Romanesque nave and the Flamboyant choir of Mont-Saint-Michel is marked (Figure 2); and the incongruity of the Perpendicular chapel of Henry VII with the High Gothic choir of Westminster Abbey is almost as considerable.

In the style-phases previous to the Age of Romanticism the intellectual experimentation of the Modern period is a familiar subject. A few illustrations will serve to recall to the reader what the historians of the Late Gothic, the Renaissance, and the Baroque have many times discussed in detail:

In the Flamboyant there was an increasing substitution of visual logic in design for organic logic. The most notable result was the emphasis on unbroken vertical lines interweaving in the tracery at the tops of the window and even in the vaulting rib patterns in church interiors. The new spirit is little less marked in the treatment of church exteriors and even more conspicuous in the elaborate but rather standardized civil architecture of the time (Figure 3). In a monument of the Early Renaissance, such as the Pitti Palace (Figure 4), or even in a High Renaissance church, such as Santa Maria della Consolazione outside Todi (Figure 5), the use of features borrowed from the antique is clearly of minor importance in the effect produced. This is even more true in the Baroque period; and in many eighteenth century works reminiscence of the past is almost entirely avoided. (Figure 6.) *

But the Late Gothic, the Renaissance, and the Baroque were only incomplete and partial expressions of Modern intellectual research and sentimental reminiscence. On the one hand they made use only in a limited and selective way of the art of the past; and on the other their experimentation was not given continuing validity by any true innovations in structure. Only in the latter half of the eighteenth century with the appearance of the Classical and Mediæval revivals and the development of new methods of construction in the nineteenth century does the Modern style enter upon a phase which is closely connected with the architecture of the present. The history of the architecture of the Age of Romanticism is, moreover, considerably less well known than that of the logical decorative development of the Mediæval inheritance in the Late Gothic, the partial revival of one great age of the past in the Renaissance, and the sophisticated balance of inheritance and experiment in the Baroque.

Paris, 15—i—29.

* The Appendix at the end of the book gives somewhat more of an analysis of the experimentation in architecture between 1250 and 1750.

PART ONE

THE AGE OF ROMANTICISM

CHAPTER ONE

THE FIRST HALF CENTURY: 1750-1800

In the year 1750 Giuseppe Bibbiena built at Bayreuth the Opera House, probably the finest achievement of the Baroque in theatre design. In the same year in France Hérè de Corny took up the unfinished work of Boffrand at Nancy and carried to completion the design of the new town, the most ambitious executed project of the manner of architecture known as the Rococo. Nor were these isolated examples. The next decades were characterized, particularly in Germany, by much building that adds to the glory of the later phase of the Baroque.

But in the same year 1750 Cochin and Soufflot were at Pæstum preparing measured drawings of the temples there; and Stuart and Revett were engaged in similar work at Athens. All over Europe there was developing an increasingly general and sustained interest in Classical antiquity. The study of original Greek monuments occasioned an attitude toward archæology both more scientific and more passionate than that of the Renaissance. The fifties are equally filled with evidence that shame for the Mediæval past was giving place to admiration or at least to curiosity. In England, where there had been even in the early eighteenth century a limited survival of the Gothic, there appeared as early as 1742 Batty Langley's extraordinary book, *Gothic Architecture Improved by Rules and Proportions*; and within the next few years Gothic garden ruins and Gothic detail of a Rococo sort were increasingly in favour. In 1753 the Abbé Laugier in France asked rhetorically why Saint-Sulpice filled his soul with no such awe as Notre Dame; and Horace Walpole gave aristocratic sanction to the already popular Gothicist movement in England by his first reconstruction of Strawberry Hill.

The previous year, 1752, in which François de Cuvilliés the younger produced in the Munich Residenztheater the finest of Rokoko theatres, Gabriel's Opéra at Versailles instanced in the same field a notable reaction from the liberties of the Rococo toward restrained and academic Classicism. This reaction had moreover already marked his designs submitted in the Place Louis XV competition of 1748. The two great Bourbon palaces begun in 1752, Gabriel's Compiègne and Vanvitelli's Caserta, illustrate the same turning back from the freer tradition of the later phase of the Baroque. This movement found in France influential expression in Cochin's attack on the Rococo in the *Mercure de France* written after his return from Greece in 1754. It is more significant still that Stuart on his return from Athens constructed with an archæological conscientiousness unknown to the builders of Gothic garden ruins an intentionally perfect Greek temple at Hagley Park, Worcestershire. In 1761 the French Academy had already discussed the technique of Gothic vaulting in connection with the restoration in Gothic style then being carried out at the Cathedral of Strasbourg. . . .

It would be possible to continue indefinitely the list of such specific events in the years just after the middle of the eighteenth century to illustrate on the one hand that the Baroque style came to no sudden end, and equally clearly on the other that its empire was already seriously challenged as it had not been previously by occasional individual reactions toward more academic correctness or by incidental dallyings with the Mediæval. The Gothic façade of Orleans Cathedral, begun under Louis XIV, hardly progressed at all until after the mid-century; Wren's Tom Tower at Oxford built in 1682, a creditable Gothic design, had been in its own day all but unique; while Vanbrugh's Mediævalist tendencies were for the most part so absorbed in his Baroque design that they were only seen in isolation by later generations when the change in taste made it possible for them to be specifically appreciated.

So also the patriotic archæological research of Dom Bernard de Montfaucon and other Benedictines in France and of chroniclers such as Dugdale and Anthony à Wood in England was as nothing beside the publications dealing with the Middle Ages, not only archæological, but literary, legal and historical as well, which began to appear after 1750. It is highly significant of the close dependence of the Mediævalist movement on literature that Thomas Gray and his friend Thomas Warton may be considered the first archæologists of the new day in England, where a line of sentimental interest in the non-Classical past may be traced down through Spenser and Milton to the first Romantic poets of the eighteenth century.

It is less easy to illustrate the change in attitude toward Classical archæology, since that had been a conventionally recognized activity since the Renaissance. But the publication in 1760 and the translation into various languages of Winckelmann's *History of Art in Antiquity* was an important sign of the times. This had an international influence on actual construction, moreover, of far greater importance than all the work of the first generation of Romantic Mediævalists. The new Classical archæology tended definitely to destroy the validity of the grammar of the orders as codified in the mid-sixteenth century and thus to break down Baroque tradition even on its reminiscent side. Curiously enough the parallel return at the end of the eighteenth century to the serious emulation of the Italian Renaissance had a similar effect.

The study of various more or less remote periods of the past, the practical efforts toward their intentionally accurate resurrection, the Romanticism in literature with which both were so closely allied, characterize quite as much the eighteenth as the nineteenth century. Not merely after 1800 but from as early as 1750 the tendencies of Romanticism are evident generally in the arts and have more and more a direct effect upon architecture.

It is less easy to determine as regards architecture when the Age of Romanticism came to an end. It is very clear that the New Tradition in architecture, the rationalistic manner of eclecticism of style beginning at the end of the nineteenth century and continuing still to-day, is very essentially romantic in the large and non-historical sense of the term. Its character is moreover definitely dependent upon points of view which began to receive general support after the middle of the eighteenth century. But since the action of Romanticism on architecture was primarily disintegrant, or at least analytical, and the successful effort of the New Tradition has been to achieve a new synthesis, there is between the two a definite break. The break may be considered to have come at a date well within the nineteenth century when the theoretical reintegration of architecture in a new style-phase, already from about 1800 somewhat vaguely suggested by the writers on the "picturesque" and ably advocated by the Mediævalists of the mid-nineteenth century, began somewhat generally to take form in actual buildings. This date may be set as early as 1875. For from then on a definite development toward the New Tradition may be traced at least in the work of one important architect, H. H. Richardson, and two unconnected transitional movements were well under way.

Admittedly in the dark night of the triumphant eclecticism of taste which concluded Romantic architecture it is difficult to find generally any solid beginnings of an eclecticism of style intelligently restrained by rationalism before about 1895.* Admittedly also there are notable isolated monuments produced by certain earlier nineteenth century architects which might be considered of the New Tradition were they not historically quite separated from it. The buildings of Soane's Bœotian manner, the more rationalistic works of Schinkel, the Bibliothèque Sainte-Geneviève of Labrouste are no more directly related to what was to follow than one to another. The traditions they exist in are not new, nor one. Precursors their designers were within the period of disintegration, pointing already the way toward the formation of a New Tradition; but fine as these and other single buildings may be, finer often than a great many works of the New Tradition *de la lettre,* they are historically of not much more significance than a large mass of work that is of very inferior quality or hardly even consciously art at all. Moreover much theoretical writing by critics and by purely revivalist architects, whose own constructions are of slight value, points quite as clearly the way on.

Since the architecture of Romanticism represented the expression of a point of view—or more exactly of several apparently contradictory points of view —and not a style or even a style-phase, its individual positive movements, such as the Gothic Revival in England, are of significance only in so far as they illustrate general tendencies. Many fantastic projects in the books of architecture of the period have greater intrinsic interest. Often at least on paper they show a much more subtle sense of quality than the revivalist productions of which the virtues were largely of a symbolical order and only fully satisfying to contemporary enthusiasts.

Nowhere do the ways of the critic and the historian more forcibly separate than in the Romantic period. During the first half century very much fine but historically unimportant work was done in which the continuance of

* Eclecticism of taste: different styles used contemporaneously but each building all in one style. Eclecticism of style: features of different styles used together on one building.

Baroque tradition prevented extreme Romantic expression. From the first there was such extreme expression more than occasionally, as even the few specific instances already cited indicated. It was in general far from fine. But the entire international manner of the *style Louis XVI* and its equivalents which produced so much excellent building represented little more than a chastening of the Baroque under direct Classical influence. Very seldom was there even in single monuments any such thoroughgoing revival of antiquity as the programmes of the age demanded and the virtues of the manner were therefore in large part those inherited from the Baroque.

An admirable illustration of this is the fact that the Classicist Adam found the compositions of Vanbrugh worthy of emulation. He sought to purify them according to his own Classical canons. But he wished to retain those Baroque qualities which he admired as "sublime" or "picturesque." In this fashion the influence of Vanbrugh, as of Piranesi, lasted well into the nineteenth century. It affected monuments as different as Wyatt's Gothic Fonthill and Crichton's Grecian Dunglass, two of the most significant mansions of the period of the French wars. The "picturesque" was beside tradition the most definite link between the Baroque and Romanticism in all the arts. The Piranesian cult of the "sublime" expressed through the colossal in architecture was equally significant. Even before the Revolution it was carried much further in France than in England and had the theoretical support of the sternest Classical critics for several generations.

But Romantic energies were at first predominantly turned toward the pen. The most characteristic productions were those in which the intelligence sought in archæology and history information about the past, and those in which the imagination—not altogether restrained in the other sort—established with this material and more particularly with the materials provided by the newly appreciated passions of man and nature a literature of sentiment and expression. To quote Christopher Hussey, writing on *The Picturesque*, it was the substitution "of emotion for reason, and of passion for decorum," initiated in England by Burke "who sponsored passion and emotion as the products of æsthetic perception," "that made possible the great poetry and the vile architecture of the nineteenth century." Hussey's study of "picturesque" building in England is one of the most generally suggestive treatments of a central problem of Romantic architecture.

The art of gardening, raised through the influence of landscape painting and the new literature from its previous subservience to architecture, became as a result of new æsthetic theories the most adequate plastic art for the expression of the essential ideas of the period. Its programme demanded on the one hand the creation of a second, and to its creators a more natural, because more "picturesque," nature. On the other hand it encouraged the construction of many buildings—not as architecture but as adjuncts to "poetic" landscape in the manner of the Italian and Dutch painters of the seventeenth century. Thus were erected ruins, Grecian and Mediæval, rustic cottages, and even entire mansions, as well as many other small edifices of real or symbolic utility classed with the rest as "fabricks." The term "fabrick" was characteristically borrowed from the landscape painters who had applied it to such architecture as they introduced in their pictures. The garden books even as late as 1850 illustrate them in vast numbers with full explanations of their complicated symbolism and of how to compose them with the landscape according to pictorial principles. (Figure 53.)

It was not because of his directly architectural qualities that Vanbrugh's work was generally influential: it was because his mansions so much more than those of the Palladian generation of the mid-century served as a well placed and much needed accent in the English landscape. They formed the "pictures" sought in the external world quite as much as on canvas in the latter part of the eighteenth and the early part of the nineteenth century. Even Blenheim was admired primarily as an immense fabrick.

Ruins were definitely more "sublime" as well as more "picturesque" than solid buildings. Architecture as subsidiary to landscape was seen through a double screen provided by painting and literature. It was naturally best appreciated from a distance. As was to be expected the quality of execution was therefore increasingly neglected. Flimsiness in false ruins was more than excusable since they fell into real ruin the sooner. Without exaggerating their importance, it is fair to say that false ruins were of all things the most fully expressive of the new points of view. Baroque building traditions were equally forgotten from the first in the other garden fabricks which marked the inception of the Age of Romanticism in architecture. As the new pictorial and literary ideas gained force and received wide adherence among those who claimed to be endowed with "taste," all those types of buildings which were thought of as having æsthetic value tended to be delivered from the hands of builder-architects into the hands of painter or poet-architects. Good construction became generally to be considered, if not a matter without importance, at least of no particular interest to the connoisseur. There was fortunately always a certain undercurrent of sounder doctrine.

The most important Romantic monument of the eighteenth century in England, Wyatt's Fonthill Abbey, was so shoddily built that it fell within a generation after its erection and is known to us only from contemporary books and prints. It is doubtless better so. For in literature and in pictures we can to-day appreciate what was engendered of literature and pictures far better than we could if we had all the crude detail and the flimsy masonry before us. It is a question of æsthetics, with which there is no need to deal here, whether "picturesque" and "sublime" edifices of this sort may be considered ever to have existed as true architecture. The theoreticians indeed long denied that they were strictly "beautiful." Very few of the earlier fabricks exist to-day to destroy the illusion that they were at least appealing or amusing. In the books they often still appear so even to the sternest critic.

The last paragraphs have treated more particularly of England where the early architecture of Romanticism has been more thoroughly studied and where the Baroque tradition was perhaps least strong. But similar developments may be traced all over the Continent and even in America. In France, Italy and Germany the extreme instances of the newer tendencies came slightly later than in England; but as the books testify they appeared with the imported English gardens well before the Revolution. Where Baroque tradition was stronger than in England it blended in the eighteenth century more successfully with the Classical Revival side of Romanticism. Thus the cult of the Mediæval and the "picturesque" in general received perhaps somewhat less frequent full expression. But there were false ruins and Gothic details of a Rococo order from the middle of the century and soon after all sorts of rustic constructions as well, for which Rousseau among others provided a sentimental *raison d'être*.

The gardens which Kléber, later one of Napoleon's marshals, laid out in 1787 for the prince de Montbéliard in Alsace were the climax of a considerable series. They contained many Gothic and rustic fabricks. Chinese and even Egyptian treatments were equally in favour for icehouses and sylvan temples here and elsewhere. Hermitages, sometimes provided with hired hermits, and tombs more usually empty, induced a gentle melancholy. When, however, near the artificial isle where Rousseau already lay buried in the park at Ermenonville an unknown visitor committed suicide, overcome by the conjunction of Romantic surroundings and literary memories, the Marquis de Girardin was sufficiently complimented to erect a second real tomb. Thus he gave a more Wertherian character to his well known properties, Englished in the sixties, whose tone had hitherto been set by a rustic village, and a ruined, or rather symbolically unfinished temple of Philosophy. From the cracked pier inscribed *à la rêverie* Frago's ladies still seem just to have fled, terrified by the violent tone Romanticism had already begun to take even at Ermenonville so soon after Jean-Jacques' death.

At Schwetzingen the grand duke of Baden had a garden constructed which vied with that of the prince de Montbéliard; and beside the finest Baroque gardens at Caserta in Italy lies the most magnificent of the *giardini inglesi,* to make room for which so many earlier Italian gardens were elsewhere destroyed. All about Paris private citizens and nobles surrounded their sober massive hôtels and châteaux with artificial landscaping. This was on occasion elaborately embellished with fabricks. There were Classical ruins in what is now the Parc Monceau; and on the estate of the architect Bélanger, whose very house indeed was marked by influences apparently François I and Flemish Late Gothic, there was an entire set of farm buildings at once rustic and asymmetrical. More generally there were cottages as at Chantilly or more or less Gothic constructions. Near Marly an entire house was designed in the form of an immense broken column.

Most significant of all was perhaps the Hameau which Marie Antoinette added to the English garden at the Petit Trianon. She had this constructed in 1783 after a visit to Ermenonville and Chantilly. The designer was Richard Mique, the successor of Gabriel as *premier architecte du roi.* He had, however, the benefit of much advice from his friend the great painter of landscapes with ruins, Hubert Robert. Robert directed also the laying out of the *jardin anglais* at Rambouillet and even designed the tomb of Rousseau. The Hameau de Trianon has lasted better than most. The construction was fundamentally solid and only the surface was flimsy with its brick and stone quoins painted on the plaster. The cottages possessed moreover certain excellent qualities of real rustic building (Figure 7). There was even more skill displayed in the irregular grouping around the lake and under the trees than in the design of the individual units.

Architecture had indeed something to learn from landscape painting. Yet for the most part the thatched cottages which English landlords were be-

ginning to erect at the end of their estates in imitation of the canvasses of
Morland and Gainsborough appear quite as devoid of all virtue as the donjon at Betz, the most considerable of French false ruins. With the exception of the Hameau of Marie Antoinette they were all the same certainly no
worse than the parallel French examples. But the sentimental and literary
connotations upon which this movement was so dependent have since quite
lost their force.

From the commanding art which it was in the Baroque period eighteenth
century Romanticism was tending to reduce architecture to a position of
subservience to gardening, to literature and to painting. Of course the illustrations just given are exceptional and the rustic and the Gothic modes
did not affect important monuments of architecture. Yet they are at the
same time highly significant. Romanticism was substituting for reasoned
appreciation of architecture, an attitude affective, emotional, and indirect
in the extreme. Curiously enough it was not specifically Romantic painting, which hardly yet existed, but painting of the Baroque period and painting which continued the Baroque tradition that had such an effect. Claude,
Poussin and the Dutch were the favourite models.

Reynolds also, surely to be considered still a Baroque painter, in his later
discourses on architecture at the Royal Academy lent powerful support
to the cause of the picturesque and the irregular. That the tide was turning
against architecture as a self-sufficient art is in a sense true. But the external influences from whatever source they came broke down the Baroque
tradition and encouraged the analytical disintegration of architecture. This
certainly prepared the way, if it did nothing more, for the manners of the
New Tradition and the New Pioneers which are considered to-day as
"modern."

But the most authentically "picturesque" fabrics are no more to be compared in quality with Gabriel's Petit Trianon, which still continued more
or less definitely the pre-Romantic graces, than the *Castle of Udolpho* with
the *Zauberflöte*. In France the Piranesian influence, the cult of the colossal
in the work, for example, of Ledoux and Brongniart, the use of the Greek
Doric, the first influences of the Italian Renaissance, all led to a barrenness
and gloominess even more likely than the gardens to encourage melan-
cholia. When the Academy of Architecture continued to protest in favour
of Baroque amenities the Revolution suppressed it as an impure institu-

tion. By the end of the eighteenth century the theories of Winckelmann on the absolute superiority of the antique found as few to refute them officially as the principles of Boileau in literature, although the Classicism of the one was Romantic and that of the other Baroque. But the principles of Boileau were openly flouted even by his defenders in the second half of the eighteenth century, and the disciples of Winckelmann modified in practice the extreme exigencies of imitation of the antique. Moreover they already dared to try occasionally the revival of other styles more satisfying to Romantic appetites and yet assimilable to the Classical Revival. And even thus early a vague suggestion of the historical, or at least the national, point of view may be found in some critical writing. Also what was to be known in the nineteenth century as rationalism, the expression of structural functions, made a highly tentative appearance still well disguised in the Classical toga.

Even if the analytical processes of Romanticism as regards architecture in the eighteenth century seldom went beyond nomenclature and symbols, they laid the theoretical foundations for a wider command of the art. Those constructions in which was attempted the full expression of some quality of which the Romantics to all intents and purposes had discovered the existence, such as the "sublime" or the "picturesque," are too often absurd. They mark, however, an appreciation that the possibilities of architecture are much wider than the Baroque had ever imagined. Even *Picturesque Voyages,* when they included buildings as well as Alps and cataracts, indicated an aggravated sensibility to architectural effects judged pictorially. This was certainly uncritical but it was healthy. It is in general terms and in retrospect that the early manifestations of Romanticism must be judged. The reader will perhaps feel in the second and third parts of the present book that even Batty Langley, or those who at least in their projects never departed from the strict temple formula, were among those who began the development of an attitude toward architecture which only the New Pioneers, the most advanced architects of to-day, are able to satisfy.

But returning again to specific monuments it is clear that the immediate effects of Romanticism were distinctly bad. Those who played safe built on the whole well; those who "advanced" built on the whole less well, even if they kept away from rustic hermitages and Egyptian icehouses. This is notably true of Thomas Jefferson, who applied the Roman temple formula in his Richmond Capitol earlier than it was done in any similarly important building in Europe. His copy of the Antonine Pantheon and his practical illustrations of the Classical orders at the University of Virginia are distinctly inferior to his own house at Monticello in which he followed to a large extent the models provided by the Louis XVI hôtels of Paris, such as Rousseau's Hôtel de Salm.

It is not the unfair comparison of the earliest "Gothick" constructions with the latest of the Rococo which is telling, but the consideration of the building of such architects as Jefferson, or of the houses of the last quarter of the eighteenth century in France published in the several works of Krafft. In such work the old and the new are usually blended with real success. But the old and the new may be distinguished, and to some extent comparatively evaluated to the distinct advantage of the former.

It is hardly before a full half century had passed that it is possible to find architecture of equal excellence which obtains its essential effects in fuller accordance with the principles introduced by Romanticism. Already there had appeared a most serious further development of ideology. Down through the Baroque it had been universally if tacitly held as in the Middle Ages that art included all the *factibile*. To the Romantics that only was art which expressed an artistic intention. In order to support the sentiment for the "picturesque" as distinguished from the "beautiful," however, it was admitted that the observer of the external world might arrange it in his perception until that perception became equivalent to an expressed artistic intention. Hence finally the conception of "picturesque beauty" became acceptable.

There was a gradual shift in emphasis which is one of the essential characteristics of Romanticism and which has been traced etymologically by Logan Pearsall Smith in *Four Romantic Words*. The centre of art was no longer in the work produced but in the "creator," who might, as in the case of the observer of the external world, never produce at all and yet share with the "genius" the joys of "inspiration." There developed a distinction—eventually of the greatest importance in painting, which ceased with the invention of photography to be necessarily a reproductive art—between scientific technics and artistic expression, of which the type was the literary-pictorial. Something had already been said with regard to the debasing influence on architectural execution this began to have from the first. But there was a more important effect in the realm of accepted even if generally unformulated theory.

Architecture was divided on this basis into "architecture"—alone an art—and "engineering"; or in more practical terms, "architecture" and "building." It is one of the greatest triumphs of the New Tradition that in its reintegration of architecture it has combined again engineering and building with architecture. It will be a further triumph of the present century if those who are here called the New Pioneers succeed in making of them once again an inseparable unity. The final synthesis will be the sounder for having been preceded by such an analysis. But nineteenth century building and engineering, although cut off in theory from architecture, produced many extraordinarily interesting monuments. They may seldom appear to the critic altogether fine. Yet even more than the most original works of "architecture" of the time they have the significance and the vigour of a really new development.

It is somewhat ironic that in the Age of Romanticism which stressed pre-eminently personality and expression much of the best work was more or less anonymous and that being done by men who did not consider themselves artists, it seldom consciously expressed an artistic intention. It was saved thus, however, the necessity of conformity to the contradictory canons of "architecture." We can to-day hardly approach emotionally the more typical architecture of Romanticism without disgust or at best amusement, although it was designed to stir the finest emotions. To the reason nevertheless it offers historically the fascination of an immensely complicated problem, as it hardly could to its builders. Even to set down as in the preceding paragraphs certain general principles of clarification without modification by innumerable exceptions is to select somewhat arbitrarily a route which has only pragmatic validity. The problem is indeed hardly thereby made much less complicated.

For example the many editions of the treatises on construction of Durand, Rondelet, and others, highly typical of the Age of Romanticism, and dozens of works on cottage, villa and rural building whose authors testify to a definite intention to "improve architecture," might seem to imply that there was no such isolation of architecture as there has been stated to have been. Nevertheless among the projects which illustrate these works those that were architecture are definitely set off from the others which were only building by the amount and the archæological character of the features of embellishment. Engineering designs, furthermore, clearly were hardly even touched by the principles which governed monumental constructions.

The nineteenth century lies so near and was a period of such considerable material expansion that the majority of monuments with which we are surrounded belong to it. In this mass it is toward the architecture that our attention has until lately been almost entirely turned, and it is the monuments of architecture which are best known. It is difficult to refer except generically to nineteenth century building and engineering with any hope of general comprehension. They were hardly appreciated æsthetically before the twentieth century. They are to-day by reaction very often overestimated.

CHAPTER TWO

THE FIRST GENERATION OF THE NINETEETH CENTURY

THE great architects of the second generation of the Age of Romanticism who appear just before 1800 were primarily supporters of the Classical Revival. They were further than their fathers from the Baroque and they were provided with a documentation that their fathers had lacked. The continually increasing flood of publications filled with drawings of Classical monuments gave no excuse for ignorance. In general, however, the architects of even the developed Classical Revival were far less exaggeratedly correct than they professed to be. They sought moreover in the work of antiquity more than temples to copy. Desiring to find other models than the peristyles of the Classical orders in Roman and even in Greek remains they were forced to invent much that never existed. Imaginary archæology, as in the case of Pirro Ligorio in the sixteenth century, justified much experimentation and even much rationalism for which there was really no ancient precedent. Although by purists and pontiffs such as Quatremère de Quincy only authentic and typical work of the ancients was considered worthy of emulation, the reign of Vitruvius began to be threatened even before 1800 from another insidious source in addition to imaginary archæology. The most serious architectural students were sufficiently affected by the general tendencies of their age to make of their Italian and even their Greek excursions *Picturesque Voyages*. Classical ruins had been among the first objects recognized as "picturesque" as well as "sublime." Archæological knowledge however had long been far enough advanced to make it certain that the "beautiful" Classical architecture had not been "picturesque" except in its choice of sites, and hardly even thus at Rome. Yet Italy was filled with structures of all dates on which Poussin and Claude had long ago put the seal of their approval; and thus the ideal at least of the "Italian Villa," that favourite formula of the mid-nineteenth century, was already born in England, France and Germany before the eighteenth century was over.

Particularly in France this new Italian influence was effectively assimilated to the Classical Revival as a sort of Renaissance-Renaissance. Percier and Fontaine in 1798 were among the very first to publish a general selection of fifteenth and sixteenth century Italian constructions. Another book of theirs published in 1812 dealt chiefly with the later and more elaborate examples. This was followed in 1815 by Grandjean de Montigny's *Architecture toscane* in which the emphasis was naturally on the major monuments of the fifteenth century. But even before this in Durand's *Précis de leçons d'architecture* of 1802 a great part of the principal structural features and of the façade compositions were based on Italian work of the greatest simplicity. Many were even definitely rustic or of Mediæval character, yet all were strictly symmetrical. Completely Italianate projects for different types of buildings were also presented by Durand frequently without any use of the orders. Only his more monumental and sumptuous designs for royal palaces and so forth were consonant with the strict revival of antiquity. By 1827 the new influence was so wide-spread and well accepted in domestic architecture that the majority of the elevations published by Urbain Vitry in the *Propriétaire-architecte*, generally after executed work, were definitely marked by it. This is only somewhat less true of the executed apartment houses and other buildings published by Normand in 1837 in his *Paris moderne*, by which date even more first-hand documents had appeared.

All this Italianism hardly modified the melancholy severity which had been developing in France even before the Revolution. The one-time Séminaire Saint-Sulpice in Paris, a fine and characteristic monument begun in 1820 by Godde, is extraordinarily stern, sober and devoid of decoration beyond the rusticated surfaces of the walls and the Bramantesque arches of the windows. Like many of the manifestations of the Age of Romanticism previous to the acceptance of the eclecticism of taste in the mid-nineteenth century the Renaissance Renaissance was for a long time most significantly a training in vision, a broadening of appreciation. Its finest productions in France are in a sense some of the plates in Durand, and in those various later *Recueils* lacking the archæological seriousness of Percier and Fontaine or Grandjean de Montigny, which offered in place of the major monuments of Florence and Rome innumerable delicate engravings of rural constructions. These latter are so authentically Romantic that they can hardly have existed exactly as drawn. Especially it seems in case of the magnificent book by Scheult that they must have been architectural arrangements on Italian themes by the "Picturesque Traveller." Never having been executed, however, they hardly constitute true architecture.

The Renaissance-Renaissance had its effects in Italy as well as in France from the beginning of the nineteenth century. But in England and Germany it arrived somewhat later and was not of any great importance until the Classical Revival was already declining. Even then it was more affiliated with the beginning of the eclecticism of taste or with the Mediæval Revivals. Nevertheless English and German architects from the beginning were somewhat less controlled by rigid Classical formulas than the French. The best monuments were freer also from the barrenness and frigid grandeur to which the French had tended to succumb even before the Revolution. The finest of them were moreover at least slightly eclectic in style and to a considerable degree rationalistic. Thus they may be considered, indeed, to have anticipated the architecture of the New Tradition.

It is the particular tragedy of the Age of Romanticism that its finest monuments either were not built as architecture: bridges, for example, and exposition halls; or were of high quality chiefly because of the continuance of Baroque tradition; or attained the dignity of really new creation by looking forward to the rationalistic manner of the eclecticism of style which did not definitely appear before the last years of the nineteenth century. It is nearly true therefore that there was no altogether great Romantic architecture as such.

The period after 1800 was not without innumerable interesting monuments which could have been built in no other age, but they are still too frequently, like the fabricks which marked the beginning of Romanticism, more significant as illustrations of new points of view than intrinsically. It is less distressing surely to read of their extraordinarily penurious construction than to observe it. Except for a somewhat limited group due to architects of great genius, their virtues are better appreciated therefore in books illustrated with line engravings, aquatints, and lithographs than in actuality. The reproducing artist was certainly able to patine delightfully walls and details that time only debased (Figures 10 and 14). Moreover he could control nature more completely than the executing architect, no matter how much a landscapist. Indeed even those extreme flights of Romantic utilitarianism, Egyptian icehouses and Swiss cowhouses, are not altogether absurd when well blended in the prints with deciduous or Alpine surroundings.

Yet it should not be forgotten that although the experiments by which the forms of architecture are changed are usually in modern times made in two dimensions first, the art only truly exists in three. Even in a period rather destitute of execution of high quality, history can only incidentally and in part deal merely with changes in point of view. The first significant accomplishments of Romanticism in actual construction appeared with the nineteenth century. Few as they were they are nevertheless worthy of comparison with earlier and later monuments.

Unquestionably the greatest architect of the beginning of the nineteenth century was Sir John Soane. His life from 1753 to 1837 covered almost exactly the period of the *style Louis XVI* and the Classical Revival. It is of course with the latter that he is usually classed. But his most characteristic works are much more widely representative of the Age of Romanticism. The designs of his youth in which he continued the Baroque-Romantic compromise in the English version notably practised by the brothers Adam are of little originality and no particular significance. Moreover in many of the ambitious projects of his later years, as in his instruction at the Royal Academy, he continued to bow to Classical canons and permitted the use of the orders in irrational profusion. But in his more individual designs he is not surpassed by any of his contemporaries, nor even by the masters of the New Tradition of which he was perhaps the earliest precursor.

In the buildings on the Tyringham estate done from 1793 to 1800 he experimented with form as much as any Baroque architect, but in a quieter and more reserved fashion. Where the Baroque architects worked in pure form as with clay, he worked as with the chisel on marble. As in the work of Robert Adam a certain connection with Vanbrugh's "picturesqueness" is traceable as is also in less degree the influence of Piranesi's "sublimity."

Soane at Tyringham avoided almost entirely the use of the orders. In the rear of the entrance screen, in the bridge and on the garden front of the house he gave a total expression of simple masonry structure and achieved a harmony of mass and line of extraordinary simplicity and elegance. In the use of detail he was exceedingly economical. He omitted mouldings all but entirely, using instead incised lines. This was an ornament for which no particular precedent existed. It provided a decoration which he developed later with considerable virtuosity, particularly on his own tomb. Even where the orders were used at Tyringham, on the front of the entrance screen and on the entrance façade of the house, they were chastened and subordinated indeed almost too completely, if they were, as the Age demanded, to be used at all. In certain other designs for mansions he attained nearly as great a purity, as for example in that for Butterton, but never such perfection of execution.

In his *Sketches in Architecture,* published in 1798 but prepared at least five years earlier, he provided certain projects of the simplest nature for rural cottages. These if built might perhaps have proved as valid in their severe character as Tyringham. His book had been preceded in this field by Plaw's *Rural Architecture,* 1785, and Middleton's *Picturesque and Architectural Views for Cottages, etc.,* 1795, both of more historical importance, as Hussey points out. Soane's designs were definitely rustic but rigidly symmetrical. In their elementary composition they were even Classical despite the frequent use of Gothic mullions. His designs for villas in the same book are still very close to Adam; but in the icehouses and reservoirs disguised as tombs he was according to his intentions more successfully original than a brief description makes plausible.

His *magnum opus,* rather than his masterpiece, was the Bank of England, now being destroyed in those very parts which were finest. He worked on this more or less continuously from 1788 until 1833. On the blank walls of the exterior there was much use of the orders. Only in the ornament of more than Greek severity did his real creative skill appear. The rooms of the interior with their thin tile vaults represented the most advanced engineering of the day. The decoration was geometrical or merely of incised lines accenting the structure. Primarily Soane was working with space, and even with light, for effects of abstract form; and he was rewarded as almost no post-Baroque architect has been. The various Consols and Annuities offices show an amazing virtuosity in varying the theme of semi-circular and segmental barrel vaults alternating with clerestoreyed domes on pendentives. As in the contemporary portraits by Ingres Raphael seems outdone, here the central churches of the Renaissance and even their Byzantine prototypes seem surpassed by an architect who did not probably even have them in mind.

Soane's models were Roman in a certain sense, but more technically than æsthetically. He was first of all an engineer seeking to obtain spacious and monumental offices, well lighted and well aired. The æsthetic effects were little related to the Roman past. The central rotunda is, indeed, rather clearly reminiscent of the Pantheon. Nevertheless it provides the ideal climax of the scheme merely as regards abstract form. Unfortunately the sculpture, although well used, was not intrinsically good.

In the loggia of the Governor's Court Soane also succeeded by his skilful avoidance of traditional proportions and by his reduction of Classical elements almost to their geometrical base in original creation. Here as in the interior his expression was definitely the outcome of Romantic points of view. He inspired awe as Piranesi had done in his *Carcer;* and he played upon the spectator, who could by this time be counted on to be a sensitive instrument, as shamelessly and as successfully as the most advanced architects of to-day, all the while remaining as they do very close to complete rationalism of structure. It is highly characteristic also that he had drawings prepared of the Bank in ruins, and indeed it would have ruined as magnificently as the Baths of Caracalla had not our own generation preferred to destroy it more neatly and completely.

In his own house, built from 1812 to 1814, which was intended as the end pavilion of a larger scheme rather than as an independent unit, there is a further development of what Soane's contemporaries called his Bœotian manner (Figure 9). The acroteria and the fret of Greek origin are the only elements reminiscent of the past on the façade; but even their form and use are quite unprecedented. The simple arched structure of the storeyed porch is decorated chiefly with his usual repertory of incised lines. It supports impressively two caryatides sculptured in the round. As in the Bank one may find such work of the school of Flaxman unworthy of the prominence he gave it. It was nevertheless as good as any English sculpture of the day and no worse than was to be had fifty years earlier or later.

The interior has much experimentation with low vaults and illustrates clearly his eclectic interest in Mediæval art, Muslim art, and in the structure of

Roman engineers rather than in the orders Rome borrowed from Greece. It is unfortunately much cluttered up by the museum he installed in it. Also his ingenious schemes of overhead lighting and intricate planning are on too small a scale to be really effective. The interior is still intact; but it is perhaps more interesting when studied in the plates of the descriptive book which he prepared in 1835 for presentation to foreign architects. The explanations of the monk's cell and of the tombs recall Ermenonville and indicate how visual effects were once reinforced by a symbolism which has become merely quaint.

The Dulwich picture gallery and mausoleum represented a larger development of the same phase of his art. Here in the technicalities of lighting, in the freedom and simplicity of massing, and in the elegance and restraint of his detail, he has been equalled by few architects of the New Tradition in the twentieth century. The treatment of the roof of the chapel showed almost as extraordinary a development of his linear ornament as his own tomb.

After this, except in certain churches designed but not executed about 1821 and in the interior of the Old Law Courts, he was less original. In seeking splendour and richness of effect he turned away from a largely imaginary antiquity and a real eclecticism of style toward the more conventional forms of Classicism and a partial eclecticism of taste. He even introduced nearly a generation later than in France a sort of Renaissance-Renaissance which did not at all blend with either his Bœotian or his Roman manner. His restraint in ornament was gone, his rationalism largely forgotten, and problems were lacking which demanded his structural ingenuity. His later work was more like that of the other architects of the later Classical Revival. It was superior on occasion only in finer proportions, more imaginative detail, and a somewhat greater structural integrity.

English connoisseurs in his day found excitement in the newly developed study of Mediæval archæology rather than in Bœotian originality. The adventurous were satisfied to encourage building in a more correct Gothic style. Soane himself seems to have been far from conscious of his real creative powers. He was even ready at least in a few projects to associate himself with the Gothic Revival. In these he was less successful however than with the rustic manner in his cottages of 1798.

There was a continuation of Soane's work in the field of rural architecture. It was nevertheless quite as frequently Gothic as rustic in manner. Malton's important *Essay on British Cottage Architecture* appeared also in 1798. His designs were both picturesque and more or less Mediæval. Laing in his *Hints for Dwellings*, 1801, combined very free and irregular planning with elevations in intention of Classical or even Grecian—to use the term favoured by the Romantics themselves—character. They were, however, definitely subordinated to the landscape. Malton's *Collection of Designs for Rural Retreats as Villas Chiefly in the Gothic and Castle Styles*, 1802, speaks for itself. The books of slightly later date by Lugar, Elsam, Randall, Gyfford, Pococke, and others testified chiefly to the consideration given to rural and picturesque building and to the rather free design of "rural retreats," and "elegant villas" even at a time when rigid Classicism is supposed to have been most completely dominant. Many of these books found their way on to the Continent, although how early it is difficult to say.

Papworth's *Rural Residences,* published in 1818, has particular interest and yet is typical of the genre as a whole. Many of the colour aquatints are exquisite; and although the Gothic designs are at this date in England of no particular interest or significance, Papworth's more purely rustic style is further developed than Soane's, his plans are excellent, and his simple free detail of tree-trunk columns, lattice and so forth is very successful on a small scale, whatever it might have been in execution (Figure 10). For his suggestions for construction display that the solid building traditions of the Baroque have been already quite forgotten. This book presents also one of the first and finest English "Italian Villas."

More similar books appeared in the twenties and thirties. That of Meason, published in 1829 and called *Landscape Architecture*, constituted a definite attempt to extract designs for architecture from seventeenth century Italian landscape paintings. It was, however, very much the work of an amateur. More influential was the series of five books by the architect Robinson published from 1823 to 1837 and in later editions. Most of his designs moreover had actually been executed. With him eclecticism of taste is already considerably developed. Yet it is controlled in general by the economic necessities of farm and villa construction and even more completely by the "picturesque" point of view. Robinson offered a very successful rural Italian manner. He was also one of the first to introduce the Swiss chalet into England. The rural Italian manner had also been favoured by Hunt, elsewhere an exponent of the Tudor, in his *Architettura Campestre* of 1827.

With Goodwin's *Rural Architecture,* 1835, dedicated to Soane, the series published during the latter's lifetime comes to an end. It indicated already the development of a somewhat fuller eclecticism of taste than that even of Thomson's *Rural Retreats,* 1827, or of Robinson's books. The different types of design offered are the same; but they are more equally favoured. Yet the Grecian villas are still more or less Bœotian. The great compendium of the period and indeed of the "picturesque" point of view was Loudon's *Encyclopædia of Cottage, Farm, and Village Architecture,* a collaborative work appearing in many editions from 1833.

Although a considerable number of the projects published in this group of books were carried out, the execution was inevitably of a very inferior quality. The books have been mentioned at some length because they are so much more agreeable as documents than the actual rural building of the day. Even John Nash, the architect of old Regent Street, had attempted the rustic. The village he built at Blaise Castle near Bristol is indeed not so shoddy as many of his. It is interesting for its actual existence; but more than the best designs in the books it is peripheral to architecture, particularly as that art was practised by Soane.

Although Soane had pupils, he had no considerable followers in the Bœotian manner. Nor is there in England any other Romantic architect of equal importance. The Grecian "Italian Villa" built for William Beckford at Lansdown near Bath in 1827 by Goodridge is very exceptional in quality. (Figure 24.) There are of course many monuments of considerable if still largely traditional excellence. Among these the National Gallery by Wilkins merits citing. It is, as is pointed out by Christopher Hussey, at once Classical and "picturesque." Since Soane had no true heirs he was historically important only in that he showed in a few buildings that Modern architecture had possibilities which had not been realized up to that time. Fortunately on the Continent those among his contemporaries who had something of the quality of his genius had also followers and therefore a more real and continuing historical importance.

In America two men, Bulfinch and Latrobe, produced buildings worthy of Soane. But Bulfinch belonged on the whole to the earlier school of those who combined with Baroque tradition a conscientious study of antiquity, rather than to the more rigid Classical Revival with its Grecian aspirations. The India Wharf Stores, built in 1808, are ascribed with much plausibility to Bulfinch. By his splendid technical treatment of industrial building—it was doubtless not considered architecture—using the best construction of the day, and depending for effect on the proportions, the spacing of the windows, and the relation of the masses, Bulfinch proved himself as much a precursor of the New Tradition as Soane. There is no more ornament than on the twentieth century German factories of Behrens and as skilful a use of structural details for decoration. The lintels, the plain string courses, and the five arches of the façade enrich quite sufficiently the good plain brickwork. The original design of the Massachusetts State Prison was of even more utter simplicity and must have been quite as impressive. This was all of granite and one of the first of a line of constructions in that stern and sober material about the markets and the water front which are among Boston's finest monuments.

Bulfinch's single serious attempt at Gothic, made in 1809, was of no interest or importance. But his granite Courthouse of the next year, now destroyed, illustrated that many formal architectonic effects, in his case still more or less Baroque, could be achieved even more successfully without recourse to ornamental decoration. In his major works he was generally dependent on tradition and even made liberal use of orders. Nowhere in his domestic building, moreover, is there any particular break with the manner with which he had grown up. The great delicacy of his detail was even at odds with those abstract qualities of his work which have been stressed here.

Latrobe, who was trained in England by the men who initiated the Grecian form of the Classical Revival there, submitted in 1805 two designs for the Baltimore Cathedral, one Gothic and one Classical. The latter fortunately was chosen. Its interior, like those of Soane in the Bank of England, was a brilliant space creation in terms of segmental vaults and domes. There is no other Romantic church to equal it in America or Europe. Yet in his other work he hardly ever departed from the temple formula and of his pupils only·Mills is of interest for his plain obelisk design of 1836 for the Washington monument.

There are, however, throughout America many little known Grecian works which might justly be called Bœotian. The Old Catholic Cathedral of Saint Louis built in 1839, and the first capitol of Missouri at Jefferson City begun a year earlier may serve as specific examples. But the general quality of domestic architecture remained excellent if definitely traditional—hence still Colonial—and peristyles were only occasionally abused.

Within the period of Soane there was in France no great virtue in architecture. The projects of the period have already been discussed, with the exception of those of more completely revivalistic character that testify chiefly to the power of the purists and the continuance of the cult of the colossal. The sad solemnity of the executed monuments is particularly distressing in contrast to the suave and graceful *style Louis XVI* of Gabriel. As early as 1780 such a church as Saint Philippe du Roule built by Chalgrin in Paris seemed already to anticipate the worst qualities of the Restoration and the July Monarchy.

But in building the further simplification of the continuing Baroque tradition and the influence of the Renaissance-Renaissance produced a rationalistic type of masonry construction more comparable to the quality of the projects in the books. As this sort of construction continued indefinitely into the nineteenth century there was always provided an admirable background for architecture, at least in Paris, when fine architecture might again appear. Although they are on the borderline between architecture and building, the arcade blocks by Percier and Fontaine that line the rue de Rivoli are the most familiar examples of the type. There were also buildings in which glass and iron were freely used. The new dome of the Halle au Blé in Paris by Bélanger and Brunet replaced in 1811 an earlier wooden covering. The delicate Marché de la Madeleine, long since destroyed, was built in 1829 by Veugny. The Galérie d'Orléans at the Palais Royal, constructed in 1829-31 by Fontaine after Percier's retirement, had like some of the Passages of the period a transparent roof. None of these, however, were exactly architecture.

Yet strangely enough one monument in Paris is fully the equal of anything of Soane's. The Arc de Triomphe de l'Etoile was begun in 1806 by the same Chalgrin responsible for Saint Philippe du Roule and finally completed in 1836, with little modification of his original design. It commands the architecture of the whole century as it commands the city-planning in which the French carried on in the expanding Paris of the nineteenth century the best Baroque traditions. If this arch be compared with Blondel's seventeenth century Porte Saint-Denis, also in Paris, it is clear that here also it was the continuation of the Baroque tradition which made possible this most successful attempt of the Romantic Age to attain the "sublime" by magnification, which had largely failed in Brongniart's Paris Bourse of 1808. The skill moreover with which its magnificent sculpture by Rude is applied is extraordinary and in its century unparalleled. It is regrettable that not again for many years in France was there equal courage and equal expression of the vigour of Romanticism. It is the *Eroica* of architecture.

The other triumphal arch of the period built by Percier and Fontaine in the Place du Carrousel was completely reminiscent of the Roman past. It was original only in the unusual delicacy of its scale and the rich polychromy which is now hardly visible. Indeed the work of these two, who were undoubtedly the leading French architects of the day, was in general somewhat timid. Their Italian interests affected them little except in the elaborate interiors for which they are best known. Their simplification of Baroque or more rigid Classical formulas on their exteriors inclined to be heavy and cold as much as the work of the earlier generation to which both Chalgrin and Brongniart belonged. Their reconstruction of Malmaison for Joséphine between 1798 and 1802 was successful in large part because the barrenness of the surface treatment was given interest by the grouping of masses of the original Baroque building. The decorations for the Sacre of Napoléon in 1804 are significant because the constructions before Notre Dame were definitely Gothic in intention. Their work on the imperial palaces was important because of its scale and as a continuance of earlier plans.

The Chapelle Expiatoire, chiefly of Fontaine's design, was built from 1815 to 1826. This, perhaps his major work, is interesting in its disposition, recalling to some extent the *campi santi* of Italy. It is nevertheless even gloomier than Saint Philippe du Roule. The detail, moreover, is coarse, lumpy and very funereal. A later royal chapel, that of Saint Ferdinand begun in 1843 by Fontaine after Percier's death, was of eclectic Romanesque inspiration. The detail was somewhat less sepulchral but even more formless than before. Although this monument represents an extreme point of Romantic originality, it is in quality very inferior even to the unexecuted design for a Gothic church that Percier had made some score years earlier for a Polish prince. It belongs, moreover, rather to a later and a different phase of Romanticism than that of the Classical Revival during Soane's lifetime. It is *troubadour* rather than Bœotian.

In Italy the first period of the nineteenth century was not a brilliant one. The advancing wings added to the Pitti Palace in the style of the original by Poccianti, a certain amount of respectable Renaissance-Renaissance building usually of a simple sort, Stern's very frigid galleries of the Vatican museums hardly constitute an imposing contribution. Pietro Bianchi in erecting San Francesco at Naples had some success in combining the dome of the Pantheon with the colonnade of Saint Peter's, and linking them by two subsidiary domes. Although this church has a real impressiveness it can hardly be considered to have the character of a new creation. In general the Classical Revival was even less fruitful in Italy than in France whose models were chiefly followed. Yet Antonio Niccolini's Teatro S. Carlo in Naples of 1815 is unexpectedly superior to Chalgrin's sombre Théâtre de l'Odéon in Paris. Valadier's arrangement of the Piazza del Popolo, done from 1800 to 1831, is splendidly formal in a day when landscape gardening was triumphant.

In Germany there was more work comparable to that of Soane. Friedrich Gilly, the son of David Gilly, one of the chief *Louis XVI* architects of Germany, made a design—unfortunately never executed—for a monumental theatre in Berlin which was most admirable in the varied interplay of simple masses. But he died young in 1800, leaving behind only the projects and the sketch books that reveal his fine Romantic talent. In the same year Heinrich Gentz finished the Old Mint in Berlin. This was a building of great severity with rational expression of plain masonry structure. It was of no great quality or particular importance, but it was of the solid type to which much German building, down indefinitely into the century, conformed as in France. As a notable example the industrial work of Langhans should be mentioned. He is of course much better known for his excellent Classical Brandenburgerthor, even more the symbol of Berlin than Chalgrin's Arc de Triomphe is of Paris.

But the most important architect of this period in Germany was Friedrich Schinkel. He was born in 1781 and was a pupil and follower of Friedrich Gilly. The fact that he conscientiously studied Mediæval building while in Italy and that he made several attempts at ecclesiastical and castellated Gothic is significant not so much because of the few buildings he produced in the Mediæval manner as because it marks him as the first nineteenth century writer to develop in part from a knowledge of non-Classical structure a theoretical system of rationalism. This was later continued and modified by Semper working largely with High Renaissance forms and according to the dominant eclecticism of taste of the mid-century. From him the system was passed on to the early men of the New Tradition.

Schinkel's most Classical buildings even were distinctly rationalistic. They were on occasion also somewhat eclectic in style although less fully so than some of those of Soane's Bœotian manner. In the Berlin Schauspielhaus the varied disposition of the masses and the magnificent expression of simple structure in the wings is only partly negatived by the dull Ionic portico and the heavily sculptured pediments above. The Palais Redfern in Berlin with its flat rustication and crude heavy cornice is indeed more magnificent than the French works of the Renaissance-Renaissance; but beside the work of Soane it lacks subtlety and elegance.

Two designs, one for a lighthouse, done in 1825, and another for a very large store or group of stores about a court, done in 1827, indicate how thoroughly and exclusively he could follow his rationalistic theories at times. Like Soane, he appears in these designs, as in the Palais Redfern, a master of the New Tradition born far too soon. He is not so great a master as Soane, but he is more important than he because of his formulated theories and because he developed an interesting school whose work falls in the next period. For he was a dignified representative of even the more extreme manifestations of Romanticism which were better carried on in Germany than elsewhere. Although his Baronial constructions were of rather inferior order his "Italian Villas" were among the earliest and best of the type. They remained still very Classical in detail, but they were free and highly picturesque in the massing. Those of Persius, who completed his master's works at Potsdam, were no finer and indeed little later; for while Schinkel did not die until 1841, Persius only lived four years longer.

There were in Schinkel's day other good architects in Germany. Peter Speeth, who was one of those who carried the German version of the Classical Revival beyond her borders first into Italy and then into Russia, produced in the Würzburg Zuchthaus of 1809-10 a monument comparable to the best of Soane's. Friedrich von Gärntner before his death in 1847 did much building at Munich in the general Schinkel tradition with reminiscences of the Italian Romanesque and the Tuscan Renaissance rather than of Classical antiquity. In his work in the Ludwigstrasse there is also the megalomania and the gloomy barrenness so characteristic of the French architecture of the time. But he really belongs as much as Persius to the oncoming generation.

Outside the countries that have been mentioned the Classical Revival produced much excellent building but few great monuments of architecture.

Many of the best edifices of Leningrad and Moscow belong nevertheless to this period. But until the appearance of the New Tradition it is unnecessary to consider particularly architecture, building, or engineering, except in France, England, Germany, and the United States, so little of it showed individual character. For example the Thorvaldsen Museum built in Copenhagen from 1838 to 1847 by Bindesböll indicates how rationalism of the order of Schinkel's, when intelligently followed even by the most rigid of Grecians, could produce a monument of some interest and excellence. But although this is somewhat exceptional for its quality it is not particularly Danish except in so far as it suggests the Danish Néo-Classicism of the New Tradition. Less good can be said of the mass of Grecian work done by Danish architects in nineteenth century Athens.

The good architects of the first generation of the nineteenth century are everywhere best to be defined as more or less rationalistic Classicists. The best of them were open even in their most Classical work to more eclectic influences. This supported them to some extent intellectually and practically in experimentation. But the buildings constructed in intentionally Mediæval style were very inferior both as regards archæological correctness —to which the designers nevertheless often aspired—and as regards intrinsic interest to the work done within the bounds of the Classical Revival. They have not like the Gothicist constructions of the third quarter of the eighteenth century the importance of marking the initiations of a new sort of sentimental reminiscence. The same holds true of the Gothic building done at this period by the men—usually more or less amateurs—who were not at all Classical Revivalists. Even more than the rustic constructions they are of distinctly secondary value, chiefly as a symbol of expanding taste. Although this Gothic work was executed in considerable quantities it illustrated less well moreover than the projects of the books the creative opportunities already provided by a wider appreciation of the past and by the new points of view that were being isolated by analysis. Yet as much as the projects they are two rather than three dimensional, in the sense that the pictorial virtues they possess in contemporary prints are hardly conspicuous in their actual presence or in photographs. (Figure 14.)

CHAPTER THREE

THE SECOND GENERATION OF THE NINETEENTH CENTURY

THE architects of the second generation of the nineteenth century had greater success in the revival of the Mediæval past than those of the first. But in their reaction from the largely unconscious freedom of their predecessors they were definitely rigourists. Their work is too often of less interest intrinsically than as an index of the development of Mediæval archæology, which was already beginning to give intellectual support to a new and more far-reaching rationalism. The architects who constructed the finest monuments of the mid-century followed for the most part rather the rationalizing Classicism to which their fathers had subscribed, inclining more and more in detail to the eclecticism of taste. The few Mediævalist buildings which are of quality comparable to those of the later Classicists, chiefly those in Germany, belong to a separate phase of Romanticism although they were erected during exactly the same years, and sometimes by the same men.

In outlying countries, such as America, much building moreover continued well down to 1850 the characteristics of the preceding period. This, although still frequently of excellent quality, was of only local significance. Paris tended to become the centre of the world of architecture as of painting, particularly under the Second Empire. Unfortunately by that time the stronger manner of the men who had matured in the thirties was being swallowed up in the Néo-Baroque, the most characteristic of the vulgar and luxuriant manifestations of the fully developed eclecticism of taste.

Henri Labrouste, the finest architect of the mid-century, was born in 1801. He was trained at the Ecole des Beaux Arts and at the French Academy in

Rome. This was, of course, the conventional education of the French architect, until lately also accepted as ideal in America. But about Labrouste gathered, on his return to Paris, all who were in revolt against the official peristylar Classicism of the day, naturally many among them men who had some desire to revive the Middle Ages. He joined with the latter in theory only, and in his work never strayed into paths which were not in a general way acceptable to the dominant Classicists.

His first major work, the Bibliothèque Sainte-Geneviève, built from 1843 to 1850, is unquestionably a monument of exceptional quality. The severity of the exterior is lessened by a certain amount of cold and elegant ornament of the sort known, strangely enough, as Néo-Grec. (Figure 19.) But rationalism had little chance for startling expression in a masonry façade clothing a functionally simple plan. It was the interior of which the two barrel-vaulted naves were supported by iron which was particularly significant. Even more remarkable was Labrouste's treatment of the reading room of the Bibliothèque Nationale. Here he covered a large square space with nine domes of glazed tile resting on an iron skeleton supported by four slim metal piers. Although the detail of neither interior has the charm or the sobriety of that of the façade of the Bibliothèque Sainte-Geneviève, they were the first considerable examples of the use of metal in architecture. They provided a brilliant demonstration that rationalism could again be creative, as in the previous generation in England and Germany, and not merely critical of the blind revivalism which would make of all sorts of buildings peripteral temples. But they showed also the lack of harmony of scale and the bad taste—there is no more accurate word—which developed generally with the loosening of Grecian restraints.

J. I. Hittorf, who alone at this time is to be compared with Labrouste, was born in Cologne in 1792. He studied at the Ecole des Beaux Arts, worked with Bélanger and Percier, and travelled in his native Germany and in Italy. His first important work, the church of Saint Vincent de Paul, begun in 1832, appears to-day very cold and harsh. For the polychrome decoration of the exterior which doubtless made it gayer was removed in 1861. To the interior he gave a rational expression based on the Early Christian basilicas of Rome, a modification of strict Classicism introduced as early as 1780 by Chalgrin at Saint Philippe du Roule. Many early nineteenth century French churches had been thus influenced in planning and general arrangement, but seldom on the façades or in the detail. This Early Christian mode was related to the Renaissance-Renaissance.

The interior of Saint Vincent de Paul was much more successful than those of Saint Philippe du Roule or Le Bas' similar Notre Dame de Lorette of 1823-1826. Like the exterior, it was once brilliant in colour, of course now much faded. The polychromy of Hittorf was justified by his investigations and those of Labrouste of the architecture of Magna Græcia. But he was surely encouraged in it by the colouristic painting of the *romantisme de la lettre* which had replaced the bas-relief style of 1800. It was even more violent on his cafés and his Cirque des Champs Elysées, built in the thirties.

This Cirque was more important than Saint Vincent de Paul in that it forced Hittorf to give architectural treatment to an engineering problem. The Grecian detail was doubtless inappropriate; but the exterior as a whole gave finely proportioned expression to the interior. In his domestic constructions, such as the façades about the Place de l'Etoile, he showed himself sober, conscientious and uninspired, producing building rather than architecture and decorating it passably according to the Classical conventions to which he remained even more respectful than Labrouste. But these buildings were just what was needed to throw the architecture of Chalgrin's Arc de Triomphe into deserved prominence.

It is Hittorf's Gare du Nord of 1851 that raises him to the level of Labrouste. Here, as in the Cirque, the Grecian detail is out of place and rather irrationally used. The symbolic idea of a station as a city gate was, however, once perfectly valid according to the principles of the eclecticism of taste. Like all such stylistic symbolism it lost rather than gained force by repetition until even the original expression has come to appear trite. But the façade in its general design nevertheless expressed magnificently an interior in which Hittorf essayed to bring engineering into close relation with architecture. Technically it remains one of the finest stations of the world, and alone among those of Paris this, the earliest, has not since required enlargement or change. The narthex, lately repainted, has an extraordinary freshness of spirit previously obscured by the grime.

The value of the work of these men, Labrouste and Hittorf, is summed up in a very few monuments. But there were certain others built in their life time in which the same tendencies are clear. Among many mediocre examples some merit special mention. In the sixties, Duc gave a fine rationalized Classical façade to the Palais de Justice toward the Place Dauphine. Just before this Duban attained almost equal success on the exterior of the Ecole des Beaux Arts. He made as well some visible use of metal in the interior. Also in the sixties, Baltard erected the strange vaguely Romanesque interior of Saint Augustin in which he continued Labrouste's use of iron-supported vaults with much less success. The influence of such constructions lived on, although it was apparently submerged by other currents. In France and elsewhere the early masters of the New Tradition profited from such examples. Richardson, moreover, had worked under Labrouste.

But the main effort of the period of the Second Empire was toward the restoration of splendour and magnificence to architecture. Rationalism took refuge in the theory of Mediævalists or in an increasingly academic worship of the plan as the essence of architecture summed up under the Third Republic in the books of Julien Guadet. Visconti and Lefuel in their extension of the Louvre had inaugurated a sort of Baroque revival. They had little creative originality although perhaps somewhat better taste than most of their generation. Garnier, the best known and the most highly considered of the Imperial group, provided in the Opéra a focus to the splendid city-planning of the baron Haussmann. The endless adequately successful building that some ten kilometres of new streets necessitated was solidly done with good stone and decorated with Néo-Grec or Néo-Baroque orders and ornament. The many plates of Victor Calliat's *Parallèle des maisons de Paris depuis 1830*, 1850, indicate the type, distinctly less restrained and less excellent than that of the previous period equally well illustrated in Normand's *Paris moderne*. To all this the new Opéra provided a climax of extravagance and a conspicuous centre of attraction. But in the history of Modern architecture it is less significant than the building about it; and the finest part is the rear that houses the offices and dressing rooms. There Garnier restricted himself to raising contemporary building in scale and variety of massing to the dignity of architecture with an economy of decorative features that brings to mind the sobriety of the best work of the early eighteenth century. His innumerable imitators, however, were never impressed by this, and strained indefinitely the licence of floridity provided particularly by his interiors.

The last particularly fine building which comes out of the Classical tradition of the mid-century—however unexpectedly and indirectly—is the Palace of the Trocadéro, built for the Paris Exposition of 1878 by Davioud. In the two theatres of the Place du Châtelet he had already shown more simplicity and a wider eclecticism than his contemporaries. In the Trocadéro he broke from all Classical restraints except that of symmetry and combined Islamic, Mediæval Italian, and other exotic features of style in a monument of real originality and creative power. It is nevertheless distinctly awkward and lacking in taste. The use of the site, the great development of the plan, were in the line of the Néo-Baroque; but the simplicity, the bold polychromy and Davioud's natural, rather than intellectual, rationalism were new. Although it came nearer than any other French work of the mid-nineteenth century in which engineering did not play a much larger part to the New Tradition, already by this time beginning, it had little traceable influence except in certain mediocre churches. It was accepted not as a demonstration of theory but as an exceptional monument of Exposition architecture.

Outside Paris the splendours of the Second Empire—except perhaps Garnier's Casino at Monte Carlo—have become exceedingly shabby. Casterman's *Parallèle des maisons de Bruxelles,* published about 1860, shows already a definite decline from the standard of the work published by Calliat. It is easily forgotten that in the period of *laissez faire* revivalism of the later years of the century, continuing even in some places down to the present day, the type of architecture known from its centre of distribution as Beaux Arts architecture is particularly the heir of the Néo-Baroque. Eclecticism of taste was, as far as practice goes, in force from the beginning of Romanticism, although each separate revivalist group through the early period of activity of the second generation of architects in the nineteenth century tried to claim that it possessed the only way of light. But before the downfall of the Second Empire eclecticism of taste was generally admitted to be in force, although the Beaux Arts manner and revivals clearly associated with it were dominant. The influence of Paris after the day of Labrouste and Hittorf was, on the whole, repressive and literally reactionary. French eclecticism of taste was distinctly inferior to that of other countries, although much more facile; and even the remains of the rationalistic tradition had become stupid and academic. The new development of engineering in the seventies was almost entirely unrelated.

Victor Laloux, to whom the last important academic monuments were due, the Gare d'Orsay in Paris and the Hôtel de Ville of Tours, is still to-day at the Ecole des Beaux Arts. Like the architects of the Paris Exposition of 1900 and the exposition architects in America down to the War, he was unable to surpass Garnier or Visconti and Lefuel. It was only possible to revise their manner in the direction of larger scale in the parts and of greater restraint, or to use the accepted term, greater refinement. But this sort of building was at its best only when it might be, at the court of Napoleon III, the expression of a splendid vulgarity; or in the case of much of Franz Josef's work at Vienna begun somewhat later, the execution of schemes and designs of the Baroque period, such as that for the Hofburg made by Fischer von Erlach in the middle of the eighteenth century. In admiring Paris and Vienna it must not be forgotten that it is largely the skilful combination of nineteenth century architecture and building in large scale city planning that we see. Laloux's Gare d'Orsay, for example, balances the rue de Rivoli, echoes the pavillions de Flore and de Marsan and completes the Louvre-Etoile composition on the Seine side. The public monuments of the Ringstrasse in Vienna form a sumptuous girdle about the inner city where so many finer Baroque constructions remain for lack of space nearly invisible. Berlin and London have analogous but less extensive effects, of which the finest, that leading up from the Mall to Piccadilly Circus, has only just been completed, although begun at least a century ago.

In England in the year of Soane's death the decision to build the Houses of Parliament in the Perpendicular style marked the beginning of the dominance of the Gothic Revival. But Barry, the architect to whom at least the general plan and conception of this monument was due, was essentially an eclectic Classicist. Born in 1795, he was with Soane among the earliest to introduce the imitation of the High Renaissance into England. His Traveller's Club of 1829 and Reform Club of 1837 are distinctly more successful than those similar constructions which Tate and the Smirkes built in the next score of years.

This broadening and loosening of the Classical Revival was a certain relief after the Grecian monuments of Piranesian inspiration, such as the elder Smirke's British Museum of 1825-1828, which immediately preceded. But in conjunction with the controlling Gothic Revival it led to an even greater lack of taste than in France. The Néo-Baroque and other phases of the French eclecticism of taste of the Second Empire were moreover imitated also on occasion with disastrous results. However, the Government Offices in Whitehall, built about 1860 in a Palladian manner, are not incorrect or unimpressive. Yet the architect G. G. Scott was a convinced Gothicist designing a Classical building only because forced to by the Liberals in power. In general by the mid-century the best English artistic talent had been absorbed by the Gothic Revival. It was moreover chiefly from Mediævalism that a later phase of eclecticism of taste developed after 1870, as well as that related transitional architecture of craftsmanship which was to prove more fruitful. Barry was the last Classical architect of individual distinction but he was by no means the equal of his contemporaries in France. Moreover, his chief work, the Houses of Parliament, is not only not Classical, but quite as much the work of his collaborator Pugin, the first of the major Gothic Revivalists.

In America in the growing cities of the East the English influence which lay behind the continuing Classical Revival and the feebler Gothic Revival, was replaced about the middle of the century by the influence of France. The bald, crude imitations of the Louvre in granite, to whose manner the name of the conqueror of the Confederacy has been lent, still retained some of the solid virtues of the earlier monuments of the century. The State Department Building in Washington, more impressive and less gloomy than the great post offices of the time, is certainly better than most similar Second Empire work in the French provinces.

Richard M. Hunt, born in 1828, was one of the first Americans to have a completely French training. He had worked with Lefuel on the Louvre before his return to New York in 1855. However he introduced many other manners of the contemporary French eclecticism of taste beside the Néo-Baroque. Although he himself handled them all with considerable virtuosity and had at least studied his documents, his example brought to an end among his ill-informed compatriots all traces of those sound traditions which had informed the Classical Revival and even continued to lend some integrity to the American version of the official Second Empire manner. The disintegration accomplished by Romanticism was therefore more complete than anywhere in Europe by the late sixties. But there appeared immediately afterward in the architecture of Richardson an extraordinarily complete reintegration. This was indeed more significant for the way which architecture was to take in the next fifty years even than the transitional revival of building craftsmanship in England and the brilliant development of engineering in France, both of which began about the same time.

In Italy the middle period of the nineteenth century was even less productive than the first. A strict Classical Revival remained more than elsewhere dominant. The reconstruction of San Paolo fuori le mura at Rome was begun in 1825 by Belli after the fire of 1823, and continued after 1833 by Poletti nearly down to the end of the Papal rule in Rome. Like the contemporary churches of France, but with more reason, it followed in general Early Christian lines preserving thus the original plan. The polychromy of the interior was sumptuous and the exterior was somewhat picturesque in outline; but the whole effect was excessively hard and glacial. Full eclecticism of taste finally came, as elsewhere, at the end of Romanticism.

The Mediæval Revival, or at least manners more affiliated with it than with Classicism, produced the best building in Germany during the middle of the nineteenth century. Schinkel's pupil, Stüler, remained, however, rigidly Classical in his Neues Museum and National Galerie in Berlin. With little of the genius of his master, he had no more success with them than Leo von Klenze, who also continued the earlier Classicism in the Walhalla, the Munich Glyptothek and the nearby Propyläon. Von Klenze's, Ältere and Neuere Pinakotheks at Munich were nearly equally dull although following the Italian Renaissance. The Néo-Renaissance—to distinguish it from the earlier and more successful Renaissance-Renaissance—received more definite formulation at the hands of Gottfried Semper. Like Hittorf, he was interested in polychromatic decoration, though his chief monument at Dresden—like those of Stüler and von Klenze, a museum—does not show it. Nor is this particularly marked any more than his later work on the Ringstrasse in Vienna, or his Dresden Opera House, all built in the seventies, by the rationalism of his writing. Theories aside, he was really no more than a competent architect of the eclecticism of taste. He worked by conviction in the Néo-Renaissance hardly more successfully than Scott who used a parallel manner at Whitehall by compulsion.

The Classical Revival, in part because of the activity of the rationalists and in part because of the necessity of coming to terms with the Mediævalists, was finally dissolved in the eclecticism of taste all over Europe and in America. It was rather within the Mediæval Revival, itself being similarly dissolved, that there resided possibilities of advance. Eclecticism of taste all but destroyed the integrity of architecture. Yet it was the conception of architecture as a separate and superior entity which had to a considerable extent made eclecticism of taste possible. Its effect on building was even more fatal. It is therefore in the building of the nineteenth century rather than in the architecture that the disintegration of Romanticism was most complete. Engineering fortunately could go its own way. Thus it was able to produce in the mid-century the only constructions whose quality is worthy of comparison with the libraries of Labrouste and the station of Hittorf, in which, morever, it had already been reincorporated.

CHAPTER FOUR

ENGINEERING AND BUILDING

BETWEEN the engineering of Labrouste and Hittorf, which was consciously æsthetic in intention and subordinated to their architecture, and engineering in general there was naturally a considerable difference. But it is impossible to say definitely that one sort is finer than the other because the problems to be solved were so very different. Disregarding hierarchical prejudice, who can say that a railway bridge is finer than a railway station, or a factory than the reading-room of a library? It is certain, however, that the embellishments of the architects where omitted are not missed.

The railroad bridges and viaducts built entirely of masonry have much the air of similar Roman works. The reminiscence however is not artistic but technical. If a dated series of such monuments be examined, such as is provided in the book of *Ingenieurbauten der Deutschen Reichsbahn*, their character will be found to remain more or less the same from those built for the first railroads down to those built since the War. In a general way perhaps those of the forties were finer in their proportions than those that followed. There is furthermore in the latest a more conscious æsthetic effort, indicative of the fact that with the New Tradition engineering became again as in pre-Romantic ages reincorporated with architecture. Unfortunately this reincorporation has not everywhere taken place so fully as in Germany, so that the particular excellence of the work of the twentieth century there, which compares so favourably with the work of the mid-century, is elsewhere less frequently found. These masonry monuments however are less characteristic of the nineteenth century and less significant than similar work in metal construction. (Figure 12.)

Metal bridges had been imagined in the sixteenth and seventeenth century. They began to be built in the last quarter of the eighteenth century. The earliest ones, however, were small in span and not particularly impressive. From the beginning of the nineteenth century there was a further development. But as in the case of the monuments of masonry it was with the coming of the railroad that engineering was first called on for great and unprecedented feats. Among the works of the forties the Britannia Bridge between Wales and the Isle of Anglesea was one of the most famous. It remains one of the finest, particularly on account of the massive treatment of the masonry supports and the entrances in a manner still quite Bœotian. There were many more large bridges built all over the world in the fifties and sixties of an even more ambitious sort. In a considerable number of these, unfortunately, the gates and supports were castellated in treatment or even more elaborately Gothic. Others, however, have no attempt at decorative embellishment and a magnificence purely in the character of engineering. In the latter part of the nineteenth century many metal bridges near cities were disfigured with even more monumental portals usually still of a quite inappropriate Mediæval character. But many more in the midst of open scenery or wild mountains achieved a delicacy and a perfection of profile of which no contemporary eclectic architect could possibly have been capable. (Figure 13.) Beyond these indeed the twentieth century has not yet gone.

These metal bridges, especially those of the cable suspension type, existed very much apart from the architecture of the time. They were little, and then with few exceptions unfortunately, affected by it; and they affected it not at all. The æsthetic sensibility of their builders in an age when æsthetic sensibility was exercised so exclusively on the forms of the past can hardly have been highly conscious. If these constructions have beauty, even a greater beauty than the similar constructions in masonry, it is in large part accidentally or *par surcroît*. If they are now much too uncritically vaunted it is on account of the *snobisme de la machine,* or the anti-intellectualism which has at present so strong an influence on all who express æsthetic convictions. But it is no act of faith in the technical creed of the New Pioneers, as some have thought, to claim that nineteenth century engineers without artistic intent readily and generally surpassed them; and the effect of the Brooklyn bridge, for example, is although perhaps "sublime" not altogether superior to criticism in detail according to the New Pioneers' standards of architectural "beauty."

Another type of construction in which engineering achieved fine effects was in the covering of interior spaces by means of metal supports. Several comparatively early French specimens on a modest scale were mentioned in the second chapter. Judging from contemporary prints, the Berlin Exerzierhaus, built probably by Friedrich Gilly or his father before 1800 with features apparently supposed to be Gothic, is also of some significance for its early date. The Galleria Vittorio Emmanuele in Milan built in 1867 by Mengoni is an immense and rather impressive covered street of the functional type of many much smaller and simpler Passages built under the Empire and the Restoration in Paris. The interior walls have the most ordinary Néo-Baroque embellishments; the façade toward the Duomo is one great Néo-Renaissance triumphal arch. The idea, the plan, and the engineering were, however, very excellent and superior to the similar examples that are to be found in other cities.

The masterpiece of nineteenth century building in metal was the Crystal Palace. This was first erected for the Exposition of 1851 in Hyde Park, London, by Joseph Paxton. He was born in 1803 and was by profession a gardener, not an architect or an engineer. Indeed the Crystal Palace may be considered the apotheosis of the greenhouse, a type of construction which had naturally enough great popularity in an age that took such a particular æsthetic interest in gardens. Many of the conservatories, orangeries, palm-houses, and *jardins d'hiver* still in existence, and others of which the designs are given in such a compendium of landscape art as the anonymous and plagiarizing *Traité de la Composition des Jardins*, 1839, are excellent examples of Romantic engineering on a small scale. They are even on occasion not ill combined with the architecture of simple or elegant villas. The Crystal Palace by its real size and the magnitude of its conception rose entirely superior to all these. Yet as in the work of Labrouste the cast detail of the iron work showed some attempt to adapt ancient forms. This was incidental in such a well-proportioned study of volume to which the linear skeleton gave an admirable rhythm. The interior in spite of the clutter of the Exposition must have been equally splendid, to judge from the contemporary illustrations in the *Les beautés architecturales de Londres.*

In 1854 the Palace was re-erected by Paxton at Sydenham outside London where it still exists. (Figure 11.) On this occasion it was effectively set in the midst of artificial landscape varied with the formal gardens which had been coming back into favour during the later Romantic period. The composition was more elaborate and more dramatic than when it was first built. But more research in expression was justified as the functional needs were on this occasion less exigent. Between Soane and Richardson there was hardly built a finer monument. It was moreover the first of a line of similar construction of which few can compare with the original. There were good examples at the Paris Expositions of 1855 and 1867, of course long since destroyed. The simpler Munich Glaspalast still exists.

The Halles Centrales in Paris built in 1853 by Baltard, the architect of Saint Augustin, represented a different type of somewhat the same order. Although of real excellence it is, however, less integrated in composition than were the smaller Italianate markets built of masonry with wooden roofs in the earlier part of the century. Of these a fine example remains in the Marché des Carmes.

Some mention has already been made of the city building of the first half of the nineteenth century, both on the Continent and in America. That industrial building—one can hardly call the factories of the time engineering —could be equally fine will be clear to any one who knows the early stone or brick mills of New England or similar work elsewhere. However, with the middle of the century a larger industrial development and the degeneration of masonry craftsmanship brought to an end this special tradition which had its antecedents even in the early eighteenth century in Europe. No longer could there possibly be intimacy or domestic scale in this type of work. But occasionally without any thought of architecture excellent work was done, particularly if there were an interesting sort of problem, or a new type of construction. Factories broad in scale and handling, with a force that makes up for poor workmanship and even for gloominess made gloomier by a half century of subjection to soot and smoke, may be seen by those who have the courage to look out of train windows as they pass through the manufacturing district of any large city. Here already at hand was the raw material with which the New Tradition was to work when it made industrial building once more consciously a branch of architecture.

The will to do so existed from the beginning of the New Tradition. Richardson is quoted as having desired about 1880 to build a grain elevator. He did make a design for a large icehouse quite unrelated to the Romantic tomb type. But it was left to such men as Wright and Behrens after the twentieth century had begun to really carry industrial architecture to execution.

There is too little of early nineteenth century industrial building left to give familiar specific examples and there is far too much of that of the later nineteenth century. Within the mass of such work the vast majority is of so low a quality as to justify after the fact the Romantic distinction between architecture and building which is chiefly responsible. On the other hand there are some single monuments, even groups of monuments, beside which most of the monuments of architecture of the century appear futile and faded. Nevertheless they are historically of little importance. For the New Tradition, which was to surpass this industrial work at the same time that it honoured it, grew out of the architecture of the nineteenth century both in theory and in practice, only reincorporating engineering and building with architecture after that had already been separately reintegrated.

The texts and the collections of pictures published in the last few years which offer only nineteenth century engineering and industrial building as the background of the specifically modern architecture of the last fifty years bear false witness. Even such an important monument as the Eiffel Tower built in 1889 just as the New Tradition was appearing in Europe is as much connected with it by the ugly ornament as by the magnificent structure. Indeed the appreciation of specifically engineering structure for its own sake, either on solid æsthetic grounds or because of the *snobisme de la machine*, is more directly connected with the New Pioneers than with the New Tradition, and dates largely from after the War.

Of the city or country building of the middle of the nineteenth century there is little good to be said. Unwilling to be quite cut off from architecture it set itself up as a sort of poor relative. Having no longer after the general disappearance of craftsmanship and sound standards of execution any worthy garments of its own however plain, it was glad to accept the cast off garments of architecture to be worn in ignorance of their proper use. For this final degeneration no one revival was responsible. Yet as long as the revivals of one Classical manner or another had been definitely the controlling régime in architecture, some remainder of Baroque tradition still existed to preserve building from utter decline, no matter how little was thought of it; or indeed rather because little was thought of it. But when in the forties various forms of the Mediæval Revival had risen generally to dispute effectively the dominance of the revivals sponsored by its divided opponents, the contradictory influences upon building were disastrous. The healthy theories of rationalism and good workmanship which the Mediæval Revivalists preached but seldom practised hardly touched building at all until considerably later.

In discussing the opening of the Age of Romanticism and the gradual establishment of pictorial and literary canons of architectural judgment the early results of what might be called the extreme anti-technical point of view have already been sufficiently illustrated. The harvest was not however at once reaped. The workmanship of the Classical Revival is in general not so much inferior to that of the late Baroque as might be expected, considering the low quality of execution already displayed in the more extreme eighteenth century manifestations of the picturesque. The worst sign was the increasing use of plaster surfaces which smoothed over a multitude of sins. This treatment was of course directly encouraged by the study of Italian buildings of various dates as well as of Roman remains other than peristylar temples. For æsthetic reasons the New Pioneers have moreover returned to it, but without imitative intent. It emphasizes abstract forms and is not necessarily dishonest, if the construction it masks is sound and clearly comprehensible. But for the Romantics it too often provided merely a means of hiding shoddy masonry and giving the effect of more expensive materials such as cut-stone and marble.

But as the Classical Revival made on the whole considerably less demand than had the Baroque on technical virtuosity, and largely avoided ornament on exteriors, there was not before about 1825 any very marked decline. This is even more true as regards the still very sound interior decoration and furniture. However as the execution of more and more unfamiliar forms was demanded of workmen, the dependence on archæological documents, usually at second-hand, became necessarily greater and the dependence on traditional training in the crafts distinctly less. Difficulties already began therefore with the introduction of more accurate Roman orders and even more with the introduction of the Greek orders well within the eighteenth century.

Eventually a specifically late Romantic nineteenth century detail came into existence in building and even in architecture. Like Romantic architecture in general it was less a definite manner than the result of new points of view which were brought to bear on many different manners. Its originality, which is unquestionable, made later generations exceedingly suspicious of originality in principle. After the reaction of the eclecticism of taste toward academic or archæological correctness at the end of the last century it may seem unnecessary to bring up this sad question. It is however an essential feature of the disintegration of architecture in the Age of Romanticism.

The originality in detail was, if not altogether unconscious, at least due in large part to the character of the documents uneducated workmen, or usually in the first place draftsmen, were expected to imitate. Even the illustrations in such a serious archæological work as Turner and Parker's *Domestic Architecture of the Middle Ages*, 1851, could be interpreted successfully only by an eye familiar with and appreciative of old work. For the inexpensive woodcut so popular for illustrations in the archæological books of the time, provided a far less satisfactory and clear means of transmitting information than the engraving used in the Baroque period. The new medium of lithography, also inexpensive, although technically capable of almost photographic perfection, was more usually called on to give to the full those pictorial and poetic effects in which Romanticism delighted. Lithography and the woodcut tended definitely to slur ornament each in their own fashion. In executed work there is much detail that seems to owe its particular character to dependence on one or the other of these means of reproduction.

This point may easily be overstressed. For the matter was by no means so simple. Both woodcut and lithographic reproductions of architecture were undoubtedly more studied by amateurs than by workmen. *Albums, Keepsakes, Picturesque Voyages* were primarily, like photographs and post cards to-day, the stock in trade of the returned traveller and the vicarious experience that consoled those who stayed at home. But they provided a certain very definite sort of training in pictorial vision. This is particularly displayed by the fact that in contemporary prints even such an extraordinarily inaccurate monument as the Chapelle d'Orléans at Dreux, begun under the Restoration and finished by Louis Philippe, can resemble somewhat similar prints of authentic Mediæval monuments. (Figure 14.) It is at least thus made to appear æsthetically plausible as it never can in photographs or in actuality.

Aquatint, which had a considerable popularity in architectural books in England for some time before and after 1800, was like lithography very effective for blending architecture with scenery and left detail even more entirely to the imagination. (Figure 10.) Its suggestiveness is to us as charming as it was to contemporaries. But we would hardly set out to copy documents thus reproduced without further information. Soane moreover in his *Sketches* warns in one case, surely among very many, that the graphic artist distorted his design as originally drawn. It was line-engraved documents nevertheless which remained probably at least down to 1850 those most generally used in practice.

Yet line-engraving, which had provided such an important and faithful means for the transmission of ideas in the Renaissance and Baroque periods, cannot be absolved of responsibility for Romantic detail. Such works as Nicholson's *Carpentry*, 1849, *The Five Orders* of *The Practical Builder*, 1841, which includes also *Specimens of Gothic Architecture*, or Brown's *Domestic Architecture*, 1842, are all richly illustrated with engravings. The plates are in many cases undoubtedly of considerably earlier preparation. But these works plagiarized one another, borrowed authors' names, changed authors' names and passed through many slightly varying editions in such a bewildering way that it is nearly impossible to date definitely the individual specimens of design. Yet they are much more significant than the compilations they make up. Thus is explained the almost Baroque excellence of certain of the plates in *The Five Orders* devoted to Classical buildings of 1800-1825. For the *Specimens of Gothic Architecture* are distinctly feeble.

An examination of these early treatises of the eclecticism of taste reveals with what extraordinary models the well meaning builder was provided. These works were influential not only in England, but to an even greater degree in America. Other works of the same sort performed a similar service of vulgarization on the Continent. Amusing as they are on occasion they have none of the exquisite character of the Rococo Gothic of Batty Langley. But in 1742 such designs are still to be considered as a late phase of Baroque exoticism in their expression rather than as the early landmark of Romanticism they represent ideologically. Despite their inferior quality the later books must nevertheless not be underestimated as sources. One can not look at the models of features of detail placed by Nicholson before carpenters, or at the "Florentine," "French," or "Anglo-Italian" villas—to choose extreme examples—which are presented so completely by Brown, without realizing that much nineteenth century building, particularly in America, which is supposed to be due solely to the ignorance and perversity of local carpenters and contractors or to the vulgarity of provincial magnates, was derived from these books directly or indirectly. For there were also local imitations such as the two series of Ritch's *The American Architect,* published about 1850, in this case with lithographs of a very low order.

Idzkowski's *Compositions d'architecture,* 1843, indicate that in other outlying regions than America eclecticism began badly. Among his designs, beautifully engraved in Paris, appear all the strangest fabrics of the eighteenth century much magnified in size. Apparently for the most part these had been erected or were to be erected in Poland. They were surely also imitated there. Even the first and most extraordinary in which all the styles of the past were pieced together in one composition had been commanded in Warsaw and may perhaps exist. It could surely never be called a fine example of the eclecticism of style; for it lacked fusion even more completely than Berlage's mausoleum project of 1889. It was moreover the apotheosis of irrationalism.

At the same time the comparatively accurate reproductions of Paris work of the same period in Victor Calliat's *Parallèle,* 1850, also were easily deformed when they served in their turn as sources, and that work itself was already far from the documents it imitated. For the most excellent and serious plates of the books of Percier and Fontaine, Grandjean de Montigny, and Letarouilly, to name but the best, give an entirely different character to Italian Renaissance detail, owing to the hardness and frigid elegance of the nineteenth century engravers, than do measured drawings made since the development of photographic documentation.

Victor Petit and others who made architectural lithographs of François I detail, presented a very curious idea of the style. In considerable part this was due to the fact that the monuments they chose to copy were not at all those which seem to us most typical or even characteristic. They preferred to illustrate work that may be somewhat ambiguously called *lithogénique* as naturally as we do that which is *photogénique.*

When photography began to provide more accurate information on the styles of the past, after about 1875, the Age of Romanticism may be considered to be over for quite another reason than has been given earlier. The possibility of direct comparison of new buildings with old without the intervention of any deforming pictorial process of reproduction made "correctness" attainable at last. It also more significantly caused an inevitable revival of the technical point of view.

But by that time nineteenth century detail existed definitely as a tradition established by the means that the last paragraphs hardly more than suggest. The introduction of the books behind the buildings throws the responsibility for distortion and originality back a step. But it does not explain them any more completely than they have already been explained more generally in the brief account of the beginnings of Romanticism. It remains somewhat a paradox that the nineteenth century which had more architectural documents than any earlier period should have produced more utterly ignorant building.

In a specific case, however, such as the origin of the fretted wooden detail known as Gingerbread, it is possible to follow the matter rather clearly. A comparison of a serious document such as Graffenried and Stürler's *Architecture suisse*, 1844, with the form the chalet manner had already taken in England in Robinson's cowhouses and farms of the previous decade, and with French and German publications of *chalets de necessité* and other park constructions of the sixties and seventies, makes the steps perfectly comprehensible by which this excrescence, owing its prestige to the Romantic cult of the Alps, was developed beyond easy recognition. The eighteenth century discovery of the "sublime" had in this case strange issue. But much Gingerbread owed a great deal also to the Tudor barge-boards of picturesque cottages designed by the less doctrinaire Mediæval Revivalists, and moreover doubtless something to eighteenth century rusticity in general. In the same way the strange skeleton bracket with which the cornices of American frame-houses of the mid-century were almost universally decorated was a reduction and a translation into wood of the Italian Renaissance console. But in the final analysis it was from the English Perpendicular that it acquired its usual droplets and not from the creative *tour de force* of some unsung genius.

It is clearly true as a generality that when the conflict between the two great parties of Romantic Goths and Romantic Grecians resolved itself in the eclecticism of taste, building by donning architectural remnants came to array itself unwittingly according to the principles of the eclecticism of style. The documents were both so inaccurate and so impure that a "French" villa, for example, as Brown's plate proves, might mean almost anything to an Anglo-Saxon, and Idzkowski illustrates what an "English" house meant to Slav. The significance of these labels lies in the facts that Romanticism was coming to believe in national rather than historical classification of styles, and that it was replacing the cult of that which was temporally distant with the cult of that which was merely foreign. The strength was already departing from straight revivalism, but not from the doctrine of imitation.

Building not being a branch of architecture was to the later Romantics even less directly than architecture itself an intellectual activity. There was no integration, no cohesion at all, except in the pictorial point of view and a somewhat arbitrary and sentimental symbolism. The same elements of varied reminiscence with which the founders of the New Tradition became creators were combined so witlessly in the building of the third quarter of the nineteenth century that the result was utter chaos.

Considering that it is the building of the last seventy-five years with which we are chiefly surrounded on account of nineteenth century growth of population and the provision for consequent multiplication of needs, it is no wonder that we look on the immediate past with little pleasure. Thus we turn still to the earlier past as to a Golden Age in the fashion of the Romantics. Moreover we generally deny the Romantics their Classical monuments of the late eighteenth and early nineteenth century because we find them too excellent to be works of a period of decline and disintegration.

With the confusion of the eclecticism of taste in architecture and its perverted reflection in building once established, it has been but futile to attempt on the one hand more and more restraint through good taste and refinement and on the other more and more safety from æsthetic error through more accurate reconstitutions of increasingly varied periods of the Golden Age, as archæology and photography have made increasingly possible. This entire movement, which still continues to some extent in America, has been but negative. The use of handbooks of the styles as of handbooks of etiquette never touches the heart; and Maya skyscrapers are as pointless as Grecian ones. Yet the positive movement of the New Tradition in architecture and its successful attempt to reintegrate building had already begun shortly after the complete triumph of the bloc system of *laissez faire* and the eventual possibility of something approaching "correctness" in the revivals.

Before concluding this account of Romantic architecture there remains to be discussed the Mediæval Revival. Since the Classical Revival has not generally been considered a manifestation of Romanticism the importance of the other has generally been somewhat over-emphasized. Yet it was, as has already been indicated, perhaps more fully characteristic. Its leaders were more than the Classical Revivalists responsible by their work for the anarchy of the later nineteenth century. They were, however, also more responsible in their thinking for the return to order.

CHAPTER FIVE

THE MEDIAEVAL REVIVAL

THE beginning of the Age of Romanticism was more definitely marked by the new interest in the Middle Ages than by the appearance of a stricter and more rigid Classicism. But the eighteenth century Gothic constructions, with the possible exception of Fonthill Abbey, were definitely of a minor and inferior order. The Mediæval Revival, if one may already call it such, was chiefly significant ideologically. Half a century later Mediævalism had gained at least many partial converts and Gothic "barbarity" had come to have as agreeable a flavour as Alpine "horror" to the majority of men. The advance in the study of the non-Classical past was encouraged by nationalism. In France, England and Germany respectively, the Gothic style was considered to be of French, English and German origin. There was with more and better documents less disparity in the accuracy with which Classical and Mediæval monuments could be imitated and there were patriotic reasons for imitating the latter.

But in the meantime the Classical Revival had become an integrated manner with its own canons of correctness. Except in England the net effect of Mediævalism on serious architecture even down to the end of the first third of the nineteenth century was little more than the general acceptance of the imitation of the Italian Renaissance as a respectable modification of the more rigid Classical programme. The Mediæval Revival was so cut off from the immediate past that even later it hardly became an integrated manner even in Germany. Elsewhere its canons of correctness, when it came to have them, were those of one century or another of the distant past, and therefore exceedingly inelastic.

There is certainly, however, no such sequence between the two sorts of revival as has generally been made to appear because of the fact that the more important and enduring monuments of the Mediæval Revival were not erected until well into the second quarter of the nineteenth century. The continuance of Baroque traditions and the greater knowledge of antiquity, as also the ease with which the limited repertory of strictly authentic ancient forms could be modified and expanded by the Renaissance-Renaissance, made it possible for the Classical Revival, taken in the broadest sense, to produce a majority of the finest Romantic buildings. Even as the development of Mediæval archæology came to vie with that of Classical archæology its effect on the mass of actual monuments remained less; and even when eclecticism of taste became generally accepted after 1850 more of the favoured manners were of a Classical than of a Mediæval order. The Mediæval Revival was not posterior to the Classical Revival; but it was always, except possibly in England in the mid-century, the undercurrent. Its great importance lies in the fact that it was a movement more intensely typical of Romanticism and that it stirred passions and opened points of view that were peculiarly new.

The Mediæval Revival produced almost no monuments as fine as those produced by revivals more consonant with what remained of Baroque tradition, and in its best productions it distinctly compromised its own more extreme programmes with certain principles of Classicism. It provided theoretical writers, however, with a stronger and a sounder inspiration and at least prepared a road which led completely away from the Baroque past. It was more disintegrant and more analytical. Doubtless because it was possible in Northern Europe to study Mediæval monuments more intimately and completely than Classical monuments, the Mediæval Revivalists in their writing made somewhat less distinction between architecture and building than the Classicists. Although their theories were generally more valid than their constructions, the latter are not entirely without a certain interest.

Even in France where the dominance of Classicism was more complete than in Germany or England there was a considerable movement that is not altogether summed up in the work of archæologists. There are moreover monuments more interesting and more significant than the later fabrics like the Château de la Reine Blanche of Batty Langley order built in the park of Chantilly in 1826, or such exotic Louis-Philippard fantasies as Fontaine's Romanesquoid chapel of Saint Ferdinand of 1843 and the domed

Gothic chapel at Dreux completed by Lefranc in 1847. (Figure 14.) The later restorations of Viollet-le-Duc at Pierrefonds and elsewhere, to all intents and purposes reconstructions, or the comparatively accurate Gothic churches, of which the best known is one of the earliest, Gau's Sainte Clotilde of 1846 in Paris, are hardly to be considered much more seriously than the Gothic castels of the *romantisme de la lettre*. One on Montmartre was built in 1835 by the comte de l'Escalopier and destroyed in 1882; another on the plain of Passy built by Bridaut must have had about the same term of existence. These castels were closer moreover to the form which the Mediæval Revival effectively took in France.

Lenoir's *Musée des monuments français*, opened in the convent of the Petits Augustins in 1791 and immensely popular from the very first, was not so much a Mediævalist as a nationalist manifestation. For Voltaire modern times opened with his own *Siécle de Louis XIV*; and the theatre costumers of the eighteenth century, when they began to attempt historical accuracy, made no distinction between the Middle Ages and the sixteenth century. Except for such fabrications as the tomb of Héloise and Abélard, still in existence in the cemetery of Père Lachaise in Paris, obviously particularly suited to appeal to Romantic tastes, it was the monuments of the sixteenth century which made apparently the greatest impression in Lenoir's collection.

While the perversity of the more erudite unquestionably led them even in the baron Taylor's *Voyages romantiques et pittoresques dans l'ancienne France*, of which the publication extended from 1820 until 1864, to study earlier and ruder monuments, amateurs in general were more charmed by the elaboration of Late Gothic churches and the prettiness of François I châteaux. Victor Hugo praised the High Gothic to the skies in the preface of 1831 to *Notre Dame de Paris*. Yet even those who found no words more exalted to express their admiration of him than *cathédrale* and even *ogive* doubtless in practice preferred the less noble later forms.

The first serious French history of the national Mediæval architecture, Arcisse de Caumont's *Abécédaire ou rudiment d'archéologie* originally published in 1830 already slighted somewhat the Late Gothic and *a fortiori* the Early Renaissance. This tendency became even more marked with later French historians. But even the Romantics did not accept the archæologists as oracles. As regards what was definitely not antique they were inclined to follow their tastes for the "picturesque," leaving the "sublimity" of the

High Gothic to specialists. Yet even the specialists often began mildly enough. As late as 1835 when in England the reconstruction of the Houses of Parliament in Gothic style was being discussed, Lassus' earliest intransigence was as a student to make measured drawings of Philibert de l'Orme's work at the Tuileries. Viollet-le-Duc in his travels in Italy still somewhat later was content merely to prefer Bramante to Palladio. Yet these two were shortly afterward the most rigidly "High" of all the Romantic Goths and hardly ever did any building which was not reconstruction. Yet had they remained emulators of de l'Orme or Bramante they might have been Romantic architects and not almost entirely theoreticians and restorers.

Just as the Classical Revival in France in practice was from soon after 1800 quite as much characterized by imitation of the Italian Renaissance as by imitation of Roman, and *a fortiori* of Greek antiquity, the Mediæval Revival was in practice pre-eminently a revival of the national version of the Early Renaissance. The development of Mediæval archæology in France with its interests increasingly centred in the twelfth and thirteenth century had little direct connection with executed building, and the significant rationalism that there is in the writing of Viollet-le-Duc found little reflection in the little new building he did. Before the development of full eclecticism of taste, and even after, High Gothic constructions in France were very few. In Paris there are only a handful of Gothic houses built before 1850. In the Place du Caire the *Maison Egyptienne* has but one storey which is Gothic. The *Maison des Gothes* at 116 rue Saint-Martin has decorations on the whole rather Flamboyant.

There were many more constructions before 1850 in Paris that were neither Classical nor Italian, of which the most extraordinary and original was a house in the rue de Richelieu. This is richly decorated with diapers perhaps intended to be Moorish. The ornament is rather fine and yet distinctly *lithogénique*. This house is however wholly exceptional among a large group. The group is distinguished by elaborate decorations of more or less *lithogénique* François I character. This ornament is nevertheless applied—as in the house in the rue de Richelieu—to the regular building formula in which the Classical Revival had continued Baroque tradition. The immense apartment house at 24 rue Linné, another nearly as large built in 1841 by Renaud at 21 Place Saint-Georges, another somewhat less extreme at 34 rue Henri-Monier and two more at the corner of the boulevard Malesherbes and the rue de l'Arcade are characteristic.

The smaller houses such as that at 5 rue Lord Byron, that built in 1841 at 9 rue de Chanaleilles, and that just around the corner from the latter in the rue Vaneau, are more attractive and distinctly more accurate. This is for the French indeed the *architecture romantique* par excellence. For this was the character which the so-called *style troubadour* of the *romanticisme de la lettre* chiefly took and it provided the actual background of the great Romantic writers. In Normand's *Paris moderne*, 1837, there is only one design which is French Renaissance, the house *dite de François I* in the avenue de Tokio erected in 1826 by Biet largely from actual sixteenth century materials transported from Moret. There are many more examples in Normand's two later volumes and a considerable number of buildings in Victor Calliat's *Parallèle* of 1850 are marked by the new fashion, although admittedly in general less than some of the specific monuments already mentioned.

This national Renaissance Revival—to distinguish it thus insufficiently from the more Classical Renaissance-Renaissance—had an even greater success in the country than in Paris. Those seigneurs of the mid-century who inherited really Mediæval châteaux were less fortunate than those of a generation earlier. Then they might have moved a short distance away, as Christopher Hussey's grandfather in England actually did, and if necessary with the aid of a little dynamite surpassed even the effect of the sham donjon of Betz in their Romantic gardens. But the stern archæologists would hardly have praised this and literary leaders as well, such as Victor Hugo, were already warring vigorously on those who demolished Mediæval monuments. If on the other hand the *pair de France* of the Restoration or the July Monarchy possessed a Renaissance château he was free and even urged to restore it so completely that it is to-day practically a reconstruction. If he were a champagne king, or newly rich by one of the processes which Stendhal or Balzac describe, there were apparently many architects to build him an ancestral château of similar style. These mysterious architects of whom as little seems to be known as of those they emulated—even the encyclopædic Elie Brault neglects them in his *Les architectes*—had considerable success as revivalists. Thanks to the restorations at least, with which the same men were doubtless also charged, it is difficult enough to tell their work at times from that which is nominally old. Its character is best studied in the photographs made of Blois during and just after the restoration done considerably later in the eighties. The old work may be very clearly distinguished from that new work which later generations of American architects have often carefully measured and drawn and photographed in the fond belief that it was original.

Under the developed eclecticism of taste of the Second Empire and the Third Republic the Renaissance Revival was able to rival the Néo-Baroque. Its best known work was the enlarged Hôtel de Ville of Paris built after Boccador's building was destroyed by the Commune; its most effective perhaps the Mairie du I Arrondissement of 1859, which balances Saint Germain l'Auxerrois. It was also brought to America by Richard M. Hunt so effectively that it came to be considered as much the style of the Vanderbilts as of the Valois.

But if the buildings of the real Gothicists were few and inferior beside those in general less known works with which the last paragraphs have dealt, Viollet-de-Duc at least was a significant theorist and developed in his writing a more far-reaching rationalism than that of any of the Classicists. Yet even Viollet-de-Duc usually avoided practising what he preached. Moreover he seems to have had little good effect upon the general development of French architecture after 1850. In one house built in the rue Berlin—before 1850, since it is in Calliat—he gave, however, a rather brilliant demonstration of the application of his theories to city building. This was much less tied by precedent than similar contemporary Gothic Revival work in England. But his simplified detail of almost New Tradition character and his exaggerated emphasis on structural elements such as relieving arches above lintels, although excellent in the occasion, was parodied afterward well into the twentieth century, as Labrouste's Bibliothèque Saint Geneviève was not. Although Viollet-le-Duc was internationally the most famous of all Mediæval Revivalists his English contemporaries are on the whole more significant. For out of the Gothic Revival there developed in England a revival of the craft of building, while out of the Mediæval Revival, even in the wide sense of the last paragraphs, there developed in France only a few rather subordinate manners of the eclecticism of taste.

Aside from that which has been particularly discussed the most successful was a sort of Richardsonian Romanesque. Those who built occasional churches in this manner had usually neither genius nor even much talent. Laloux, more particularly a late continuer of the Néo-Baroque, was nearly as successful as any in his church of Saint Martin at Tours. One monument alone stands out, the Sacré Cœur, and that was completed only in 1910 by

Lucien Magne, elsewhere a follower of the Art Nouveau, although it was begun just after 1871 by Abbadie, to whom the general design of all but the tower is due. The site, the highest point of Montmartre, is unequalled even by that of the Arc de Triomphe or the Trocadéro. Thus this strange white edifice of somewhat eclectic Mediæval inspiration and considerable real originality seems to float over Paris like the image of a celestial city of white cloudlike domes, an auspicious sign to Catholics and quite the reverse to anti-clerical politicians. It cannot be said to anticipate the New Tradition so definitely is it a direct product of the last phase of Romanticism. Those who have approached it have only found disappointment in its coarse detail and awkward arrangement; and it is notorious that Abbadie in order to justify his considerable originality restored to an extent equivalent to reconstruction the old church of Saint Front of Périgueux in imitation of the Montmartre basilica. Lassus and Viollet-le-Duc were less outrageous even in what they did to the Sainte Chapelle.

In concluding the account of the Mediæval Revival in France it should be mentioned that Viollet-le-Duc, although he was one of the few architects among the archæologists of the mid-century, was not the only one who drew from the study of the Middle Ages intelligent ideas on the architecture of the present and the future. Merimée, de Laborde and de Voguë all went so far as to interest themselves in the possibilities of the use of metal. This is far more than can be said for Ruskin in England. But it was Viollet-le-Duc particularly who laid down general principles. Moreover he, more than any other, made the study of the Middle Ages respectable in France among architects. He was unable to break the official system of Classical education; but after his day it was less exclusive. Official Mediævalism would surely have been no improvement, if one may judge from the damage something equivalent to it has done in the field of restoration even since Viollet-le-Duc's day.

The labours of the Mediæval Revivalists in America were even less productive of good buildings than in France, and the movement before the time of Richardson was but a reflection of the Gothic Revival in England. Upjohn's Trinity Church, built in New York in 1839, nevertheless, compares very favourably with the best English work. Renwick's immense Saint Patrick's, however, built in the mid-century, is cold, awkward and lacking in scale or dignity. In America, more than even in England, the effect of Victorian Gothic architecture on building was disastrous. Yet it was in the Victorian Gothic that Richardson first worked on his return from Paris, and even his Romanesque Revival was only because of his creative ability a first manifestation of the New Tradition and not merely a parallel branch of Mediæval revivalism in general. In the hands of his followers it became indeed like the similar movement in France, but a bloc within the system of the eclecticism of taste. It was moreover very shortly cut off by his death and that of Root, who alone might really have continued it as a developing phase of the New Tradition.

Regrettably it must be stated that the architecture of the last half of the nineteenth century in America, outside Richardson and the men after him who belonged consciously or unconsciously to the New Tradition, was perhaps even more generally worthless than elsewhere. Engineering and industrial building was no better than in Europe, and city building was definitely worse. The general influence of the English architecture of craftsmanship arrived hardly before the twentieth century except in the Eastlake form with its Néo-Gingerbread. The increasing restraint of the nineties which followed was little less futile than in France.

America, however, has produced the last Romantic Mediæval Revivalist, Ralph Adams Cram. He retains all the fervour of the 1830's and '40's and a certain distinction as an historical and archæological writer. Yet even his Cathedral of St. John the Divine in New York now in process of completion will doubtless despite its correctness and its scale seem to foreign visitors of a not distant future as incredible as Lefranc's Orléans Chapel. It will unfortunately be less easy for them to study it in contemporary prints. Feininger would hardly choose it for his woodcuts and Wanda Gag finds the Gingerbread of New York Elevated Stations more *lithogénique*. It does not appear that the visitors who come to see skyscrapers have been aware of its existence; at least their impressions are not recorded. The French, however, have politely listened while its architect compared it to their own work of the thirteenth century, perhaps even in a hall decorated in the manner of the Exposition of 1925.

The Mediæval Revival, in Germany, being even less than in France concerned with the Gothic, was vastly more successful. The French, Latin in culture, found in their own Renaissance a compromise which did not shock too greatly their Classical training, and yet at the same time appealed to that Nordicism which in Romantic literature had been early exploited in

Ossian. The Germans, having only artificial Latin culture, found in Italy everything that appealed to the Mediæval side of Romanticism as well as all that appealed to the Classical side. Chateaubriand, it is true, grew fervid before the spectacle of Greece, quite as much as before the spectacle of the Middle Ages; and his Christianity was of a somewhat pagan order. Sainte Beuve stated somewhat later that it was to be Romantic to seek antiquity at its Greek sources. But the Classical Romantic par excellence was Goethe. Not only did he somewhat indirectly fill a second tomb in the marquis de Girardin's park; he also with more serious consequences sent a whole century of Germans off to follow the paths of his *Italienische Reise.* This had produced at once as well as a book that extraordinary and symbolic portrait by Tischbein at the Städel Institut at Frankfurt in which the sage of Weimar sits with a sheet thrown over his ordinary clothes upon an antique fragment against the background of Alban hills. The sage himself moreover made picturesque sketches, even with fabricks. Later the *Italienische Reise* developed the work of painters as different as Böcklin and von Marees and very nearly all the best architecture of the mid-nineteenth century. Potsdam, which had been a second France in the Rococo period under Frederick the Great, became a second Italy under Frederick William IV.

There was of course some activity more parallel to that of Viollet-le-Duc in France and of the English Gothic Revivalists. Cologne Cathedral was completed very plausibly in the original style and G. G. Scott was called from England to build the Nicolaikirche in Hamburg. There was also much unfortunate restoration of old monuments. But the tone of the Mediæval Revival as of the Classical Revival was set by Schinkel. Although he was already almost as much an eclectic of taste as an eclectic of style, his Mediævalism was largely Italianate. Yet he made a design for a domed Gothic mausoleum, that was very effective on paper. It was however somewhat dangerously like the Chapelle d'Orléans and certainly quite as inaccurate. He had also worked in the English domestic Gothic Revival manner as well at Babelsberg. His followers furthermore sometimes built Tudor cottages.

The most extraordinary manifestation of English influence, however, was in the premiated and executed designs for the Maximilianstrasse in Munich. In the competition of 1851 the programme set by Maximilian II required the invention of a new style. By reaction against the universal Italianism a rather eclectic Perpendicular was offered and strangely enough accepted. It was gay rather than gloomy; but it was much less excellent as architecture than the Tuscan and other Italian forms with which von Gärntner had in the previous quarter century built the Staatsbibliotek, the Ludwigskirche and the University in the Ludwigstrasse. The road to the Wagnerian horrors of Ludwig II lay definitely open. But in general Bavaria and the rest of South Germany were as Italianate as Prussia.

Ludwig Lange was a prominent architect who worked in several cities in Germany and in Greece. He was born in 1808 and was after 1847 an influential professor of architecture in Munich. His work was very typical of his generation, well massed, rational in the general composition and not badly built. But it was as vulgar and awkward in the usually Mediæval Italian detail as the contemporary French Néo-Baroque. Heinrich Hübsch, born in 1795, was a far superior architect of the same general order. His activity was particularly centred at Karlsruhe. He achieved a more integrated manner than Lange, and was both more sparing and more successful in his use of detail. His churches were particularly dignified and impressive; but his city building was also excellent. Even his unusually ornate theatre in Karlsruhe had a real character due to the frankness with which he expressed the plan in the exterior massing. Many of the railroad stations built in South Germany in this period followed his manner rather successfully. They lack the significance of Hittorf's Gare du Nord and the polychromy of the brick can never have been effective; but that at Munich and that at Würzburg are rather excellent, particularly in contrast to those of Berlin.

While the Mediæval Revival was in France chiefly Mediæval in being nationalistic and the Gothic Revival in England also preferred those styles of the past which were most definitely English, in Germany there was not until rather late in the nineteenth century much imitation of the specifically German past—not even, as has been said, of the Gothic, although it still generally was held to have been of German origin. Yet the chalet manner which like all the rest had first been introduced in mild and elegant form by Schinkel was surely at least Bavarian or Tyrolese quite as much as Swiss. Chalets in general, and Gingerbread derived from the chalet manner, became distinctly popular. In the mid-century the latter was even used in the decoration both of the cottages that were "English" and the villas that were "Italian" with unfortunate results. However, in the summer palace built for Maximilian II at Berchtesgaden by Lange, the chalet character was less marked than in some of the villas about Berlin designed by architects who continued more directly the Schinkel tradition. For these sometimes wore Gingerbread with all the courage of a Prussian in *Lederhosen*.

Fortunately, however, the rather brilliant group working particularly at Potsdam for the kings of Prussia, built more generally extraordinarily sound Italian villas. Their Tudor cottages and Oberbayrisch chalets are somewhat incidental. Hesse, Stüler and Hitzig were all pupils of Schinkel continuing various of his manners through the mid-century. As has already been said, Stüler, for example, was on occasion in his museums a rigorous Classicist and the others in city building preferred something more Grecian to the picturesque Italian manner with which alone they had great success.

The best of the group was Ludwig Persius, born in 1804 before Hitzig and after Hesse and Stüler. He died very young in 1845 in Rome. He was also eclectic in taste, finishing Schinkel's English castle at Babelsberg, adding wings to the Rococo palace of Sanssouci, and building Classical churches and Moorish mills. But in his more characteristic constructions, of which there are many in the royal park at Potsdam, he showed himself the great genius of the Italian villa manner and an intelligent precursor of the eclecticism of style. His power-houses, his dairies, his gardeners' houses, even his Early Christian Friedenskirche, are truly fine works of Romantic architecture. (Figure 15.) They do not, like the constructions of the other men, need to be studied in contemporary plates, such as those of the *Architektonisches Skizzenbuch,* 1859, in order to be fully appreciated. Yet Persius was completely a picturesque architect, and the relations of his buildings to their surroundings and those surroundings themselves were always carefully and indeed skilfully studied. Von Arnim was still another man who aided Frederick William IV to mark Potsdam no less effectively, if very differently, than Frederick the Great a century earlier. He used more detail than Persius but it was of excellent and rather original character.

Beside the Mediæval Revivals of the continent which compromised so generally in executed monuments with the Classical Revival, the Gothic Revival in England appears of an extraordinary intransigence. It was much complicated in architecture by parallel developments hardly distinguishable from it in religion and sociology. In the mid-century it became exceedingly difficult to tell whether one should build in the Gothic style because it was, as the case might be, Roman Catholic or Anglican, or because workmen are made miserable by the necessity of working on Classical buildings. But by 1850 it was almost universally accepted among the leaders in every walk of life that one must build in Gothic, and disputes were chiefly about such details as whether a two light window was not dangerously symbolical of the Socinian heresy. Even the Socinian Unitarians, however, built in Gothic, avoiding of course three-light windows.

It had not always been thus and the productions of the early Gothic Revival are, if vastly less correct, the more agreeable for having been taken less seriously. (Figure 53.) Neither Batty Langley nor his imitators at Vauxhall and in the shop fronts and the furniture of the mid-eighteenth century did much direct harm to the established Palladian architecture. Their work was at least light and diverting as the vagaries of the Rococo had been. Few indeed can always distinguish Chinese Chippendale from Chippendale Gothic and if in a given case one decides on the latter the design in the books will very likely be labelled Turkish or Indian.

Those who attempted more elaborate constructions in the second half of the eighteenth century were for the most part dilettantes concerned chiefly to amuse themselves and mystify the public, typical *milords anglais*. They demanded of Classical architects, such as Chambers and Adam, Mediæval mansions that should be much more mansions than they were Mediæval. This was done quite consciously and openly by Payne Knight, one of the two great writers on the "picturesque," even at a somewhat late date. Wyatt, just before the beginning of the nineteenth century, began to give a certain sort of monumentality to the lordly "Gothick taste." Contemporaneously the first ecclesiastical attempts were made with infinitely less success. Being suspected of Popery they met with little general approval. There were some grounds for this. Bishop Milner, the learned author of the *History of Winchester*, who built in that city in 1792 a Gothic chapel, was a Roman Catholic. His architect was J. C. Carter, his chief contemporary rival as a serious archæologist. The chapel still exists, but it is hardly the product that might have been expected of such a collaboration, nor an æsthetic menace to Protestantism.

The younger generation in the first decades of the nineteenth century did not advance much beyond the later works of Wyatt, such as Belvoir Castle, extensively remodelled about 1825. Nash had built castellated or Baronial mansions in Ireland as well as the rustic cottages earlier mentioned. However, neither he nor Wyatt's nephew, Wyatville, added much more than bulk to Windsor Castle. Even the term "Baronial" seems to have been an invention of Walpole's as the manner itself would suggest.

Other typical monuments showed either, like Cundy's Hawarden Castle of 1809, the extreme barrenness and gloominess by which the Baronial manner was usually marked, or like Porden's Eaton Hall of about the same date, an extravagance based on Perpendicular ecclesiastical building. For in England, as later in France, the national style of the sixteenth century was favoured. The elder Smirke, also, like earlier Classicists tried his hand in both the Baronial and the Tudor. But "the revived taste for Mediæval architecture was yet caviare to the multitude," in the somewhat trite simile of Eastlake, the first historian of the Gothic Revival and the inventor of Néo-Gingerbread.

After Sir Walter Scott reached the height of his fame it became more widespread. For it was generally known that he lived in a castellated house. This was built in 1812 by Atkinson in the Baronial manner—indeed, unusually effectively, with markedly Scotch character, so that many later visitors have doubtless thought it old. Gothic, as the books already mentioned which were published in Soane's lifetime indicated, became something to apply to villas in order to achieve the "picturesque." More important for the developed Gothic Revival were the vast quantities of publication of real Mediæval work in the first quarter of the nineteenth century. The better architects of the twenties and thirties were primarily archæologists, who applied their incomplete knowledge to occasional churches. These stand out only by comparison with the excessively low standard of what is called Commissioner's Gothic. This was used, extraordinarily enough for economic reasons, in many new churches built by the State at this time.

The real Gothic Revival began in the later thirties with the building of the Houses of Parliament and the appearance of A. W. Pugin. He was a fiery and worthy champion; yet like Milner somewhat handicapped by his conversion to Rome. The later Gothic Revival produced vast quantities of controversial literature, but only a small amount of building which is correct and not altogether without intrinsic value. Even eighteenth century Baronial was preferable to nineteenth century Decorated. But the even originally *lithogénique* Decorated was in general the most favoured for imitation. The triumphs of the movement were summed up in Eastlake's *History of the Gothic Revival,* published in 1879. It is not without interest to compare this account with *The Gothic Revival* by Kenneth Clark. Writing in 1928 the latter finds singularly little good to be said of even the most accurate executed monuments.

In spite of its perverse vigour this very English manifestation was distinctly less successful in the quality of the work produced than the Mediæval Revivals of the Continent. For even the Early English had been in its own day vaguely Victorian, or at least restoration has made it appear so. When in the mid-century the experiment of borrowing from the Italian Gothic had been unwisely launched by Ruskin, it became indeed difficult to tell serious architecture from the most vulgar sort of building. Yet curiously enough the renaissance of craftsmanship which developed later in the period of transition from the Age of Romanticism to the New Tradition in architecture was to be, aside from theory, the best product of the continuing Gothic Revival, by that time considerably dissolved in the general eclecticism of taste.

The Palace of Westminster—that is the Houses of Parliament—was begun in the Perpendicular style in 1837. On it Barry, the best and at the time the most eclectic of the later generation of Classicists, had as collaborator Pugin, the real leader of the Gothicists. It has already been once mentioned in connection with the former. It is probably, as Clark rather implies than states, the best monument of architecture of the mid-century produced in England by either Classicists or Gothicists. It marked, moreover, the triumph of the Gothic Revival in England.

Those who are further interested in a movement so little productive of good or original buildings will find it fully treated from opposing points of view in the books of Eastlake and Clark. For paradoxically enough it has been more thoroughly studied than any other phase of the architecture of Romanticism except the earlier Classical Revivals—usually when thus studied not considered directly Romantic at all. Rather therefore than to continue the discussion of further actual executed work, the account of Romantic architecture may be more fairly concluded with a significant example of the writing of the Mediævalists in England; particularly as the writing of Viollet-le-Duc and others on the Continent has merely been mentioned.

CHAPTER SIX

THE ARCHITECTURE OF THE FUTURE: 1857

THE quotations which form the bulk of the present chapter are taken from G. G. Scott's *On Gothic Architecture*, 1857. The section which he devotes to the future of architecture is on the whole more instructive as to the prospective vision of the mid-century in England than anything in the works of Ruskin, the greatest critic of the period, or of Pugin, its most conscientious and perhaps its greatest architect.

For Ruskin was not an architect nor, except in the Old Testament sense, a prophet. He was so exceedingly categorical that all who are not entirely beguiled by his style must be frequently irritated by his extraordinary belief in the validity of the Bible as a guide to æsthetics. Moreover he tended to involve his architecture with his socialism. He nevertheless remains one of the few great critics of architecture. It is his permanent value indeed that makes his writing so incompletely representative of the time.

Pugin was of course very much an architect. But with him architecture was distinctly entangled with religious controversy. He was nevertheless in his ideas the most original of the English Gothic Revivalists. To him is due the first presentation of the most of the theories of Ruskin and other later writers. Scott always acknowledged him as his master. Yet many proposals of his chapter on *The Architecture of the Future* would surely have roused Pugin's ire. While Pugin was a stormy petrel and the founder of a movement, Scott was a practical and materially successful man who spoke as the head of a movement already generally accepted. He was indeed an astonishingly busy architect, producing from 1840 until his death such a steady stream of buildings that he must have had difficulty in finding time to write. It cannot be said that his books are more important than those of Ruskin or Pugin; but they are certainly more urbane. Even though his ideas were seldom original they were perhaps therefore more widely representative of the intelligent theories of the Mediævalists, not only of England, but of the Continent as well. His writing was moreover directly concerned with architecture and hardly at all with religion or socialism. Also it avoids the more dogmatic rationalism of the Mediævalists who could not see beyond a thirteenth century vault.

Scott felt assured that the forward looking men within his own movement and those among the opposing Classicists were really seeking a new architecture. "We differ in this—that one thinks the false step"—the Renaissance of the sixteenth century and the succeeding related style-phases— "must be retraced before we can get into the right groove, and that the indigenous style of the race"—as a Romantic nationalist he of course held the Gothic to be that—"must be our *point de départ,* the other views this as a repetition of the original error and holds that the point from which the future is to start must be that (however false) at which we now find ourselves.

"The peculiar characteristic of the present day as compared with all former periods is that we are acquainted with the history of art. . . . The Roman, it is true, was conscious of his copyism of the Greek." But "it is reserved for us, alone of all the generations of the human race, to know perfectly our own standing point, and to look back upon the entire history of what has gone before us, tracing out all the changes in the arts of the past as clearly as if every scene in its long drama were enacted before our eyes." It should be remarked that this is but "reserved" to us. Such complete knowledge— as the insufficiency of the present study of Romantic architecture particularly indicates—we can only approach as a limit. Scott feared that our unique position was a "hindrance rather than a help to us as artists." This was perfectly true in his day and for long afterward. For less thought was given to the "standing point" than to the arts of the past whose long drama was moreover in general very ill interpreted.

"In all periods of genuine art no one thought much of the past,—each devoted his energies wholly to the present. Their efforts were consequently *concentrated.* . . . " All the same, unless there were to be a return to the vandalism which in fifth century Greece filled up the foundations of the Parthenon with the art of preceding centuries, or which in the thirteenth century in Western Europe tore down Romanesque cathedrals ruthlessly in order to replace them with Gothic, this *"concentration"* had to be foregone. It is a price that has to be paid for catholicity of taste and intelligent men have in the long run become reconciled to paying it. Universality of historic sense is one of the most valuable and durable inheritances from the **Age of Romanticism**, and Futurism, which hardly touched architecture, is now forgotten. "It is self-evident that it"—the architecture of the future— "must receive much of its colouring from this peculiar characteristic. . . . It is for us to guide that influence"—of our knowledge of the past—"by subjecting it to our intellect."

Scott was aware that "the first natural effect of working with this vivid *panorama* of the past placed constantly in our view" was to make architects "content to pluck the flowers of history without cultivating any of our own." Indeed a decade later we find Scott himself simultaneously building Glasgow University in Early Decorated and St. Pancras Railroad Station in Venetian Gothic—that is the façade. There was as well some excellent engineering. But it was much less an integral part of the whole than in Hittorf's Gare du Nord, or, indeed, in many less important stations with small artistic pretensions.

But Scott's theory was better than his practice. "We have to lay down a plan for the future—to choose a distinct course and to follow it with determination; and, having fixed on the line we will take, to develop and enrich it with our utmost energy—using information of other minds as a means of amplifying and giving scope to the art which it is our aim to generate, and never suffering it to allure us from the path we have selected." This is an amazingly good description of the programme of an architecture really eclectic in style as the manner of the New Tradition which succeeded the eclecticism of taste proved to be. Indeed Scott himself makes in a footnote the distinction between the so-called eclecticism—the eclecticism of taste—of "choosing for each building just what style" the architect "may fancy"—which was in truth the method of Scott quite as much as of the rest of his contemporaries—and the real eclecticism—the eclecticism of style —"in the sense of borrowing from all we know of art elements wherewith to enrich, amplify, and render more perfect that style we have laid down as our nucleus and groundwork."

Later Modern architecture moreover has united "the two great natural principles of construction—the lintel and the arch"; while it has "embraced, and that heartily, the two leading forms—the round and the pointed arch," quite as he urged. Of much greater significance was the brief paragraph in which he insisted that "in great engineering works, other curves, as the ellipse, the cycloid, etc., are admissible, as mechanical conditions may suggest, and though unpleasing on a small scale where it is obvious that other forms would answer, they always seem to satisfy the eye where they are demanded by mechanical laws," and that "our architecture, then, must embrace within its pale all these forms of arch." The reincorporation of engineering and *a fortiori* of building with architecture was taken for granted by a Mediæval Revivalist in theory as it would less naturally have been by a Classical Revivalist. The reverse was however at least as frequently true in practice, as the work of Labrouste and Hittorf indicates.

In the matters of roofs and windows Scott expected the greatest freedom to prevail despite his own natural preference for high pitch and mullions. It may appear that in a discussion of the future of architecture "freedom" is a safe guess and that the fulfilment of this could hardly redound to the credit of Scott as a prophet. However, it should be remarked that whoever writing in the Early Renaissance prophesied freedom for windows and roofs would have been wrong. So incidentally, it seems certain, would be any one thus prophesying to-day.

As to ornament Scott was in general misled by the general nineteenth century delusion that all representative art must more and more approach nature. In such a passage as follows, however, where he was thinking technically rather than philosophically, he came closer to foreshadowing the type of ornament which eventually prevailed.

"I need hardly say that all disputes between flatness and relief, and between natural and conventional drawing, would vanish with the advent of such a style. It would probably be seen that every variety of treatment from the simple outline to the most perfectly finished painting, has its place; and that, while no circumstances will excuse the caricaturing and deforming of the human figure—the visible exponent of the image of God—it will still appear . . . that different architectural positions will dictate greater or less degree of severity and rigidity of treatment, or will leave it free and unfettered." In the face of Mediæval religious art the theological reference must appear rather curious coming from an avowed Mediævalist. Yet although Scott was the author of a *Plea for the Faithful Restoration of Ancient Churches,* he would appear hardly to have approached them except for the purpose of reconstructing them with what to-day must appear as perverse unfaithfulness.

Scott considered polychromy to be a "noble field for development and invention" that must be "worked out afresh: at present it seems to be in a state of hopeless confusion, but . . . is far from being as hopeless as it appears. . . . We need a master mind which can grasp the principles of all great art and which out of the immense fund of material left us by the Greek, the Roman, the Byzantine, the mediæval, and the oriental decorators, can sift out all that is good . . . and out of it generate a perfect style worthy of the highest efforts of which art is capable and embracing every kind of coloured decoration of which architecture is susceptible." In actuality this led to the appalling Albert Memorial which Scott built six years later. More intelligently carried out it proved nevertheless to be an excellent programme.

Scott's architecture of the future was of course to be formed about a nucleus of the "pointed styles" from which it was to differ "not only through expressing the ideas of a new age, but also from its comprehensiveness." For "a living art has marvellous facility for the admission of incongruous ideas and of harmonizing them with itself." It was, however, distinctly not the High Gothic of their respective countries which served the founders of the New Tradition as a nucleus. This was specifically recommended by Scott; but it was rather the Romanesque for Richardson, Berlage, and Fischer, for example; rationalized Classicism for Wagner and Perret, and still other styles for other men. Scott's more general plea that "not only the different varieties of the architecture of Western Europe should be laid under contribution but the great Eastern branch of Christian Art be brought to aid our own," was a more useful proposal.

To this retrospective element of inheritance from the past "will be added, or rather on this foundation will be built the creations of the *prospective* element. . . . All the changes in the state and feeling of society which have taken place, or are yet to arise (unless indeed such changes be vicious), must be provided for. All inventions and discoveries must be brought under tribute and every new material or mode of applying it must be made subservient to the one great end." The style of the future "must be also universal in its applicability," but "its root must be in the temple. At first sight it would, unhappily, appear that, however earnestly we might wish such to be the origin and growth of our future architecture, nothing could more thoroughly belie the spirit of the age whose God, as Mr. Owen Jones tells us, is *Mammon*." Alas, earnestness was unavailing and Mr. Owen Jones was somewhat supported. The root of the new architecture was in no church, hardly even in Richardson's Brattle Square, but more definitely in Berlage's Amsterdam Exchange and Wagner's banks.

"The style must embrace also"—in addition to architecture—"engineering works,—as bridges, viaducts, and railway constructions . . . warehouses and factories . . . agricultural buildings and labourers' cottages." All this indeed came true. By the very process of "making any one of these buildings affect the character of another," which Scott disapproved, a later manner has already been born which has its roots in the engineering works and labourers' cottages toward which he was thus patronizing. What would Mr. Jones say and how would Mr. Scott feel with regard to this architecture of the New Pioneers? Indeed, in the popular ideology of protest the Machine has replaced Mammon, and Henry Adams already included in his *Prayer to the Virgin of Chartres* a subsidiary *Prayer to the Dynamo*.

The architecture of the future was to be "eminently practical," in keeping with the *"practical character"* of the age, and *"straight forward."* "It must not strive unduly after artistic effects—it must avoid fantastic and strange forms; it must have a simple primary aim at utility; at, in the first place thoroughly and in the best way providing for the object for which the building is erected; and, secondly, at expressing that purpose in its architectural aspect; superadding to this so much of beauty, of artistic form, and of picturesqueness, as is evidently consistent with its purpose, and as naturally results from the forms which convenience dictates."

In this case Scott would seem to have looked too far ahead. The preceding passage is truer of the architecture which is succeeding the New Tradition. He who was to design the Albert Memorial might also have been expected to realize that a manner which was free to borrow elements from the entire past would produce unexpected hybrids such as the "fantastic and strange forms" that Germany delighted in during the years of Expressionism just after the War. Further in this connection Scott makes the complaint against the young architects of his day which has since been made against those of the early twentieth century: that they "laboured to produce intentional queerness and artistic ugliness." This form of vituperation is still much used even against the Baroque as well as generally when the timid desire to impugn the good faith of the bold. It was nevertheless not unjust with regard to certain architects of his day, such, for example, as Frank Furness of Philadelphia. Even the somewhat fuller and more serious explanations already offered here, moreover, will not seem to dispose so neatly of the building of Scott's day and the succeeding quarter century.

Scott's architecture of the future was to be as well the leading exponent of a "great and catholic system" by which all the arts should be upraised. Indeed, as he had already recommended in speaking of ornament, the New Tradition came in its decorative detail to make the fullest use of painting and sculpture. As independent arts, however, they reacted definitely against this reassertion of their dependence, usually disowning in the course of their search of "purity" the modern ornamental work which was willing to reassume that position of subservience to architecture that much of the finest sculpture and painting of the past had naturally held. Nevertheless, there has been a parallel development in these arts of architectonic qualities. Through the various forms of Cubism this eventually was to be partly instrumental in determining the character of the manner of the New Pioneers during its inception in the years of the War and immediately afterward.

As to the way in which his architecture of the future was to come, Scott was not far wrong. "The two great schools of architecture"—Classic and Gothic—"will probably run on for years collaterally. In each there will be a servile and a developing party and in each the latter will be ever gaining the ascendancy." Finally with the introduction of new materials and inventions, the renewal of detail and of colouring, "they will unite in a style infinitely more Gothic than Classic." The result of this fusion actually was by analogy more Late Classical than Mediæval; yet in that the New Tradition was to be generally picturesque and lacking in fixed rules, even his extreme conclusion was not altogether unjustified. In adopting Ruskin's suggestion of the Italian Gothic as a compromise nucleus Scott certainly made a serious error. The use of Italian Gothic in England was perhaps the least fertile in good building of all the stylistic flirtations of the nineteenth century. Italianate Mediævalism was only successful in Germany. Even there it was seldom Gothicist and the "streaky bacon" polychromy was no more admirable than in England.

Scott's lack of support was hardly—as he protested—what delayed for almost half a century the appearance of a really new manner. In 1857 a considerably fuller eclecticism of taste than that of the first half of the nineteenth century was only beginning to finally exhaust the energies of Romantic revivalism. On the whole, however, Scott's outline was valid. The further examination of architecture of the New Tradition will indicate how much a prophecy his programme actually was.

It is particularly significant moreover that Scott was willing to accept, at least tacitly, that a new architecture demanded a really new æsthetic and that this æsthetic would not necessarily agree with any past æsthetic or even with the common denominator of all past æsthetics—if that be not zero. Romantic æsthetic theoreticians never dared go so far. In a sense there had not been since the end of the Baroque any general set of coherent judgments of architecture which could include fairly all the new tendencies actually being manifested. The establishment of a solid new æsthetic system wholly distinct from that of the Baroque required much conscious or unconscious analytical investigation. The foundations of such new systems are never laid without a more or less long and tedious undermining of the previously existent structure.

By an ever widening process of disintegration, the Age of Romanticism eventually destroyed the validity of the Baroque æsthetic which had long continued unconsciously. The next coherent style-phase, the New Tradition, was to perform along much the lines of Scott's *Architecture of the Future* a first and rather loose reintegration both in principle and in practice. The latest phase, the manner of the New Pioneers, is even perhaps the first of a truly new style. For it is carrying reintegration so much further that its æsthetic system is already more definite in form than that of the Baroque and comparable rather to those of the great styles of the earlier past.

PART TWO
THE NEW TRADITION

CHAPTER SEVEN

THE TRANSITION

THE Age of Romanticism came to no sudden end. Indeed, as we are in America too well aware, the full eclecticism of taste in which it had culminated by 1850 still to some extent continues. The date 1875 somewhat arbitrarily set in the opening general discussion of Romantic architecture was still within the period of transition. Richardson it is true between 1870 and his death in 1886 raised single-handed his Romanesque Revival into an integrated and eclectic architecture, filling it may be remarked the general requirements of Scott's programme. In retrospect his work appears to belong more to the New Tradition than to the final phase of Romanticism. But the New Tradition made no general appearance before the middle of the nineties, and even a decade later transitional movements were still producing among their finest monuments.

Several of the best architects working in the second half of the nineteenth century, such as Richardson, Cuijpers, and Wagner, precursors at least and even to a certain extent founders of the New Tradition, are better studied not in isolation but in connection with the national development of twentieth century architecture in America, Holland and Austria. On the other hand the two chief transitional developments, that of architectural craftsmanship in England, and that of metal construction in France, are related generally rather than specifically with what followed. The one constituted primarily a reintegration of building; the other a reintegration of engineering. In the work of Richardson in the seventies, however, there was already that reintegration of architecture itself with which the full New Tradition opened some twenty years later in Holland, Austria and Germany.

In the year 1851 two significant events had occurred: the first construction of the Crystal Palace in London, and Maximilian's competition for a new style of architecture in Munich. The former initiated the line which the transition was to take in France; the later, despite the mediocrity of its eclectic use of the Perpendicular, suggested vaguely the line which the transition was to take in England. In the first case there was a direct continuance, as the constructions at the Paris Expositions of 1855 and 1867 sufficiently indicate. In the second case there was of course none. The building of the Maximilianstrasse is distinctly inferior to that of von Gärtner or von Klenze; and Anne at least nominally, certainly no Wittelsbach, was the royal patron of the renewed craft of building in England.

In 1859, two years after the appearance of G. G. Scott's book, William Morris built the Red House; almost certainly without particular thought of the *Architecture of the Future*. The architect was Philip Webb, and the manner for reasons somewhat *ex post facto* soon came to be called Queen Anne. This has been considered very justly as the first modern country house. It was free and comparatively organic in planning, distinctly picturesque in general composition, and as moderately eclectic in the minor architectural features as had been some of the simple or elegant villas published in the books of the first half century. Unlike them, however, it represented a highly intellectual æsthetic effort; and even more unlike them, it was the excellence and good sense of its construction which was chiefly remarkable. Despite the somewhat Mediæval effect which was intended, sash-windows were used as being more practical. The execution of the brick walls and the tile roof was of the best order, renewing dead but authentic traditions. The simple detail was excellent in craftsmanship.

The decoration of the interior, in which Morris had the assistance of his friends the Pre-Raphaelite painters, was not only very rich but quite the best of its day to be found anywhere. It was indeed in the preparation of the furnishings of his house that Morris began that revival of the English decorative arts which had in the nineties such an important influence on the Continent. His furnishing although more or less Mediæval in inspiration was very different from that which Pugin just before his death had prepared for the Exposition of 1851. Pugin's interiors, of which the character may be judged from those in the Houses of Parliament, had marked the furthest triumphant of the Gothic Revival. Being sanctioned by the impeccable Albert himself this triumph finally destroyed all lingering eighteenth century traditions of design in furniture and decoration. Even in France the *style troubadour* of the thirties and forties had done the work of disintegration less completely. Even in the next decades, despite her Scotch descent, Eugénie does not seem to have amused herself with the design of plaid oilcloth as did another empress at Balmoral. Eugénie's apartments indeed were in what came to be known in America as the "Louis Styles."

Morris was a poet, a socialist and a Mediævalist; but he was also a practical man. A Morris chair may even to-day be preferred on mechanistic grounds to the latest metal furniture of the New Pioneers. Morris's ornament moreover is usually preferable to the Art Nouveau of which it unwittingly aided the inception, as also to the later Expressionistic and geometrical efforts of the New Tradition. Even for the vulgarizer of Morris's idea, Eastlake, whose *Hints on Household Taste,* first published in 1872, wrought such particular havoc by introducing Néo-Gingerbread in America, there is some little good to be said if he be studied at the source. He was a liberal rather than a literal follower of the Gothic Revival of which he was the historian and some of his designs previous to being executed in Manchester or Birmingham were simple and free renderings of excellent traditional forms.

In France the reintegration of engineering did not begin so early and it had much less effect on the building arts in general than the revival of craftsmanship in England. In many ways the situation in Paris, still very much an artistic capital, was typical, however, of conditions in the rest of the world. There is much even in what Gromort writing on the period of 1870 to 1900 in his *Histoire abrégée de l'architecture au XIXe siècle en France* that is true of England. A considerable quotation, in which he, as a professor in the Ecole des Beaux Arts, denies its utter futility, may serve moreover to give balance to an account otherwise perhaps too negligent of the continuing eclecticism of taste in architecture.

"The great periods of the past came to be appreciated not *en bloc* and without discrimination, but by retaining from them the forms which best expressed their preoccupations, their preferences, their *spirit*. The idea of what was Classical was more and more widened and the eclecticism of inspiration permitted thenceforth the search for character, thanks to a constant variety.

"Thus naturally the period of the last thirty years of the century has been reproached for not having any style of its own and for having limited its efforts to resuscitating all styles at once. Surely there is in that some injustice; for twenty or thirty years are very little in the evolution of a country's art, and the renewed study of very diverse styles ought not to be without effect in aiding powerfully the slow elaboration of the *elements*, up to then far from precise, which are to be those of the architecture of the future. There was then, in my"—that is, Gromort's—"opinion, a very fruitful period of transition, free of preconceived formulas, and ready as occasion might demand to direct its ardour and its ingenuity toward new researches, such for example as the use of laminated or rivetted iron.

"A sort of fever of study, stimulated it would appear by the development of the mechanical arts, took possession of artists and constructors. On all sides, their attention was solicited: some sought to utilize ceramic facings, others tried to improve the arrangement of *apartments*,—neglected for more than a hundred years" (*sic*),—"or to acclimate for modest country houses, the frequently agreeable manner of English *cottages*. Certain building programmes took on a quite unexpected importance: school laws necessitated the building of many primary schools, high schools, and colleges; banks, and department stores made necessary quite new compositions frequently very fine. . . .

"To tell the truth, the expansion of efforts in so many diverse directions was not without affecting adversely the value of the individual results. Everywhere there was an absence of directive principle, a lack of mutual comprehension between the best intentioned groups of architects. But the sum of labour was not entirely unproductive and it is not by pure chance that a whole generation of architects in the first years of the twentieth century have been able to adapt themselves, with a facility equal to the exigencies of the situation, to an entirely renewed architecture. Doubtless because of their very diversity the somewhat hasty realization of the last quarter of the preceding century aided more efficaciously the development of contemporary art than could have done a hundred years of better co-ordinated research, if that research had been limited by an æsthetic as exclusive as that of the period of Louis XVI, of the Empire or of the Restoration."

In the seventies Richardson was already able to pass beyond this confusion, discovering perhaps unconsciously a directive principle, and achieving valuable individual results. A less lenient critic must therefore find this apology excessive; particularly considering how few architects in the early twentieth century in France were truly able to adapt themselves to an entirely renewed architecture. To return from the general to the specific, however, there can be no question that the important French constructions in metal of the period were of the highest interest.

The Bon Marché department store, built in Paris in 1876, is the earliest on a large scale that has not previously been mentioned. It was significantly the result of a collaboration between a great engineer, Eiffel, and a poor architect, Boileau. It is impossible to say to whom the credit should be given for its very successful adaptation of metal and glass to a building not simple like an exposition hall but very elaborate in function. It may be accepted on the other hand that the thin lifeless ornament, which was so freely used, was wholly due to Boileau. It is this ornament which makes it to-day so difficult to appreciate the work at its full worth. The day was still a quarter century off before there was any real renewal of ornament or the ability to use it as in the past without hampering those larger effects of arrangement of parts which were already here understood. In the Main Exhibition Hall of the Paris Exposition of 1878, also by Eiffel, there was in the latter connection a definite advance; particularly since in a temporary building the glass and iron construction was as freely shown on the exterior as on the interior.

Neither of these monuments were finer by any means than the Crystal Palace or the best of Labrouste and Hittorf. Yet they represented a more extensive and more skilful use of metal construction and they were distinctly of superior importance to similar work done in the intermediate period.

Another large department store of the same general type, the Printemps, was built entirely by an architect, Paul Sedille, still before 1900. There is on the exterior perhaps somewhat more respect for the metal construction than at the Bon Marché although the general design follows quite as definitely the Beaux Arts manner. The interior was elaborately decorated with a sort of proto-Art Nouveau ornament, more positively offensive than that of Boileau at the Bon Marché. Although the beauty of the engineering as such suffers by it, it represented an attempt to fuse the architecture with the engineering and its scale was better related to that of the whole composition.

The next group of similar constructions were built after the twentieth century had opened. The finest was surely the store in the rue Réaumur by Chedanne. Here the metal work was entirely exposed on the exterior and there was very little use of ornament. The mark of the period is seen in the occasional bending of the verticals to conform to the naturalistic æsthetic of the Art Nouveau. Guthon's Bazar de la rue de Rennes was an amplification of Chedanne's work. It had more ornamental pretensions and the construction was thereby somewhat more deformed. The largest of all of this concluding group was the Samaritaine, built by Frantz Jourdain in 1905. Here the construction is perfectly regular and clear. Yet except on the rear it was seriously disfigured by faïence panels of an appalling mustard yellow. There were also naturalistic roses of gilded metal and other curvilinear excrescences which were encouraged to climb freely over the structural forms. Some similar department stores were constructed along these lines in other countries, but few of them have the significance of the best French work.

The vast galleries of the Paris Exposition of 1889 showed no very great change from earlier examples of similar temporary engineering construction except in a more extravagant polychromy. But Eiffel's tower still stands as one of the greatest monuments both of the nineteenth century and, in a sense, of the nascent New Tradition. Although, it filled a very different function, it was in the direct line of later nineteenth century metal bridges, such as the Garabit viaduct which Eiffel had built four years earlier. (Figure 13.) Moreover it looked forward quite as definitely to the engineering architecture of the New Pioneers which is succeeding the New Tradition. With the last it was connected chiefly by its ornament. This ornament in 1889 was not strictly speaking Art Nouveau, but it represented a similar attempt at original creation with naturalistic and curvilinear forms.

There was little else of much significance built in this period in France. In the Paris Hôtel des Postes of 1887 the rationalizing Classicism of the mid-century was continued by Julien Guadet, the chief doctrinaire of the Ecole des Beaux Arts. This was not even of the quality of Duc's Palais de Justice built a generation earlier. Victor Laloux, the prince of later eclectic architects already several times mentioned, illustrated somewhat later in his Tours railway station that he could handle the contemporary engineering manner with as great facility as the Néo-Baroque in his Hôtel de Ville or the Néo-Romanesque in his church of Saint Martin, both also in Tours. In spite of the rigid bipart division of the façade it was moreover more successful than either of these. It was also distinctly superior to his Gare d'Orsay in Paris, if that be judged independently as a railway station. For the latter was magnificent only as part of a much larger city-planning composition, by no means due to Laloux.

The period of transition in France concludes with that reign of the Art Nouveau in decoration which left its mark on the later department stores. The Art Nouveau was crystallized in France by the work of Henry Van de Velde. In his own house at Uccle in Belgium in the early ninetics he had sought to develop a suitable contemporary manner of furnishing. He was much influenced by Morris in this work and he achieved an even greater success with simple rational forms devoid of decoration.

Van de Velde was brought to the attention of Bing, a German art dealer in Paris. Bing had prospered with the sale of Japanese objects in the eighties; but Japonisme was declining, and he was desirous of providing a suitable background for the objects from Morris' workshops he had already begun to import. Bing called Van de Velde to Paris in 1896 and gave him the opportunity to install four rooms in his Maison de l'Art Nouveau in the rue de Provence. Unfortunately Van de Velde attempted to combine with his rationalism in these interiors a very imaginative and unprecedented curvilinear ornament.

Van de Velde's rooms were not at first favourably received in Paris. In the next year he was called to Germany, returning to Paris only in 1911 to provide the first designs for the Théâtre des Champs Elysées after the Art Nouveau was well over. The introduction of the Art Nouveau into Germany was the least of Van de Velde's services to twentieth century architecture there. Although it left its mark on whole quarters of Charlottenburg and Hamburg it was soon obscured by other more important developments in which Van de Velde was equally concerned.

Van de Velde as early as the building of his Darmstadt School at the beginning of the twentieth century was indeed one of the most important precursors of the New Pioneers. It is the greatest injustice that his name should have become almost entirely associated outside Belgium and Germany with the unfortunate venture of the Art Nouveau. For to-day as head of the Institut Supérieur des Arts Décoratifs in Bruxelles he still remains one of the most distinguished as well as one of the most advanced architects to hold such official and influential position.

After Van de Velde's departure for Germany the Art Nouveau soon developed much further and more widely in France. Naturalistic foliage pseudo-organically used was combined with a considerable reminiscence of the Rococo, and even a continuance of the Japonisme of the eighties. The rationalism which lent validity to Van de Velde's Art Nouveau as to Morris' Mediævalism was quite forgotten and the manner developed almost entirely as a form of ornament. This was applied with equal inappropriateness to cut-stone or steel skeleton façades, even by men of such considerable talent as Frantz Jourdain. The use of faïence polychomy in the crude and sickly tones that the æsthetes of the eighties had first set apart as "artistic" was also developed.

The best known works of the Art Nouveau were the Paris subway entrances which are less small pieces of architecture than enlarged *objets d'art*. However ridiculous the movement may appear in retrospect, it cannot be denied that it had much in common with Néo-Impressionist painting. As a setting for the immense mural of Steinlen it can still be appreciated in the interior of the Taverne de Paris. The characteristic curved line of the Art Nouveau is moreover found recurrently in the music of Debussy. *Pelléas* is far more Art Nouveau than Mediæval as stage designers seem hardly to appreciate. The strange colour schemes seem often to have been determined by the red hair of Sarah Bernhardt, and they still serve on occasion to suggest the perverse glamour of the latest epoch which is now definitely past beyond recall.

The Art Nouveau was not, however, the movement which was destined to initiate that general development of the minor arts which came later to the support of the New Tradition. As in the case of the Néo-Gingerbread and the Japonisme of the late seventies and the eighties, it pointed the way beyond archæological ornament and decoration; but it did not establish a tradition. Like the earlier and more authentic Gingerbread of the fifties and sixties it was still a strange hybrid belonging to the degenerescence of Romanticism rather than to the new manner of sound eclecticism of style. Yet this new manner was already making a general appearance in serious monuments of architecture, usually under very different and much less novel auspices. The Art Nouveau only disfigured the Paris monuments of engineering of the transition to which it was applied.   Except through Henry Van de Velde it was little associated with a revival of craftsmanship.

But the latter revival in England, begun so auspiciously under Mediæval influences, continued soberly repairing rather effectively the damage which the Mediæval Revivals had done in the mid-century as they finally destroyed Baroque traditions.   Moreover while in France there was no reaction from the continuing degeneration of craftsmanship, in North Europe generally where there was less experimentation in structure and in ornament there was increasing thought of execution.   The craft movement undoubtedly first started in England with Morris' Red House.   But it developed, to some extent independently and to some extent due to English influence, in Scandinavia, Germany and Holland.

The writing of Pugin and Ruskin of course had preceded the work of Morris and even prepared the way for it.   Much of Ruskin's moralizing, for example, went toward the development of craftsmanship.   When he urged honesty he urged good building.   When he inveighed against the use of metal and the machine, the very means by which the French were first to pass beyond the impasse of Romanticism, it was because they encouraged the easy elaboration of the worst sort of ornament.   Yet it must be admitted that the immediate effect of Ruskin's writing was not to improve craftsmanship.   The attempt to revive the Italian Gothic indeed led it further astray.   As the contemporary Oxford movement seldom induced directly a more spiritual life but rather swathed it in gaudy Italian trappings, so Ruskin's preaching led not often to good craftsmanship but more generally to a swathing of construction in equally exotic garb.   Nevertheless against the continuance of degeneration a first ineffectual counter movement was established.   With William Morris this counter movement came to more actual achievement than in the Oxford Museum begun under Ruskin's direction, but never completed as regards the decoration.

After the Red House the revival of craftsmanship in architecture became somewhat more general.   Norman Shaw, Nesfield, Belcher and others made in their country houses a concerted attempt to renew autochthonous traditions.   They were less eclectic at first than Webb had been and often very conscientious Mediæval Revivalists.   But in the manors of Norman Shaw, even the most exaggeratedly feudal, the workmanship was always extraordinarily good.   He at least attempted to train workmen artificially as craftsmen where old traditions were entirely lost. Already in a house built in 1864 he more or less gave up rigid stylistic revivalism and began to depend more completely on the virtues of good simple building. In another house built three years later Nesfield based his architecture of craftsmanship on the building traditions of the early eighteenth century rather than on the building of the late Middle Ages. It was thus that the movement became associated with Queen Anne. Shaw followed in this new direction. He went, however, even further, developing in his New Zealand Chambers of 1872 a manner in which late Mediæval and Classical features were freely combined in great profusion. From then on a considerable eclecticism of style marked the Queen Anne.

But the further the Queen Anne got away from country houses, the more elaborate it became; and the more elaborate it became, the more it tended to divide itself up again according to the principles of the eclecticism of taste. The significance of the elaborate version known as Free Classic was that it carried even into the general Classical Revival the new standards of good workmanship. In the last quarter of the century all over Northern Europe and even in America, thanks more particularly perhaps to photography as has already been suggested, the new standards of execution came to be applied to all sorts of revivalism. They even gave revivalism in England and America a new lease of life.

In the country houses of the eighties and nineties the line of Webb's, Shaw's and Nesfield's houses of 1859, 1864 and 1867 was better continued. Architectural features were very largely dispensed with, detail was reduced to a minimum, and the effect achieved depended as in the Red House on the picturesque expression of irregular functional planning and the exquisite use of local materials. The revival of brickwork advanced very rapidly and was paralleled with a revival of stonework which American imitators have after a generation hardly yet equalled.

Many architects built such houses and many still build them to-day. Moreover there has been both in America and on the Continent much more or less successful imitation of them. In such a vast quantity of work, all of excellent quality within its limitations, it is hard to mention specific examples, or even specific architects after the first. Moreover this work remained into the twentieth century wholly traditional in spirit, although the reminiscent architectural features are frequently only of the slightest importance.

As very generally in the New Tradition elsewhere, the borrowing from the past hardly goes beyond a Mediæval effect in the picturesque grouping of masses, or a Baroque effect in a more symmetrical grouping. The ensemble is so clearly functional and expressive of the type of life for which such houses were and still are built that it is often little more than the similarity of that life with the life of the past which seems to appear in the stylistic expression. Yet they lack that eclectic stylization which marked the general New Tradition. They have remained for the most part transitional, still subscribing nominally to the principles of the eclecticism of taste.

Mackintosh and Voysey in Scotland alone attempted about 1900 a certain conscious eclecticism of style. The former indeed had certain relations with the opening New Tradition in Austria as his Glasgow School of Art illustrates. Their work is however not of prime importance.

The best known and even perhaps the most typical of later English architects working in the manner of the transition is Sir Edwin Lutyens. He was born in 1869 and began to work in 1888. His houses in the nineteenth century still kept close to traditional formulas. But the inherited detail was of slight importance and seemed inherently associated with the craftsmanship, as it had in the case of the first men to build thus in the fifties and sixties. At Orchards, Godalming, of 1899 there was already no direct reminiscence of the past except in the mouldings about the entrance door. The general massing and the use of varied materials was nevertheless very suggestive of old work.

In the Deanery Gardens, Sonning, built in 1900, Lutyens may almost be said to have built all unwittingly the finest house of the New Tradition. (Figure 18.) It is surely one of the finest pieces of traditional craftsmanship produced in the twentieth century. The quality of the plain brickwork and the plain oak beams at the great bay-window, the fine balance of the irregular masses, the skill displayed in the entrance arch of many brick orders, an architectural feature suggestive but not imitative of the past, the perfect adaptation of the plan to contemporary life, have hardly been equalled.

Regrettably, as the century continued Lutyens, taking his essential craftsmanship for granted, began to add more and more reminiscent features, Tudor or Georgian, until he became hardly distinguishable from any other eclectic architect of his day in England or America. After a series of houses fine despite his increasing Palladianism, and still marked even by a limited eclecticism of style, he surrendered completely to revivalism in building Heathcote, Ilkley. In Chussex built in 1908, however, he displayed that working on a small house and with limited means he could on occasion by the simplification of his Georgian formula achieve nearly as fine a result as he had done with his simplification of the Tudor formula at the Deanery Garden. Although they have more traditional features the same is true of Nashdon and Folly Farm, both on a much larger scale.

Beyond the best of Lutyens no other English architects have gone in this manner. Those who have lately begun to copy the New Tradition of the Continent moreover have thus far not succeeded in developing a really national version. The promise of Soane and the Crystal Palace has not at all been fulfilled. The country houses from the Red House down to the present day in the transitional manner of the reintegration of building are practically all England has produced of good post-Romantic architecture. How definitely a product of Romanticism this manner still is, it is hardly necessary to point out. But it is a far finer product than the earlier Gothic Revival out of which it grew.

Craftsmanship and limited avoidance of borrowed architectural features were not enough to renew and reintegrate architecture any more than the structural and ornamental experimentation of the French transitionalists. The one prepared building for reincorporation with architecture while the other prepared engineering. But in Europe it was in Holland, Austria and Germany most particularly that architecture itself was first generally renewed. In America the New Tradition has been more isolated in the mass of twentieth century construction.

The general description of the New Tradition itself has already been postponed beyond the actual moment of its first appearance in the seventies in America and in the nineties in Holland, Germany and Austria. Yet outside these countries, whose transitional movements are best considered as opening their national versions of the New Tradition, there remains still one name to mention: that of Gaudì (1847-1921). In the unfinished church of the Sagrada Famiglia in Barcelona, on which he began to work in 1884, he attempted the creation of a new style by the purposeful distortion of Mediæval forms. It has been without issue and it is surely neither fine nor important. It was however a sort of precursor of some of the more extravagant work of German architects of the New Tradition under the influence of Expressionism.

An apartment house in Barcelona also by Gaudì, built well within the twentieth century, illustrated a phase of the transition to the New Tradition somewhat similar to that of the Art Nouveau in France. Yet in its use of poured concrete it was of some structural importance. Except for its marine ornament it bears considerable resemblance in principle of design to Mendelsohn's Einstein Tower of 1921. Gaudì's park architecture represents the extreme point of the imitation of the effects of nature which had been frequently recommended in the Romantic treatises on gardening.

CHAPTER EIGHT

THE ESSENCE OF THE NEW TRADITION

THE New Tradition in architecture appeared as soon as architects turned from the eclecticism of taste to the eclecticism of style with the intention of founding a rational and integrated manner. To all intents and purposes Soane and Schinkel very early in the nineteenth century had already done this in single monuments. But they and such of the other Romantics as made similar attempts failed to establish their innovations. All fell back readily into the revivalism from which in intention they had hardly altogether departed. There was therefore in architecture no such transitional movement as those in building and engineering.

Yet in Gromort's treatment of late nineteenth century eclecticism of taste it is easy to see how that served in a sense as such a transition. It was the sort of training needed to familiarize architects widely with all the various architectural motifs which the past had developed. This the earlier and more exclusive revivals of Romanticism had done only in very incomplete fashion. Moreover, by the last third of the nineteenth century Classical and Mediæval archæology had made somewhat more clear the nature of architectural motifs and their original functional significance. The rationalizing Classicists had already applied such knowledge to the Classical elements from as early as 1800 in some cases. The Mediævalists had at least considered doing so with the Mediæval elements by the fifties. As has been indicated, this was effective in connection with building rather than with architecture. Scott, for example, in his practice did not pass much beyond the Mediævalist equivalent of the peristylar temple formula with which intelligent Classicists were long finished.

The early Romantics found in the non-Classical and non-national past only a pleasant flavour of fantastic unreality. But by the last quarter of the nineteenth century the widening of the field of archæology had made Egyptian, Indian, Islamic and other non-European styles nearly as functionally comprehensible as those of the Classical and Mediæval past. For example Mr. Owen Jones, who was mentioned by Scott, made a study of the Alhambra and also published a universal *Grammar of Ornament* which ran to many editions. The eclectics of taste made, it is true, less use of exotic styles than the early Romantics. But they were prepared to do so when occasion demanded with at least a certain plausibility not inferior to that of the Classical and Mediæval Revivals.

As Scott pointed out, such general interest in the architecture of the past, such wide possibilities of emulation had never existed before. The Late Gothic had known and had been influenced only by the immediate High Mediæval past. The Renaissance and the Baroque had considered only Classical antiquity. With the Age of Romanticism a change appeared. One after another and several at a time there were revivals of different periods of the past. Yet still generally in theory the Romantics believed only in the revival of one period or another; or, at least, only of such different periods as were closely related in character. Thus there were sharp struggles between the two chief factions, the Classicists and the Mediævalists. The resolution of their differences along symbolic functional lines was the accomplishment in theory of the eclecticism of taste. It quite destroyed that sense of style which the best Classical Revival and Mediæval Revival architecture of Romanticism had somehow been able to preserve at least until 1850. It restricted sound traditional building to the English Mediævalist revival of building, and constructional experiment to engineering. It obscured those abstract qualities the early Romantics had discovered and called the "sublime" and the "picturesque." The principle of freedom and catholicity of reminiscence was, however, firmly established. Thus the nineteenth century at the conclusion of the Age of Romanticism, regularized its relation to the past. In so doing as regards architecture it also more or less completely cut itself off from the present.

The model town in America after the War still possessed churches of High Mediæval style, banks of Greek or Roman form, houses Late Gothic or Georgian, and public buildings Renaissance or Baroque. The whole as regards architecture was completely heterogeneous. As regards building it was usually perhaps somewhat superior to that of the last half of the previous century. The engineering was moreover as expressive of contemporary conditions as the architecture permitted and unconsciously at times in factories and garages even rather fine. The churches were as nearly forgeries of Mediæval monuments as money, skill and the religious prejudices of particular sects permitted. The best of the houses were often—but less often than in England—excellent examples of traditional craftsmanship. The public buildings were considerably constrained by the attempt to fit elaborate modern needs into ancient shells. In the schools, gymnasiums and swimming pools architecture was almost as forgotten as in the factories and garages. Only the window enframements and the entrance features of the façades reflected the period of the past the whole was supposed to emulate; the rest was good, bad, but more usually mediocre building and engineering. Popularly the value of a monument was in exact ratio to its accuracy as a forgery. Gothic power stations and industrial chimneys or Renaissance hotels at impossible scale were accepted, however, as *tours de force*. They were supposed to be productive of harmony, the very quality which the incoherent and symbolic functionalism of the eclecticism of taste made impossible.

As regards architecture the New Tradition replaced eclecticism of taste with eclecticism of style. From the nineties this is clearly evident in an increasing number of important buildings. For once the past could be seen as a whole and not as a set of closed and contradictory systems, it became possible to imitate an effect of mass from the Romanesque and to support it with Baroque detail—to offer an extreme example. On occasion this eclecticism of style was so little fused that it is obvious to the most casual observer. From the beginning, however, the founders of the New Tradition in various countries succeeded in blending their borrowings so subtly and in so prominently incorporating with their architecture the finest craftsmanship in building, as well as to some extent contemporary methods of engineering, that the public was persuaded there was no reminiscence of the past at all. From this fact appears to derive the appellation "Modernist" frequently given to the architecture of the New Tradition. More timid architects easily avoided startling the public by combining their reminiscences in such a way that the resultant amalgam appeared superficially to belong to some accepted formula of revival, treated in the occasion rather broadly. Yet in retrospect there is very little difference in the dependence on the past of those who early announced themselves as the creators of a new architecture and those who remained respectful, as Soane for example had earlier done, toward some principle of single or multiple revivalism.

Ventures really more far reaching in intention, such as the Art Nouveau, failed as completely as Romantic attempts to achieve an architecture which was merely "sublime" or purely "picturesque." The Art Nouveau had a certain intellectual support. A purely linear ornament was quite conceivable and yet it had never existed. The ornament of the past was known to have been frequently derived from the stylization of natural forms. It was, however, over-cerebral at its best and out of the hands of Henry Van de Velde it rapidly degenerated. It was far less adapted than the eclecticism of style to the decoration of revived building. For the revived building was traditional. It offered no effects of sufficient scale to include contemporary engineering. Engineering was moreover in 1900 still much more subsidiary in the general mass of production than it later became. Previous to the general adoption of ferro-concrete construction architecture was still largely tied to the use of traditional materials. Metal except in certain types of buildings had no more important place than it had had in the mid-nineteenth century.

But eclecticism of style as such would have been no more successful than the Art Nouveau, as such Romantic projects as that of Idzkowski in the forties and that of Berlage in the eighties illustrate, had it not implied distinctly more. It was primarily a summing up of the experiments in form of the last five hundred years, and even of the parallel experiments in form of earlier periods. Like the Late Gothic which did not merely continue the earlier Mediæval style; like the Renaissance and *a fortiori* the Baroque, which were far from exact in their recall of the antique, the New Tradition stylized what it borrowed in a way not without analogies in the new stylization of nature which the painters who came after the Impressionists were developing at the same time. After the first also there was much less a repetition of the original varied borrowing followed by a new stylization than a continuation and evolution of the manner of the founders. It was thus that the New Tradition became truly a tradition.

This tradition of architectural forms furthermore was given solidity by the reincorporation of building and to some extent of engineering. It was not therefore like the Art Nouveau a matter merely of theory nor a matter merely of detail. It was a reintegrated architecture, in intention as all-inclusive as that of any pre-Romantic period. It gained moreover very definitely from the analyses of the Age of Romanticism. Romantic vision had discovered and set apart certain values which were retained, or more exactly were for the first time adequately achieved.

What the Romantics built to be "picturesque" was in general at best only quaint. What the Romantics built to be "sublime" was too often absurd or of such a derived and literary symbolism, like the descent from the Alps to Gingerbread, that the relation is nearly incredible. The New Tradition provided much more nearly a "picturesque" architecture than anything in the Age of Romanticism which did not anticipate it. The word indeed constantly rises to the lips in the presence of the best early twentieth century monuments. It is better restricted to the earlier period, however, if it is to be used with critical exactness, or at least as far as possible to such matters as definitely have their individual roots in the earlier period, as in the case of the irregularity and the relation to the landscape of country houses. Even its greatest admirers are chary of calling the skyscraper "sublime." Yet that æsthetic quality as distinguished from the "beautiful" in the eighteenth century is more clearly present in the twentieth century German industrial architecture than even in the Arc de Triomphe, and it is indeed often suggested by the best skyscrapers as well. By keeping it *entre guillemets* it is a valid critical term, if its special origin may be thus currently recalled.

Thus set down, the essence of the New Tradition has a falsely simple air. It appears in retrospect as much a formula as the best of the Classical formulas of the nineteenth century, different chiefly in being less exclusive. But much less than they was it arrived at as a formula and then later applied. Indeed, with the Art Nouveau many of the most creative men of the day in which the New Tradition was initiated went at first far astray. The New Tradition is a formula only historically, existing on *a posteriori* analysis. It found and still finds very different explanations from those who established it, as well as from those who do not approach it in sequence as the reintegration of architecture after the Age of Romanticism. It is very possible, for example, to minimize the eclecticism of its formal experimentation, increasing proportionately, as is for the developed manner not unjust, the importance of new methods of construction. One may even deny its "sublimity" but not its "picturesqueness," despite or even because of the ambiguity of the term. Moreover in different countries and with different architects the formula was arrived at very differently. The results are therefore notably different in exactly the same way that Wren's work differs from that of Borromini or Bramante's from Boccador's. But after 1910 the formula was in general established by one means or another and the New Tradition very definitely a real tradition, if a comparatively broad one. Not good building became traditional, but the special sorts of good building used by the founders; not engineering—which is by nature anti-traditional—but certain ways already initiated of using engineering in architecture.

By 1910 the New Tradition had reached maturity, and although the analysis of later monuments may be made in terms of elements borrowed from the past, it is more accurately made in terms of the work of the founders. One finds in general not such and such a combination of Archaic Greek and Late Gothic features or of Japanese planning and Maya ornament, but rather Dutch fantasy modified by the more geometrical manner of Wright, the Néo-Rokoko detail of Hoffmann in combination with the brickwork of the English, or the engineering of the French joined to a formal expression based on Berlin néo monumentality.

It was particularly in ornament that the eclecticism of the New Tradition was manifest, although that ornament was not only stylized but reduced— that is much simplified—in order both to give it original character and to bring it within the capacities of contemporary craftsmen. But the ornament of the New Tradition has already begun to fall out of use to some extent. The reasons for this increasing avoidance of decorative embellishment are of such general significance that they merit particular treatment. The question, however, goes some distance back into the past and is only fully resolved in the manner of the New Pioneers which is succeeding the New Tradition.

In Modern architecture previous to the Age of Romanticism it is difficult, as was done by the Romantics in principle, to distinguish engineering from building or either from decorative embellishment. The lack of detail on the Pitti Palace or an eighteenth century French château was comparative. Detail existed in the exquisite mouldings as truly as in the orders or the carved ornament of more elaborate monuments. Moreover, the work of architecture was still, as in the Middle Ages, the result of co-operative effort. The execution of even these mouldings presupposed trained and even sensitive hand craftsmen. This is in general quite as valid as regards the architecture of the further past. Not, it is true, under the developed Roman

Empire, when engineering and embellishment became more or less separated and the latter was done mechanically by ill-trained and insensitive crafts-men; nor for the early monuments of the ancient East in whose construction the individual workman must frequently have been used like cogs in a wheel.

Already, however, in the Late Gothic a new point of view began to make its appearance. As detail became more elaborate it also became more mechani-cal. The virtues of architecture existed primarily in the design of the master builder and the quality of the detail as such was in some degree incidental. The use of detail—and even good detail—was still presupposed; but it was already conceived as an embellishment. To this the existence of many empty niches, for example, appears clearly to testify.

Against this the Renaissance at first reacted. Much opportunity was again offered for individual creative expression in decorative detail. Yet elab-orate ornament, or even particularly excellent ornament, was notably un-necessary to Brunelleschi in his finest works. From such ornamental free-dom the High Renaissance turned at least in theory toward the conception of the craftsman as a machine for the correct production of the Classical orders. This conception continued into the seventeenth century Baroque. Its freedom in detail other than the orders did not at all require real excel-lence of execution. Such detail existed solely as a function of the whole and its intrinsic quality was, therefore, of small consequence.

The later Baroque, particularly in France, was the last stand of the indi-vidual craftsman. Both in the more elaborate and in the simpler version detail, even if it were no more than mouldings, became of very great impor-tance with the change to a more intimate scale. Only traditionally trained workmen with a real feeling for the work could carry it out altogether satis-factorily. The difference between the work of Paris and that of the provinces is often for this reason very considerable. This also to some extent creates the difference between the Rococo done by the French in Germany and the Rokoko done by the Germans.

The opening of the Age of Romanticism marked a new development of the post-Mediæval point of view toward the craftsman. This amounted in time to a definite and complete change, although it came very gradually and was long masked by unconscious continuance of old methods. No longer, how-ever, was detail intrinsically of even as much importance as in the Late

Gothic or the Baroque. The idea of detail of one sort or another alone was of serious consequence to the Romantic mind. All detail thus became merely a trophy or a symbol. This was to some extent already true in the case of the Classical orders, but not more generally.

The direct vision of architecture which came to dominate during the second half of the eighteenth century took account chiefly of masses, volumes and relations, even if according to pictorial canons. But the early Romantics also saw indirectly according to literary and archæological principles. Thus the consequences of the new vision were double, as has already been pointed out. Workmen were forced to struggle not only with the inherited Classical orders in which they were at least trained, but also with newly discovered versions of these and with more abstruse archæological documents in the hope that the desired effect of reviving the past could be achieved thus mechanically. Yet on the other hand standards of execution in detail were forgotten since architecture was characteristically to be seen only blurred as through a fog. Detail did not need to be, in the terms of the period, "beautiful," that is regular and intrinsically of high quality, so long as it accomplished an effect which was "sublime"—hence superior to the criticism of parts—or "picturesque." In the latter most typical case indeed intrinsically good detail might even have been considered actually undesirable for it would have interfered with the irregularity of the whole and set the work of man so completely apart from the landscape that the most lithographic eye could not fuse them.

The two rather opposing ideals were only fully satisfied by real ruins whose ancient and authentic "beauty" had been rendered "sublime" or "picturesque" by the action of time and nature. Their combination as they came nearer together in the nineteenth century resulted in the utter degeneration of detail, reaching its extreme point between 1850 and 1875, which has already once been discussed. What is here significant is as much the fact that the combination of the pictorial and the archæological point of view also caused an extraordinary multiplication of detail as that it brought about this degeneration of detail. If a certain amount of reminiscent detail was considered worth-while as a trophy of erudition, according to nineteenth century quantitative standards twice as much was twice as worth-while. As it was never seen clearly but only impressionistically, twice as much certainly made a greater effect on eyes which had lost with the sense of quality of execution the power of appreciating in actuality the expressive texture of undecorated plain surfaces which they so much enjoyed when it was sufficiently exaggerated by the graphic artists or by time.

Thus, as the critics of the time occasionally noted, the most insignificant building often became as richly endowed with architectural features as a cathedral or a palace. The solid virtues of many of the simpler published projects in the books of the first half of the century disappeared for lack of adequate execution when they were built: otherwise the designs had to be loaded with ornament in execution in order to make palatable in reality that which engraved or lithographed must have had as much charm and real quality to the men of the day as to us. (Figure 10.) In terms of currency there resulted an inflation of detail of which any street largely built between 1859 and 1900 is the sad witness. For the world was flooded with vast quantities of detail each item of which was nearly valueless.

The route toward deflation took several forms. For some time the soundest was that pursued particularly in England. The revival of the craft of building accomplished at least a revaloration of the small change of detail. The latter eclecticism of taste attempted a more general revaloration which proved to be more or less futile. Providing draftsmen with accurate photographic documents and training workmen artificially to follow the draftsmen's paper designs for detail accomplished only a more and more complete duplication in the contemporary paper currency of the gold coinage of the past. The results were usually more like the Greek drachma than the British five-pound note.

The New Tradition profited in its turn by the lessons of both these attempts. After the fiasco of the Art Nouveau had displayed the impossibility of really creating an ornamental currency on *a priori* principles the masters of the New Tradition on the one hand made the most of the possibilities of detail the revival of the craft of building provided. On the other hand they sought in their ornament borrowed from the past not the exact repetition of documents but stylized and reduced forms which the post-Romantic craftsman was capable of executing adequately. Both a Doric column and a Romanesque capital for example were impossible with contemporary means of production. But neither a simple column nor even a comparatively elaborate capital were, provided they were not brought into real competition with the work of the past by the obvious intention of direct emulation.

Moreover since the earlier revivals of the nineteenth century had particularly favoured the fully formed styles of the past, failing so very obviously even in their intended replicas because there existed a wholly definite standard to which they could not possibly attain, even the men at the end of the nineteenth century who were only working toward the New Tradition began to imitate periods of transition in which detail had no fixed norm, or when two norms existed in conflict, as in the Early Mediæval styles or the Early Renaissance. From this the step to full eclecticism of style was easy and was immediately taken in the twentieth century when the arbitrary symbolical value of detail had somewhat diminished.

Stylization and reduction gave the new detail a certain coherence. Stylized and reduced forms still recalled or suggested to the sophisticated observer the various styles of the past without attempting directly to vie with the works of any one of them. Eclecticism of style thus provided for a time a far wider revalorization than had the revival of the craft of building, at least when the importance of fine execution was as adequately recognized. This was of course sometimes equally recognized by some of the eclectics of taste who understood the pseudo-economic parable of the five-pound note.

But the ornament of the New Tradition, as has been said, rapidly became subject to a formula, or rather a set of national formulas. Although these formulas had at first a certain originality they staled very rapidly with repetition. The later attempt to rejuvenate them by ever more exotic borrowings from the primitive arts of the past did not succeed in giving any further validity to the original principle. The miracle of the new creation which had occurred once could hardly be repeated often. The current imitation of the French formula in America is particularly indicative of the impossibility of continuing the ornament of the New Tradition, now that it has been already sometime established, without arriving at once at an inflation as serious as that of revivalistic ornament. In general while the work of the followers of the New Tradition is more sure than that of the founders, it lacks the force and conviction they alone as true innovators could give it.

Fortunately at the same time increasing interest in the study of mass and proportion, also along eclectic lines, tended to support the abstract pictorial and psychological points of view inherited from Romanticism. It became consciously admitted that ornament was of minor importance and less central to the problem of style in architecture than had been accepted generally by the literary and archæological theorists of the nineteenth century. The more clearly the new youth of ornament was seen to be artificial and the more certainly its bloom proved almost as impermanent as that so quickly tarnished of the Art Nouveau, the more desperate were the attempts at first to find more exotic and novel forms. Expressionism in the broadest sense was the last concerted programme of renovation. But neither its exaggerated distortion of reminiscent forms nor its geometrical experimentation along the lines of the Art Nouveau have had any continuing success despite their continuing use. The zigzag has become as tiring as the sinuous curve and its intrinsic interest is even less.

Thus in the last years without changing its more general principles the New Tradition has come more and more to discard ornament. It has sought its eclectic effects of mass for themselves in simplified and reduced form, lending them secondary interest by balance of surface textures, frequently without recourse even to mouldings. This version of the New Tradition does not, however, constitute in itself a separate and later manner since its fundamental principles remain unchanged. Although devoid of decorative detail, it resembles only superficially the succeeding manner of the New Pioneers, who from the first recognized the impossibility of ornament. With this it has indeed to some extent merged, particularly in Germany and Eastern Europe, borrowing features from the latter manner as freely as the primary version of the New Tradition borrowed from the styles of the past. But it is not profitable to attempt a separation of the New Tradition into three versions, that of the founders, that of the followers, and that which is already rather superficially close to the New Pioneers.

Once established and formulated, the New Tradition may be more accurately considered to have continued without real development wherever it has penetrated. For such development as there has been toward greater emphasis on engineering, toward greater simplicity and the reduction of reminiscent elements, has led too directly toward the essentially different architecture of the New Pioneers. It is moreover to be found quite as much in the work of the founders as elsewhere. If one were to distinguish three versions within the last thirty years it would be necessary to find that almost every architect of the New Tradition had had equal success in two and many in all three. The New Tradition, although far from over, may therefore be considered in general terms as pre-eminently the single dominant manner of architecture of the first quarter of the twentieth century since the continuance of the eclecticism of taste is negligible except in bulk. The story of this manner of architecture of the first quarter of the twentieth century is far too complicated and too rich in individual personalities to be told further thus. For the architecture of the Age of Romanticism, the use of generalities was at once more possible and more necessary.

CHAPTER NINE

THE NEW TRADITION IN AMERICA

At least four different versions of the New Tradition, taken in the broadest sense, may be distinguished in the American architecture of the twentieth century. Of these four versions the skyscraper particularly, and very justly the work of Frank Lloyd Wright as well, have received more attention than the development in America, along the same lines as in England, of a domestic architecture of craftsmanship on the one hand, and the appearance in the last few years of an overt modernism unrelated to the work of Wright and usually borrowed from Europe on the other.

The domestic architecture of craftsmanship is of importance as a transitional manifestation. Yet its use of reminiscent features has often been so considerable that the work is not to be differentiated except in honesty of execution from the most sterile productions of the continuing eclecticism of taste. The simplification and dependence on the values of good handwork is usually less than in similar English work. The tendencies toward eclecticism of style of such architects as H. T. Lindeberg, Theodate Pope, or those of the Philadelphia school suggest merely the recall of transitional styles of the past; and the craftsmanship of American architects is in general at once more conspicuous and less naturally achieved than for example in contemporary work by Scandinavian architects now coming to be well known in America through the presence of Saarinen at Detroit. Nevertheless many American architects remaining nominally within the Georgian or the Tudor revivals have produced twentieth century houses acceptable to the general taste of the country that are quite as fine and as contemporary not only as those of England but even as those more conspicuously "modern" in other North European countries where eclecticism of style has been carried much further. (Figure 17.) In general, however, although this manner has existed at least from the beginning of the century it was not sufficiently distinguished from revivalism nor taken seriously as an architecture early enough to provide a nucleus of style creation. Like the equally transitional work in England it constitutes primarily no more than a reintegration of the art of building; wherever there have been considerable architectural pretensions the manner has succumbed to the revivalism of the continuing eclecticism of taste. To-day it is probably too late to look for a further real development. For America has become conscious of foreign "modernism"; and original creation is now all but impossible along these lines, for that reason and because the day of the New Tradition is probably coming to a close.

This version of the New Tradition, however, has been from the first sounder, and despite the relation to England more autochthonous, than the practice so conspicuous in the last few years of imitating the detail of continental contemporary building exactly as the revivalists imitate detail of the past. This is the form in which the New Tradition is at the moment most prominently before our eyes in the large cities of America. Skyscrapers such as those of Ely Kahn, or Holabird and Roche, or the new telephone buildings in many different parts of the country thus doubly dependent on the New Tradition, are generally very little more excellent than many of those which in their ornamentation imitate the styles of the past. Even the later designs of Goodhue, although the result of more conscientious and fundamental study, do not succeed in the attainment of qualities which were not inherent in his earlier traditional building. Parallel manifestations of overt modernism on a smaller scale are even more obviously incidental and secondhand as is illustrated even by the work of the more independent, such as Barry Byrne, Chase McArthur, and Wright's son, Lloyd Wright, who were "modernists" even before the foreign influences became general. Such work in their special cases and more generally is of interest chiefly as a sign·that the period of revivalism is nearly over in America rather than for its somewhat accidental connection with the skyscraper whose size after all makes detail, however intrinsically interesting, of minor importance. This, the Barclay Vesey Building of Ralph Walker notably demonstrates.

Even the skyscraper has belonged to the architecture of the twentieth century chiefly through its engineering and its inherent effects of what the eighteenth century would have called "sublimity." McKim, Mead and White, Cass Gilbert, Carrère and Hastings, Arthur Harmon, James Gamble Rogers, the imitators of Saarinen's Tribune Tower project and all the others who have given one or another sort of "architectural" coating to the skyscraper have only succeeded in obscuring the unconscious æsthetic achievements of their engineers. The more studied the shape of the mass, the more skil-fully adjusted the ornamentation by the architects, the more surely is the integrity and the scale of the engineering lost. Only in construction or at night can even the "sublimity" be adequately appreciated; and then as by the Romantic traveller before ivy covered ruins or cloud hung Alps, not at all as by the critic before a fully developed form of architecture. (Figure 22.)

The temporary relation of the skyscraper to the creative New Tradition in America is best seen in connection with the work of the Chicago precursors of Wright. Its possibilities, barely envisaged in the present century, re-main to be developed by the New Pioneers in the future. As individual monuments there are so far hardly any skyscrapers whose value as archi-tecture is comparable to that of productions on a much smaller scale by Wright and a few others.

The same is in general true of American factories. Only the Larkin Soap Factory of Wright has an expression in design truly integrated with the engineering, the others display the futility of attempting to leave æsthetic expression to the surface without truly affecting or being affected by the economic and functional principles which determine the development of the whole. (Figure 21.)

It is particularly in the work of Wright that the history of the New Tra-dition in the twentieth century is summed up in America. But Wright comes at the end of a line of architects to whom consciously or unconsciously he has owed a great deal. Not only his own master Sullivan, but first of all Richardson prepared the way for him at a time when the New Tradition did not exist in Europe. Richardson moreover, even without considering the period in which he worked when the general level of architecture was exceedingly low, was surely as great an architect as Wright.

H. H. Richardson was born in Louisiana in 1839. After receiving his degree at Harvard, he was in Paris from 1859 to 1865 studying at the Ecole des Beaux Arts and working under Labrouste undoubtedly the best master he could have found at the time. On his return to America he was one of the two men in the country who had the benefit of such a thorough European training. Ironically enough he did much to develop the practice of sending American architects to study in Paris. For this and the introduction of French teachers and methods into the first American architectural schools which were founded at this time did much to turn almost an entire later generation of architects toward Beaux Arts revivalism.

But Richardson never used the knowledge of the Beaux Arts classical formulas which he had imbibed at the fountain head, although they were perhaps more popular than any others in the large cities of the East just after the Civil War. In his first building done the year after his return, Unity Church in Springfield, Massachusetts, he worked within the formulas of the Victorian Gothic then universally dominant in American ecclesiastical architecture.

His next important building was the Brattle Square Church in Boston designed in 1870. Here he anticipated by almost a generation the characteristics of the mature style of Berlage in the Amsterdam Beurs considered in Europe as one of the earliest works of the New Tradition. His rationalism and his special Mediævalism were well satisfied in a manner which his fellow-countrymen accepted as Romanesque. To the archæologist it has only very incidental connection with that style. His effects were obtained by the scale and the severity of the picturesque massing and by the use of originally varicoloured stone. There was practically no decoration except in the frieze of trumpet blowing angels about the top of the tower. The chamfered edges at the frames of openings, the rather shapeless mouldings, the fortunately infrequent capitals had the crudeness which was at the time falsely associated with the Romanesque; but as with Berlage's similar detail this is incidental to an architecture in which experimental rationalism and even eclectic reminiscence—for there are incidental echoes of other styles than the Romanesque—were so brilliantly combined. The road from the Bibliothèque Sainte-Geneviève to this church was a surprisingly short one and the relation to the picturesque Italianism of the Age of Romanticism was also rather close, although he doubtless knew very little of either the Prussian or the South German work of the mid-century.

In his next great building, Trinity Church in Boston, with greater conscientiousness toward the Romanesque he produced a monument more reminiscent, less eclectic, less experimental, and altogether less noteworthy in design. It has nevertheless been accepted as his masterpiece. Its prominence—which caused his acceptance after its completion in 1878 as the leading architect in America—and the experimentation with polychromy in the excessively rugged stone work of the exterior and in the now gloomy interior are historically the chief reasons for its importance. The murals and glass, even though they were the work of LaFarge and others of the best American painters of the time, fell far short of the vision which Richardson must have had of a richness such as that of Saint Mark's. Like Gilbert Scott who had, twenty years earlier, advocated more experimentation with colour in the development of modern architecture, Richardson was incapable of carrying his vision into execution. But he began a revival of the crafts dependent on architecture and set for the time an extraordinarily high standard, comparable even to that of Morris.

In the next decade up to his death Richardson had more work than he and his atelier of pupils could handle. For a time he seemed to have created single-handed an American architecture, strangely enough without any particular connection with American traditions except in his occasional buildings in wood.

In his public buildings such as railroad stations and libraries he was less constrained by the canons of the Romanesque than at Trinity Church. In the finest of these he succeeded in expressing in vigorous design and with excellent craftsmanship of brick or various stones rational and simple plans, often using reminiscences of the early French Renaissance as freely as of the Romanesque. Of these works Sever Hall at Harvard with its rich brickwork and almost complete freedom from reminiscence represents one pole. Austin Hall, also at Harvard, with its elaborate columns and arches and Auvergnat polychromy represents the other. In his larger city buildings of intermediary order such as the Pittsburgh Courthouse and Jail he achieved a sense of large scale and impressive force that has hardly been equalled since his day. Even his more definitely François I work is much superior to that of the Renaissance Revival in France.

In the Marshall Field wholesale store in Chicago, a building devoid of all ornament, he produced of solid masonry an edifice which to those who were able to understand the relation of construction to expression pointed the way for the first and finest skyscrapers. As architecture this was more successful than the contemporary Paris works of engineering. It may stand beside the best industrial buildings of Germany, built a generation later, as a New Tradition monument of the first order.

In city houses such as the parsonage of Trinity Church he was all but free of the Romanesque and manipulated his brickwork with more virtuosity than even the Dutch had up to then obtained. Unfortunately the rich interiors on which were lavished the finest and most varied materials and the best craftsmanship of the day have sadly dimmed and the execution must ever as in the case of Trinity Church have fallen far short of the creative vision. As the creator of a New Tradition he did not have the resources of later generations in Europe. But he had developed a rich foliate ornament hardly at all bound by Romanesque or Byzantine tradition which most of his imitators were only able to caricature.

In his country houses of wood, he was quite unconstrained by the past. He sought and found an ideal naturalistic solution of the problem of the shingled house on the New England shore or the Western plain. (Figure 16.) No buildings were ever more American than these nor more ideally adapted to their time and their purpose. Because he understood the importance of construction and execution he was able truly to create as architecture the "picturesque" house which three generations of Romantic builders had signally failed to translate from projects into reality.

But Richardson died in 1886 at the age of forty-eight. The style which was accepted and continued by the country as his was not his freer manner but the more definite Romanesque Revival exemplified in Trinity Church or Austin Hall. There has been no greater tragedy for American architecture, not even in the death of John Root five years later. For Richardson was cut off at a time when he might have gone on with the development of his own style and have eventually made it really intelligible to the country at large, so that its acceptance would have been the acceptance of the New Tradition.and not merely of another revival.

The dominance of Richardson was not of course complete. Especially in New York various Beaux Arts revivals particularly exploited by Hunt were more important and the dependence on Paris already well established. But the new cities of the West followed Richardson generally and it was in Chicago that the school of Richardson found its most significant continuance. The year before Richardson's death Colonel Jenney of Chicago introduced in the Home Insurance Buildings the first true skeleton construction in metal which was to make possible the skyscraper. Three years later in the Tacoma Building of 1888, also in Chicago, Holabird and Roche produced the first building entirely supported by a metal skeleton. With all its awkwardness and its ornament—which was second-rate Richardsonian Romanesque—this first real skyscraper has never been equalled as frank expression of functional structure: all the way that skyscraper design has travelled since has been from the point of view of rationalism along a false route. It is for this reason that the later course of architecture in America must be so largely traced outside the field of the skyscraper; and it is for this reason also that this building, doubtless not felt to be "artistic" by its designers, is so much more important than the buildings of Sullivan. For they lay to one side of, but still on the false route. They provide, however, the transitional links between the unconscious New Tradition of Richardson and the conscious New Tradition fully developed by Wright.

John W. Root, however, was the architect who might have been the immediate successor of Richardson. Yet he did not have time to build the masterpieces of the Chicago school: skyscrapers altogether fine where that of Holabird and Roche had been chiefly important as indicating the route to be followed. Root was born in Georgia in 1850 and died in 1891 at the early age of forty-one. After studying art in Liverpool he took his degree in Civil Engineering from New York University. In Chicago after the fire he formed a partnership with Burnham. The latter was after Root's death more than any other responsible, perhaps somewhat unwittingly, for turning American architecture from the free Mediævalistic and experimental tradition of Richardson into the straight channel of correct Roman and other "Period" revival.

Root had worked in New York with Renwick, the Gothic Revivalist, but in his own work in Chicago he kept definitely within the Richardsonian tradition. His great Monadnock building, the last large building built of solid masonry, was even more bald and elemental than Richardson's Marshall Field Building and depended for its effect on the sloping chamfers of its corners and its heavy bell cornice. This was one of the earliest American buildings to attract the attention of the Europeans who sought some new leadership in style from across the Atlantic. In the Rookery, as befitted a man much more an engineer than Richardson had been, he gave the first valid solution of the modern office building plan; while in his ornament there, working from the Richardsonian Romanesque, he developed a more definitely eclectic manner which was to be taken up and carried further by Sullivan and Wright. Even in his most completely Romanesque building, the Chicago Club, he showed that he understood the true relation of Richardson to the Romanesque and did not fall into the error of his fellow followers in the East of merely making a large and unintelligent draft on archæology, or returning as the Western followers so generally did to the vagaries of ignorant mid-nineteenth century building—their interpretation of freedom.

At the same time in order to handle the tremendous commissions for sky-scrapers for which the office was called on, Root's partner Burnham developed the intricate organization of the American architectural office which has made of all but a few of our later architects not individual crea-tive artists but factory managers. The importance of this step was very great. It brought about the increasing dependence of American architects on their draftsmen and hence encouraged the endless repetition of tradi-tional detail requiring no original designing in which all draftsmen were instructed. It is impossible to say whether many of the outstanding archi-tects of America since this development of office organization could have designed a building: it is very clear that few of them have ever directly done so.

What more than anything else sets Wright and Sullivan apart from their contemporaries in America is that they were as Richardson had been, as the best twentieth century architects in Europe were at least during their creative period, architects in their own right and not merely regisseurs controlled by the draftsmen they must work through. This is a vital point of difference between those forms of the New Tradition with which this chapter began. The craftsmen architects more usually work largely in their own right; the others for their detail send the draftsmen not as previously to the books of the past but to the books of the present.

What the World's Fair would have been had Root lived to be its chief de-signer we can not know. Surely it seems, if we may judge from his ideas for rich polychromy, and if we may presume a further development of his limited eclecticism of style and of his rationalism on a large scale uncon-trolled by outside considerations, that it might have been of extraordinary magnificence. But when Root died in 1891 Burnham called in Hunt and

McKim, Mead and White from the East bringing the day of the Richardsonian Romanesque to a close. The introductory phase of the New Tradition in America was finished before it had at all begun as a tradition in
Europe. But the fact that a new style-phase had appeared in America was
hardly known outside the country even in later years when Europeans sought
it here all but in vain. Richardson and his following had for a brief time
created a manner from which more generally was to be hoped than has in
a generation come to pass.

It was the young men who had followed Richardson's advice and gone to
the Ecole des Beaux Arts, revivers not even so much of the noble past as of
a somewhat restrained form of the Classicism which had attained its culmination under Napoleon III, who came to dominate American architecture.
The later course of the conscious New Tradition in America has been not
the story of the party in power but of a small and limited opposition. That
the White City of 1893 was not altogether an hallucination, a delusion of
grandeur, and a sort of white plague, Fiske Kimball has perhaps displayed
in his account of American architecture. As we have seen in Europe the
New Tradition achieved its full development only when the freer rationalism
dependent on Romantic Mediævalism was fused with another more formal
rationalism issuing from that sounder sort of Classicism to which with the
exception of Richardson's work and that of certain Germans the finest productions of the nineteenth century had been due.

In America there was never such a fusion. Against the perhaps excessive
vagaries of the Richardsonian Romanesque and its offshoots there was a
sharp reaction toward the taste and the refinement which revivalistic Classicism in its Roman, its Renaissance and its Baroque or Georgian forms,
was held to offer. To Sullivan and Wright there was no possible attitude
toward this largely sterile reaction but intransigence. It was their mis-
fortune that active rebellion was necessary as a protest against blind conformity. They were much less able therefore to attain that balance and
serenity which is frequently found in their great contemporaries abroad or to
influence the general character of the architecture of their generation in
America.

Louis Sullivan was born in 1856 and he did not die until 1924, but his own
work was relatively unimportant in his later years beside that of his pupil
and follower Wright. Sullivan was educated at the Massachusetts Institute

of Technology and then went to work in Philadelphia for Frank Furness. Furness was an extraordinary architect of the mid-century whose buildings in their all but complete originality and independence illustrate how generally unfitted the earlier generation in America, devoid of sound training, and without any wide knowledge of the architecture of the past, was for stylistic experimentation. All the same in his youth there was perhaps no better office in America in which Louis Sullivan might gain courage to believe that anything was possible to the architect who willed it.

Before going to Paris Sullivan also worked for a year in Chicago with Jenney, the builder of the Home Insurance Building already mentioned. Here the optimism and the immense building activity after the fire exercised as much of an effect on him as had his work with Furness. It was as a convinced innovator in theory that he set out for the Ecole des Beaux Arts for what was to have been the completion of a really thorough training. But he was already too intransigent, too far developed to submit to academic discipline. He returned to Chicago after a year convinced that there alone a new architecture might be created. This was perhaps unfortunate, for the training of Guadet, the tradition of Labrouste, would surely have been healthy for him. It might moreover have been more possible for him to influence his contemporaries had he understood their gods.

But the early work of the firm which he founded with Adler shows hardly at all the originality that was to be expected. To-day his first buildings appear, but for a certain facility in the ornament and a certain attempt to express the structure, far less fine or important than the contemporary work of Root. Only in the eighties did he join his Chicago colleagues in following the Richardsonian Romanesque. Then, however, he produced in the Auditorium Building one of the great monuments of the manner. Here he also showed himself for the first time as the prophet of a new ornament. While the exterior remained definitely a product of the Chicago Romanesque school, in the interior there appeared at once those naturalistic and those geometrical patterns to whose development Sullivan was to devote his major energies. Wright has specifically denied that Sullivan's ornament owed anything to Richardson. It is possible that it did not directly or consciously. It nevertheless could hardly avoid going on from much the point at which Richardson left off. History is frequently superior to such denials of fact without impugning in the least the sincerity of those who make them.

In the Wainwright Building in St. Louis, built in 1890, the year before Root's death, Sullivan attempted definitely in his exterior design to establish a formula. Despite his introduction of intermediate vertical piers of equal weight between his supporting piers, Sullivan produced here what has since been considered as the norm of logical treatment for tall buildings of steel construction. Anxious as he was to express his "Idea" that form follows function it must to-day appear that in the Tacoma Building had already been provided a far more satisfactory solution of the problem. Moreover the elaborate ornament, in which he was perhaps more interested than in his expression of structure, was out of scale with so large a building; and his heavy cornice was later discarded by all but his Classical opponents in the design of skyscrapers. It has been said of Sullivan that he was an architect of one building, this Wainwright Building, for his other later buildings there and in Chicago, Buffalo, and New York follow it very closely.

Far finer, however, was his Transportation Building at the World's Fair, in which his ornament was more justified by the plaster construction, his rationalism less pretentious, his general design more varied, and unconsciously more in the tradition of Richardson. Here the ornamentist was free to display his extraordinary talent and to enhance his patterns with rich polychromy. The Hotel St. Nicholas in St. Louis built the same year illustrates also how much more successful he was outside the skyscraper, particularly if it be compared with his St. Louis Union Trust also of the same year.

After the Columbian Exposition and the general triumph of the Beaux Arts trained Eastern architects, Sullivan had fewer clients and less opportunity to work on large city projects. His later buildings were chiefly small banks in the prairie country, of which that at Owatonna, Minnesota, is particularly fine, as well as houses, and tombs. Indeed in such tombs as that of the Getty family in Chicago, or in that of the Wainwright family in St. Louis built somewhat earlier in 1892, jewels of ornament and simple massive form, he was nearly at his best. It seems clear that in spite of his extraordinary virtuosity and his ambition to express in his ornament the American democracy as Whitman has tried to do in *Leaves of Grass*, he was not an architect of the calibre and certainly not of the general appeal of Richardson and Root. To a large extent the reaction away from him was justified, and the Classical Stanford White in the conservative East—as it was then called with some justification as regards the arts—produced in the Boston Public

Library based on Labrouste's Bibliothèque Sainte-Geneviève, nearly as fine a monument of the New Tradition as any work of Sullivan's without consciously breaking with the principles of revivalism.

In the latter part of his life, Sullivan devoted much time to the vain task of proselyting for his theory of form following function and of free ornament. His *System of Architectural Ornament* was illustrated by plates in which his theory was carried to its furthest point in a naturalistic fantasy entitled *Impromptu* and a Euclidean fantasy entitled *Awakening of the Pentagon*. In this particular line his most important follower has been Claude Bragdon. The latter has supported his fourth dimensional design schemes on theosophical grounds; but he has in his buildings seldom shown any very definite renewal of even three dimensional form. Fortunately this was not the only continuance of Sullivan's ideas, which were carried much further by his pupil Wright.

Frank Lloyd Wright was born in 1869. After graduating in civil engineering from the University of Wisconsin he went to work in the office of Sullivan. Already in his first house built in 1893, there are visible certain elements of his own style as independent from that of his master. The loose planning, the blocklike forms, the horizontality are already conspicuous and the young architect is from then on clearly a greater innovator and a greater architect than his master who became more and more preoccupied with ornament and its perfect finish.

Of the series of houses built previous to the War, all under the same general inspiration and with the same general effects, certain are particularly notable for their exceptional quality or because they mark particularly the several special tendencies in his work. These were built largely around Chicago, but certain fine examples are in Buffalo and Rochester as well as in different cities of the Middle West. At the same time, although his major work was done in large suburban houses of the type so extensively built in the age of Roosevelt and Taft, he was called on as well to do churches, factories, warehouses, and other varied projects. His continuing experience gave him particular mastery in residence building but he was nevertheless at home in whatever type he touched. Like Richardson his style is so strong and so much his own that it is all-inclusive.

Among his houses the first perhaps which is intrinsically notable is the Willets house in Highland Park, Illinois, built in 1901. Here the symmetrical repose, the breadth of handling and the simplicity of the treatment of the ordinary American stucco-covered timber frame display him as a great composer making of a current vernacular construction a real monument of conscious and intellectual art. Far finer however is his Larkin Soap Factory Office of 1903 where a more specialized function caused the creation of more startlingly original forms. The mechanically perfect brickwork of this gave scale to the imposing masses. The placing and the shape of the windows was masterly both from the point of view of the technics of the admirable interior and of the abstract form of the exterior. The capstones and the simple ornament that crowned the piers were admirably related to the whole. There was not yet a building in Europe that showed more completely the possibilities of the New Tradition in the industrial field. (Figure 21.)

In the Oak Park Unity Temple of the next year somewhat the same scheme was applied to poured concrete construction. The absence of the fine brick surfaces, the greater use of abstract ornament make of this a less unsuccessful monument than the Larkin Office, although the choice of material was significant and it was used with eminent rationalism.

In the Ross house of the same year Wright did for American wood construction what he had done for stucco construction in the Willets house. Here was a worthy successor of Richardson's wooden houses but much bolder, more positive than they. At the same time he was building many houses of brick. Of these the masterpiece was the Robie House in Chicago with its long horizontal bands of wall surmounted by long groups of small windows and capped finally with the widest eaves and the longest roofline he had ever achieved. The effect here is indeed exceedingly mannered but it expresses an admirably functional plan and it has a three dimensional organization of planes that is absolutely unprecedented. Here Wright seems almost to have pushed beyond the New Tradition and foreseen thus early some of the effects of the New Pioneers. (Figure 20.)

In his own house at Taliesin, Green Springs, Wisconsin, the irregularity of the rough local stone, the interminable extension of the roofs and the diffuseness of the plan quite destroy an effect which was no doubt intended as a further advance along the lines of the Robie house. The houses that led up to the Robie house such as the Heath house in Buffalo, despite the trivial patterns in the leaded glass reminiscent of Sullivan's geometric dallyings, are far finer. In the Coonley house of 1911, at Riverside, Illinois, he had considerable success in enlarging the formula of the Willets house. It is an important and on the whole a magnificent work. Unfortunately the coloured diaper with which he sought in the upper walls of the house to vary the universal whiteness of the stucco is, like his leaded glass patterns, out of keeping with the dignity of the whole. Wright had less than Sullivan the skill of the ornament designer. Fortunately he has been ordinarily more chary in its use.

In the Midway Gardens of 1913 Wright was freer to be fantastic and decorative. In his alternation of plain brick, concrete slab, and all-over patterned surfaces, he was as successful as even de Klerk in Holland. In his broad symmetry, his well placed accents and the three dimensional interplay of geometrical elements, in part structural and in part ornamental, he justified completely his preoccupations with ornament and created in the unlikely form of a beer garden one of his greatest works. Regrettably the interior was not up to the exterior and the ornament in detail was of a peculiarly awkward and ill-understood Cubism which foreshadowed some of the worst efforts of the German Expressionists after the War.

It is pertinent to remark here that his house interiors also were never worthy of his exteriors despite the extraordinary thoroughness with which he studied their design and the excellence of their plans. His rooms were dark, uncomfortable and generally at once cluttered and monotonous. His efforts to make them light and playful only increased their self-conscious fussiness and their self-righteous stodginess. Beside them Richardson's appear those of a master decorator. Yet they were at times very close indeed, but for the failure of some spark to give them real life, to the interiors of the New Pioneers to whose principles, not for many years to be fully articulated in Europe, they largely conform.

The Imperial Hotel at Tokio done in 1916 has been Wright's largest commission. Yet the design, despite its admirable plan, is redundant, overburdened with unskilfully exotic ornament, and except where the quality of the materials is well brought out, vastly ineffective. The interiors on which Wright expended apparently a considerable effort are incomparably worse than those however Louis XVI of any coëval Ritz.

On his return to America Wright began to work in California. The Barnsdall house of 1917 is also one of his least successful buildings. The poured concrete smoothly surfaced enhances the monstrous weight of the design. The ornament of unparalleled inappropriateness, suggesting whittling rather than moulding, has only the virtue of being well placed and of lightening somewhat an almost pyramidal gloom. Yet the handling of the elaborate plan is admirable in the relation of the house and its adjuncts to the meridional landscape. Wright's worship of nature has led him to accomplish in the general effect a harmony in the direct line of the picturesque of the early Romantics. In his return to the experiment of 1904 in Unity Temple with monolithic construction the wealth of his clients permitted in this case full play to his intemperance in ornament. This had perhaps also been encouraged by direct contact with the Far East. Thus in his positive "modernism" he produced a major work in many ways less satisfactory than the houses of the better Néo-Spanish architects of California such as Myron Hunt or George Washington Smith, at least negatively restrained in their nominal borrowing from the past.

In the Millard house at Pasadena built in 1923 he evolved a new method of construction which permitted to his love of ornament its finest expression. The house has double walls of pre-cast concrete blocks with steel reinforcement in the cement mortar joints. If the surfaces which define his brilliantly studied masses are to be broken by the joints of the blocks there is no reason why the blocks themselves should not be cast with repeating patterns—especially as those patterns, occasionally cut through to form grilles, are simple and admirably suited to the process of manufacture. They give in the bright sunshine a richness of texture that is astonishing. Almost never as in the Millard house and several succeeding houses about Los Angeles has Wright so succeeded in bringing into harmony his various discordant tendencies. The relation of the work of man to the natural surroundings is more perfect than ever before. His rationalism and his command of pure form are as conspicuous—although less technically Cubistic —as in the Robie house or the Larkin Factory, and his ornament is subordinated to the whole scheme as it had never been before. (Figure 23.)

It is fortunate therefore that Wright has been not only an architect—that is a designer and creator of buldings—but also an engineering technician. In his latest system of using concrete and steel he provides for the use of the machine and the standardization which he has always urged as a writer. Architect and engineer—for such despite his training is the order—he is also one of America's most prolific writers on architecture. His occasional papers, *In the Cause of Architecture,* appearing in the Architectural Record have urged even more vehemently than his own little known constructions the adoption of an integrated and national new manner, of which his work has remained in his own land all but the sum.

For among those Americans more or less his followers there have been few to really continue or develop his work. His son and Chase McArthur have both in very different ways attempted the fusion of a structure resembling somewhat that of the New Pioneers with an expression based rather on the Spanish architecture of California. Barry Byrne, as his project for the Cathedral of Cork in Ireland notably illustrates, has come closer and closer to German Expressionistic Mediævalism. Neutra alone is a worthy disciple of Wright. He is an Austrian and moreover definitely a New Pioneer. Wright's more general influence around Chicago was over even before the War. It is indeed there to-day that he is least appreciated and there that the use of obviously foreign detail on skyscrapers has become at least as frequent as in New York.

Wright's theories are curiously incomplete and even in part contradictory. He has learned very little the lesson of Ford and he has but a limited sympathy with the spirit of the machine as such. His approach to a pure architecture is complicated with the Nature worship and the ecstatic and individualistic democracy of Whitman. There is moreover an orientalism which appears as much in his writing as in his work. These influences, inherited in part from Sullivan, undoubtedly weaken more than occasionally his intellectual and logical command of his problems and they lend support to his cult of ornament and embellishment as essential to architecture.

Much has been written, and vigorously denied by Wright, of his dependence on the Far East. In spite of his denials Wright is unquestionably eclectic in style and his eclecticism in opposition to the revival of European styles by his contemporaries in America has thrown him back consciously or unconsciously on the Far East, the Ancient East, and the Maya of Mexico. In the Wisconsin camps designed at the same time as the California work the substructures are the same in method of building and in scheme of design as those used on the Pacific, but the exotic wooden superstructures suggest rather the nostalgia of the Ancient North.

Too much has been set down in negative criticism. It remains to be said in conclusion that he is, without qualification and without the support of any worthy colleagues or important American followers, the greatest American architect of the first quarter of the twentieth century. Of his international influence the later architecture of the New Tradition in Holland offers the most definite testimony.

CHAPTER TEN

THE NEW TRADITION IN HOLLAND

THE direct international influence of Dr. H. P. Berlage has been less important than that of Wright. But within Holland the New Tradition is almost
entirely dependent upon him and has brilliantly developed the many tendencies inherent in his personal manner into a general national style that
has been admired and emulated by the rest of the world. He is unquestionably to be considered with Wright, whom he has done so much to bring
to European attention, as one of the major architects of the early twentieth
century.

Berlage was born in 1856, three years after van Gogh, the best known of
modern Dutch artists. His period of training fell therefore within the lifetime of the second generation of rationalizing Classists, Labrouste and
Semper, of the great nineteenth century Mediævalists, and of those men
in England who developed from Romanticism a domestic architecture based
on craftsmanship. Berlage's work also reflects more than that of the other
founders of the New Tradition the architectural background of the mid-
century.

The specific forerunner of the New Tradition in Holland was Dr. P. J. H.
Cuijpers, born in 1827 and dying only in 1917. He restored and built many
Catholic churches throughout his life, but he is best known as the architect
of the Rijksmuseum and the Central Railroad Station of Amsterdam. In
his ecclesiastical building Cuijpers was as whole hearted a Gothic Revivalist
as any in England. But he sought also as did the more intelligent Mediævalists elsewhere, at least in theory, to return to national building methods

—which meant in Holland exposed brickwork—and by use of decoration dependent on handcraftsmanship to regain the honesty and autochthonous quality which the various Classical Revivals had all but destroyed. He provided even in his most completely reminiscent work a tradition of sound building in brick which has been the central point of interest in the architecture of Berlage and the Amsterdam school.

Cuijpers's earliest non-ecclesiastical constructions are of little merit. The houses built in his native city, Roermond, in 1851 reflect as much as the contemporary Maximilianstrasse the domestic architecture of the early Gothic Revival in England which had had such a pervasive international influence in Northern Europe. Later in such work he turned rather toward the forms of the sixteenth century in his own country. But while he achieved a greater coherence between his general design and his building methods his work was not altogether free from wooden excrescences of Gingerbread or Néo-Gingerbread order.

The most successful of his later houses was the Bovenkerk manse of 1875. There is in his own house and other houses built in the Vondelstraat in Amsterdam about this period a further development of functional planning and an almost entire dependence on the expression of structure for the architectural effect. These houses are less reminiscent than the contemporary domestic building of Richardson. Yet because of the awkwardness of the detail and the uncertainty in free form of a man trained to work within historical ecclesiastical formulas, they are distinctly less fine and more closely related to that general mass of building with which this period of the nineteenth century is so gloomily associated.

In 1876 Cuijpers began the Rijksmuseum, his most important work. Here, according to the revivalistic principles of the contemporary eclecticism of taste, he justified his considerable eclecticism of style by basing the expression on the national transitional architecture of the sixteenth century. In general design this immense building is regular and sober. Its impressive effect is due rather to the excellence of the massing and the fine execution than to its rich and varied minor architectural features. As in the work of Richardson the sumptuousness of the use of sculpture and painting has sadly dimmed with time. Except possibly in the circle of Morris in England, however, really good or even interesting minor art was nowhere to be obtained in the seventies.

In 1881 Cuijpers began the Central Railroad Station in Amsterdam in collaboration with the engineers van Gendt and van Asperen. The train shed due to the engineers is no more excellent in itself or better fused with the front portion of the building than in other stations of the time. The monument as a whole is distinctly less fine than the Rijksmuseum which it resembles so closely. After the completion of the station Cuijpers devoted himself again chiefly to restoration and church building. Thus his work of the seventies and eighties had no immediate issue.

Berlage in the eighties was strongly influenced by the Néo-Renaissance of Semper which controlled at Zurich where he was educated; and like so many of the architects of the Age of Romanticism by more general memories of his travels in Italy. His first buildings are commonplace attempts to clothe modern offices rationally with Renaissance forms.

The first effect of the work of Cuijpers on him was to turn him toward eclecticism. In a design for a mausoleum done in 1889 all the styles of the past were joined conglomerately as in the fantasies of half a century earlier and with even less attempt at fusion. But in 1893 in the insurance offices on the Damrak in Amsterdam he began to use the Romanesque as a nucleus of crystallization in the same way Cuijpers had used the national sixteenth century style. The building was, however, of stone, not of brick, and Italianisms were still prominent. There was moreover by reaction against his earlier Renaissance formalism a definite *parti pris* for the novel and the irregular. Such exotic vagaries of experimentation particularly in detail had become widespread in Europe as well as America in the eighties and were paralleled by the contemporary passion for Japanese art. Outside Holland however this movement in the eighties of which Eastlake's Néo-Gingerbread formed a part led to no more continuing accomplishment than the original Gingerbread and brought in its return a sharp reaction toward Classical restraints.

If Berlage was able to develop directly from this exotic manner of the eighties into the full New Tradition it was because he inherited from Cuijpers an appreciation of the necessity for sound and honest building and because behind all his experimentation was a directive principle, a sort of will to style creation. He substituted for the intellectual discipline of the Mediævalists which had been archæological a new discipline which was mathematical. Beneath even his early extravagance in detail there was not only a clear and rational structure but also a solid geometrical framework which was able to carry much which in particular was worthless quite as in the case of certain Baroque building.

Most other experimental architecture of this period was seen to be devoid of real value as soon as the temporary virtue of mere novelty in the parts lost its effect and the barrenness of the whole was revealed. Unfortunately the architects who followed after in their reaction from innovation returned usually to copying good detail of the past, avoiding the pitfalls of experimentation by depending on that which was surely safe however lacking it might be in life. Had they realized that the awkwardness of the work of the eighties was intrinsic and necessary in the earliest stage of style creation, the New Tradition might have developed more generally and more rapidly but doubtless no more effectively. For the mass of the weak lends no real support in the work of formulation which must be done inevitably by the few who are strong.

The period of Berlage's training, the influence behind and about him are important to bear in mind in the study of his early work. For that work forms the transition internationally between architects such as Cuijpers and Richardson who were in varying degree Mediæval Revivalists and the architects of the developed New Tradition who began to appear in numbers with the opening of the twentieth century. Berlage, indeed, as an early founder of the manner has continued to be hampered by the lack of taste characteristic of the period of his formation.

After the Damrak insurance offices of 1893 the first true phase of his personal manner began to appear in executed buildings. He continued to be dependent on Romanesque forms; but he achieved increasing freedom in planning and in general design. More and more he obtained his effects through fine proportion and the use of good brickwork rather than by the elaboration of carved stone detail. The buildings whether city offices or suburban houses are much more irregular than those of Cuijpers. When several of them were enlarged ten or fifteen years later, as for example the insurance offices in the Kerkplein at the Hague, he regularized them considerably, seeking symmetry as definitely as he had earlier avoided it.

The work of the nineties reached its culmination in the Amsterdam Beurs (Stock Exchange). Berlage's first design of 1885 for this had been very definitely related to the Rijksmuseum and Railroad Station of Cuijpers in the nationalism of its Late Gothic and early Baroque reminiscences. But the series of designs of 1897 which led up to the finally executed design of 1898 were Romanesque in inspiration and increasingly simplified and rationalized. Embellishment was largely omitted from the exterior as unnecessary to elevations and masses which achieved their interest from the rigid geometrical proportioning of the essential utilitarian features.

This building, finished in 1903, was unquestionably Berlage's masterpiece and it marked more than any other one monument the appearance of the full New Tradition in Europe after some quarter century of preparation. It was, however, very close to Richardson's finest work. Moreover the simplified bevelled detail of the stone work and the way in which the minor arts were called on made its relation to the general manner of the preceding half century very plain. Yet such a continuance of the practices of the Mediævalists of the mid-century were far healthier and more architectural than the linear and Art Nouveau ornament which was becoming so general in France and Germany at this time.

Here for the first time appeared a consciously reintegrated architecture: the first manner of the twentieth century with its rationalism of function and structure, its dependence on fine execution in traditional building materials and its limited irregularity. This latter was held in check by an increasing approach to symmetry now that the principle of non-Classical picturesque composition had finally become acceptable in monumental architecture. Moreover the principle of the new eclecticism of style was clearly established. The specifically Romanesque features were reduced until they were hardly recognizable and features suggestive of other epochs of the past were introduced as well. The essential was that all these borrowed features which recalled more or less distinctly the past were fused and merged with one another and with the direct expression of function and structure. In the interior the metal work of the roof was exposed and combined harmoniously and logically with the masonry of the walls as Cuijpers had not done in his Railroad Station. Thus engineering became again a part of architecture in the way that Labrouste in particular had anticipated half a century earlier in the Bibliothèque Sainte-Geneviève.

The houses built by Berlage at the turn of the century also show a change. They are on the whole simpler and more regular. At the same time the

Diamond Cutters Building in Amsterdam of 1898 shows on a smaller scale than the Beurs all the major virtues and the minor vices of Berlage's architecture. (Figure 27.) The next important project, that of 1907 for the Palace of Peace in the Hague, marks no very considerable development. It is however distinctly more symmetrical and more aggressively massive paralleling the increasing monumentality characteristic in German architecture of this period. The design for the Beethovenhuis of the next year is of much the same type.

Toward 1910 Berlage turned rather toward the development of surface plasticity as opposed to monumentality and toward a further simplification of façade treatment omitting more and more decorative accessories and particularly detail in cut stone. The vast city-planning schemes on which he was called to work at this time may well have thus effected him by turning his attention from single buildings to complexes of buildings. The houses in the Transvaalstraat and the Ringkade at Amsterdam illustrate this socialization of a talent which had previously been happiest at the highly individual treatment of single outstanding monuments.

It was at this period that the finest younger members of the Amsterdam school began to work independently and to develop for themselves this phase of Berlage's work. At the same time he himself not only turned from individual office buildings to apartment housing in the city, but in the country he began to build large groups such as the dairy farm de Schipborg at Zuidlaren of 1914, with a distinct advance in clarity and serenity of expression similar to that of the best English productions of the architecture of craftsmanship.

In 1912 after a voyage to America Berlage returned to Holland much impressed with the work of Frank Lloyd Wright which had already received publication in Germany in 1910. His lectures on Wright's work introduced in Holland an influence which was general and marked on the younger men. Indeed it served later in part to aid the New Pioneer Oud in breaking away from the Berlagian school.

Just before the War in 1914 Berlage provided a most interesting demonstration of his versatility and his ability as in the Beurs to reintegrate engineering with architecture. In Holland House in London he gave very admirable free expression to the terra cotta facing of steel construction, the problem which at the same time in the American skyscraper was becoming so hopelessly involved with Late Gothic reminiscence. This is a work comparable in quality if not in size or significance to the Amsterdam Beurs. (Figure 28.)

The years of the War were occupied with the planning of the Southern extension of Amsterdam in which his followers had an opportunity in the individual blocks or sections of blocks to work harmoniously together and to produce along his general lines one of the finest of twentieth century city quarters. This work is still being carried on.

In the design for an immense museum in the Hague done after the War he seems to have been to some extent influenced by the work of his followers as well as by Wright, particularly in the treatment of the new methods of construction then coming into use in Holland. But neither this nor the magnificent scheme of 1922 for the development of the Hofplein in Rotterdam were built. The next actually executed building, an insurance office in the Hague, designed in collaboration with A. N. van Gendt in 1925, shows like the London offices of 1914 an attempt to find a rational and original expression of a new type of construction, in this case a reinforced concrete frame with brick filling such as is used so much in America, thus far without any architectural success. But the effect was somewhat weak and trivial and less clear and simple than in the large projects of the preceding years. However the Christian Science Church in the Hague built in the same year in which he covered his concrete construction with a plain shell of brick in order to emphasize the geometry of its form showed that he had not lost his mastery. And finally in his civic designs of 1927 for the Mercatorplein in Amsterdam he succeeded in quite fusing his individual manner with the later reduced style of the general Amsterdam school.

While Berlage is the earliest of the modern architects of Holland, setting with his Amsterdam Beurs the standard which those who have come later have set out to attain, it is only in theory that he sums up the whole New Tradition there. The school of Amsterdam whose members are all in large part his followers and even before that his own contemporaries, of whom the most individual was de Bazel, have expanded his work in different directions and produced a vast mass of work of which much may even appear finer than that of Berlage who was the first to set out upon the new path. Perhaps the most influential in distinguishing the work of the Amsterdam school from the mere imitation of Berlage was M. de Klerk in his work in the extension of Amsterdam just before and during the War. On the basis of Berlage's rationalism and his dependence on fine brickwork, de Klerk developed a highly personal style which became at once very popular with the younger generation of architects in Holland. His buildings, arranged in blocks or even in groups of blocks, are monumental only in size and are largely devoid of any features which resemble traditional architectural features. At the same time the massing and grouping shows a certain dependence on tradition.

The great quality of his manner rests in the amazing skill with which the brickwork is used to enhance the effect of the surface by variations in the direction of the course and the size and the shape of the brick. There are even for strong emphasis occasional planes hung with roof tiles. The focal features, whimsical and generally curved in plan, are used to break up the functionally regular design with abandon and even with humour, something that is hardly found elsewhere in architecture.

But not only are the wall surfaces rich like textiles, the windows which break them so piquantly are similarly varied in shape and size and reduced in scale by means of small panes and prominent muntins. Thus by the brick texture and the strategic placing of windows and abstract ornamental features the flat surfaces of these buildings are given a life and plasticity which is seldom found in the more solid and more monumental work of Berlage even though it was suggested and even sought by him as early as the Beurs.

The extreme point of the fantastic in the work of the Amsterdam school was the Scheepvaarthuis of van der Meij built in 1913, where no plain surfaces are left in the riot of textures and abstract embellishment. But de Klerk himself was increasing in sobriety down to his death in 1925 and his peculiar power of manipulating brick surfaces was most fully manifest where he indulged it least. Very like that of de Klerk is the work of P. Kramer although he has been on the whole more definitely eclectic in style and he has avoided from the first the more excessive whimsicality which was at once the hall-mark and the vice of de Klerk. On a reinforced concrete structure Kramer has hung his curving brick wall surfaces like curtains to obtain magnificent but not always logically defensible effects. This he did most notably in the department store de Bijenkorf built in the Hague in 1927. More than de Klerk he has depended on sculpture and decorative embellishment and in so far he is closer to Berlage.

The Amsterdam Office of Public Works has built large numbers of schools and other public buildings in a somewhat simplified version of the manner of de Klerk and Kramer. At their best the buildings of these anonymous architects are as fine or finer than those of their well-known contemporaries. They testify to the strength of the New Tradition as a tradition in Holland. In them functional necessities have held exotic tendencies in check and the specific effect of the fine brickwork, the plastic surfaces, and the oddly shaped windows is more telling as in the later work of de Klerk for restraint in its use. (Figure 29.)

An interesting and individual architect affiliated with the Amsterdam school is W. M. Dudok to whom a great number of buildings at Hilversum is due. Like Kramer he has studied buildings of the past for his effects of mass and like the Amsterdam Public Works Office the functional necessities of school building have kept him from the wilder humours of de Klerk. In his later work particularly there has been a somewhat greater frankness as to the underlying structure and a tendency to approach the more definitely Cubistic effects of the New Pioneers. But a comparison of his project for the Rotterdam Beurs with that of Oud makes it clear that these tendencies are incidental and part of the general movement of the New Tradition toward simplicity already specifically remarked in Holland in the case of Berlage and de Klerk; although in Dudok's case carried further to the point of constituting a transitional manner. (Figure 30.)

The names here mentioned by no means exhaust the list of important Dutch architects of the early twentieth century. For Boeijinga, Mertens, Baanders, Staal, to name but a few, have produced buildings as fine as those of whom there has been particular discussion. Moreover a Catholic architect, Kropholler, has been able like de Bazel, whose Netherlands Trading Corporation Building is one of the most impressive and original buildings of Amsterdam, to develop more or less independently of Berlage from the tradition of Cuijpers. But on the whole the New Traditionalists of Holland either have followed Berlage directly or the more extravagant version of his manner most typically represented by de Klerk and Kramer. Only lately has the influence of the New Pioneers begun to break down somewhat this universal conformity.

All sorts of city buildings have been produced in quantities with especial success in the development of domestic construction on a large scale. In the country "picturesqueness" has found in Dutch architecture of the New Tradition its apotheosis. The houses are very irregular in plan, of brick and timber with heavy thatched roofs, thus they melt into the landscapes very much more successfully than the rustic constructions of the Age of Romanticism whose builders sought the same effects, but usually left their attainment to the aquatinter or the lithographer.

The New Tradition in Holland has indeed remained generally close to the non-reminiscent tendencies of Romanticism of which it is perhaps the most noteworthy heir. Beside the work of Frank Lloyd Wright the Dutch work appears more versatile but it is more definitely tied than his to the immediate past and offers unquestionably less inspiration for the immediate future. The New Tradition in Germany and Austria has been more successfully eclectic and except for the period of Expressionism less fantastic. In industrial architecture it has moreover produced buildings which are to be compared with the best work of Wright and the Dutch.

CHAPTER ELEVEN

THE NEW TRADITION IN AUSTRIA AND GERMANY

IN Germany and Austria the New Tradition appeared as in Holland just before 1900. During the twentieth century it has been very nearly as completely dominant. Until after the War, however, the German and Austrian New Tradition remained more definitely eclectic. It was also less a development from the experimentalism of the eighties and more related to the formalist reaction toward a more correct eclecticism of taste with which in America Sullivan and Wright were unable to make any terms whatsoever.

The specific event, comparable in significance to the construction of the Amsterdam Beurs, which marked the beginning of the New Tradition in Germany was the calling of Henry Van de Velde in 1897 to Hagen-in-Westphalen to build the Folkwang Museum in recognition of his success in Paris the year before. But Henry Van de Velde was by no means a German Berlage; and it was not this Museum finished in 1901 but the linear decoration of his interiors at the Dresden Exposition of 1897 which had at first the greatest influence. His architectural ideas were, however, sounder than his decoration and the quality of his building usually high. His effect on the German New Tradition was primarily to crystallize it. He himself stood always somewhat apart; on the one hand in his rationalized craftsmanship closer to Morris from whom his own incentive had come; and on the other in his experimentation with abstract form independent of eclectic reminiscence foreshadowing the manner of the later New Pioneers.

In Austria the first synthesis of the New Tradition was due to an architect of an earlier generation, Otto Wagner. It is in the work of his pupil and follower, Josef Hoffmann and his German contemporary, Peter Behrens, that the tendencies of the new manner were to find their most typical national expression. For although Wagner in time broke quite away from revivalist traditionalism the marks of his training in the sixties remained in his work. Hoffmann was able from the first to show in the handling of the new ideas which were really Wagner's a mature mastery which the older man lacked.

Wagner was born in Vienna in 1841 the year of Schinkel's death. He died only in 1918. In his studies in Vienna and Berlin he was influenced like Berlage later at Zurich by the Néo-Renaissance forms in which Semper had interpreted the rationalizing Classicism of Schinkel. It was in the nineties in his stations for the Vienna city railroad that Wagner first showed any particular tendencies toward a new manner. Even in these, his rationalism of structure was obscured by a considerable amount of detail of Néo-Renaissance or Néo-Baroque order and a rather heavy and traditional monumentality. There was however a certain suavity and polish due to the Classical tradition which was notably lacking in the contemporary work of Berlage who had by then broken so sharply with his Néo-Renaissance training.

In later work, such as the Vienna Postal Savings Building and the Steinhof church of 1906, Wagner continued to use formal symmetrical schemes of design. But he retained otherwise from the Classical formulas only the cornices and the simplified suggestion of columns and pilasters. In a period of structural transition, when new building and engineering methods were just beginning to be admissibly combined with serious architecture, it is not unnatural that the expression he achieved had a somewhat tentative and incomplete character. The insistence on the fact that his marble plate surfacings were not more than surfacings for example made them appear too demountable. Trying to renew ornament in the early years of the twentieth century without following the curvilinear Art Nouveau, he turned particularly to simple geometrical formulas. Although this gave his designs an harmonious integrity, it made them also thin, stringy and rather monotonous.

These developments came only after he was sixty and he was unable to give them the creative vigour which had informed his earlier work. Wagner was one of those artists who are born too early; but his influence in Vienna was of great importance, especially as he became in 1894 a professor in

the Academy of Art. Moreover, the frequent publication of his projects from 1891 served to carry his ideas beyond the boundaries of
Austria.

Wagner's earliest important follower, J. M. Olbrich, was born in 1867 and
died in 1908. He was a more international figure than Wagner and open
to other influences. His Secessionsgebäude of 1899 in Vienna was not unrelated to the early manner of Van de Velde; but it was more traditional
in composition. Later when he went to work in Germany he was more chary
of ornament and at first rather geometrical in his forms as his Exposition
building of 1901 at Darmstadt particularly illustrates. In the last year of
his life the Mediævalistic Tietz department store in Düsseldorf and a soberly
Classical villa outside Cologne indicated that he was strongly influenced
by that néo-monumentality in Berlin which was already generally modifying
the last wave of the eclecticism of taste in the direction of the eclecticism
of style. Up to the time of his death Olbrich clearly had not formed a really
personal manner. It was left to Josef Hoffmann to bring to its fulfilment
the Austrian New Tradition.

Hoffmann was born in 1870 and studied under Wagner at the Vienna
Academy of Arts. Even in his earliest executed work he showed an assurance and an integrity of style that both Wagner and Olbrich lacked. Wagner had arrived at a new synthesis by a continuing reduction and rational-
ization of Classical formulas very much as Soane had done a century
earlier; and Olbrich had been content to substitute for this new synthesis
others which were being tentatively offered in Germany in the first years
of the twentieth century. Mediæval formulas as well as Classical formulas
have served Hoffmann; and the past as a whole has been more of an inspiration than the specific influences of his contemporaries. His work represents
to a considerable extent a reaction away from the formal coldness of Wagner
and Olbrich toward the "picturesque." Thus he achieved in Austria where
the first version of the New Tradition had issued from the later Classical
Revival of the nineteenth century a more complete balance than Berlage
whose developed style, although tending in time away from the irregular,
had been nevertheless almost entirely dependent upon Mediævalism after
he reacted against the Néo-Renaissance. In Wright moreover there had been
no connection with Classical tradition and hence in considerable part a lack
of that urbanity of expression which particularly distinguishes Hoffmann.
Hoffmann's close relation to the minor arts has also had a notable effect

on his work. Under his leadership, decorative ornament developed according to the principles of the eclecticism of style to a brilliant virtuosity. The suavity and polish of Wagner was enlivened by the most varied borrowings from the past, subtly stylized and skilfully fused. But this Néo-Rokoko, so suited to the Viennese temperament, is more applicable to craft objects and interiors than to exteriors. Austrian architecture of the New Tradition generally appears to be but the chief of the minor arts. It is too often fine only on account of the exquisitely executed ornament and not as in many works of Berlage and Wright, despite crudity of detail.

In Hoffmann's earliest houses at the opening of the twentieth century his feeling for the "picturesque" appears clearly, although in the Parkersdorf Sanatorium of 1905 he used the contemporary geometrical ornament of Wagner. In this, however, the massing was more complicated and less regular than with Wagner. It depended primarily for its effect, however, on fine craftsmanship, as it was architecturally very simple.

The large Stoclet house at Brussels built in the next five years also still has much of Wagner about it. The walls are covered with marble plates and the angles are emphasized by gilded mouldings. But the somewhat cold and still rather Classical general design is enlivened by much irregularity and by many free ornamental features of interior rather than exterior scale. It is very much decorator's or exposition architecture. At the same time it marked a notable step in the general development and acceptance in Europe of the New Tradition. Hoffmann succeeded moreover in fusing much better than was done in other large continental houses of the time the free planning of the English houses of the transition with a very conscious and highly formalized modernity.

In the years up to the War Hoffmann's manner grew more rugged and architectonic. Using less sumptuous materials he succeeded in avoiding somewhat the appearance of interior scale on his exteriors; and in both interiors and exteriors the combination of fine craftsmanship, well placed and well designed detail, picturesqueness and extreme polish reached its most typical expression. Now that he was freed from the direct influence of Wagner's later work, Hoffmann was able to regain something of the impressive monumentality of Wagner's work of the nineties. But he did this with far simpler means, handled as they could only be handled by a man to whom twentieth century architecture had already become an established tradition.

Particularly fine were the Austrian pavilions at the Rome and Cologne Expositions just before the War.

After the War Hoffmann went on from the same point at which he left off. But his major activities were for several years in connection with the Wiener Werkstätte which had at this time their greatest international influence and popularity. Furniture, textiles, wallpapers, cigarette cases, whatever Hoffmann and his associates touched, they succeeded at least temporarily in giving a new delicately eclectic life to.

In the Vienna workers' apartment houses built in 1924-25 Hoffmann was forced by economic conditions to reduce very considerably the amount of ornamental detail. There was also a definite increase in symmetry. He avoided, however, the dryness and coldness of Wagner's later work and when he turned to individual villas again his decorative virtuosity appeared little diminished, if perhaps healthily chastened, by his experiences with the post-War world.

His Austrian pavilion at the Paris Exposition of 1925 was doubtless his masterpiece. Certainly it was, with the possible exception of the Swedish pavilion, the most finished work in that extraordinary gathering which resumed and even in a sense concluded the New Tradition. It was perhaps the last completely fine contemporary building in which ornament and the tradition of the past in reduced eclectic form had a logical and necessary place; and in which handcraftsmanship was so naturally and perfectly used that it did not appear anachronistic. (Figure 33.)

Hoffmann has had many pupils both in architecture and in decoration. In the Vienna Academy of Arts he has been for some time the outstanding professor. His influence has not been limited to his pupils. From Holzmeister through Strnad, Wlach and Frank the architects of Vienna have followed him very closely. (Figure 31.) Moreover, as in the last few years Hoffmann in his teaching has sought in extreme simplicity and the expression of new methods of construction to turn away from even reduced eclecticism, he retains like Van de Velde a more direct connection than Wright or Berlage with the younger men who are reacting rigorously against the New Tradition. The only architect of Hoffmann's generation who stood apart was Adolf Loos. Even before the War by his building and more particularly by his writing he was quite as much as Van de Velde a precursor of the New Pioneers.

In Germany as well as in Austria Hoffmann's manner has profoundly influenced the New Tradition. In theatres Kaufmann particularly, Wilms and others have developed a very elaborate sort of Néo-Rokoko. In domestic building many architects whose own individual tendencies in other types of construction have been very different, such as Fahrenkamp or Bonatz, have effectively emulated his delicacy and his craftsmanship. The important work of Heinrich Tessemow, even before the War, had arrived moreover at a great simplification of the New Tradition rather parallel to some of Hoffmann's latest designs and very different from the more aggressively architectonic and monumental manner than general in Germany.

Within the New Tradition as a whole there exist many focal points. Of these the versions of Wright and Berlage are perhaps the most intrinsically important. Their manners, derived on the whole from rationalized Mediævalism; the more definitely traditional architecture of craftsmanship in England, America and the Scandinavian countries; and the Classically derived ferro-concrete functionalism of Perret in France are all perhaps less central than the version of the New Tradition exemplified by Hoffmann and those Austrian and German architects who have followed him. But there have been in Germany other focal points of which one at least has been of equal importance. This is represented by the work of Peter Behrens and of those innumerable architects who have emulated his impressive constructions either as his followers or by developing along similar lines.

Behrens was born in 1868 and studied first as a painter in Karlsruhe, Düsseldorf and Munich. He began to execute buildings at about the same time as Hoffmann and under somewhat the same influences. The house he built for himself at Darmstadt in 1901 was a somewhat monstrous experiment derived apparently from an undigested Mediævalism. From this he reacted toward the Classically derived style to which Wagner was just giving form. Exposition buildings of 1905 at Oldenburg and Düsseldorf and of 1906 at Dresden and Cologne, a crematory of 1907 and several houses of which the finest were the latest, built in 1909 and 1910 on the Hohenhof at Hagen-in-Westphalen, represent this phase of his development. Departing like Olbrich and Hoffmann more and more from the rather thin manner of Wagner he achieved a simplified and regular expression that was nevertheless already more definitely eclectic. It was also the more solid and the more vigorous for the influence of Van de Velde.

But there were other forces in German architecture in the first decade of the twentieth century which left their mark generally on the New Tradition in Germany. Muthesius' *Das Englische Haus* published in 1905, made known to Northern Europe the free planning and the simple expression of craftsmanship which had marked the English domestic architecture in the past as well as its intelligent revival by the craftsman architects of the preceding half century.

The work and the teaching of Theodor Fischer in South Germany also derived from nineteenth century Mediævalism. Fischer was born in 1862 and after studying in Munich he worked with Wallot on the Berlin Reichstag, the most extravagant of late nineteenth century Néo-Baroque buildings in Germany. But already in his Bismarckturm on the Starnbergersee of 1897 he had purged himself of all but the aggressive monumentality of Wallot and was basing his expression on a free rendering of Romanesque forms. In the Ulm Garnisonkirche and the Stuttgart Kunstgebäude, both of 1911, he achieved in connection with modern methods of construction a manner more rugged and less influenced by Classical tradition than that of the Viennese or of Behrens up to that time. His housing projects executed in the next few years marked him also as a forerunner in a type of building which was to have after the War an extraordinarily prolific development in Germany. For this indeed he rather than Hoffmann or Behrens set the dominant type.

In Berlin there was an even greater tendency toward monumentality. In the work of Ludwig Hoffmann, born in 1852 and since 1896 city architect, this was related to a modified continuance of the eclecticism of taste. Hoffmann's buildings had from the first tendencies toward eclecticism of style and the frequently profuse reminiscent decoration was always more or less mannered and related rather freely to his general design, which was only nominally Classical or Néo-Baroque. Alfred Messel, born in 1853 and dying in 1909, developed an analogous treatment for large city buildings based on Late Gothic forms. But his work was much richer and more vigorous than the similar attempts which followed Cass Gilbert's Woolworth Building in America. In Messel's Wertheim Department Store in Berlin, built in 1904, he used on the Leipzigerplatz and the Vossstrasse façades a wealth of stylized reminiscent detail to clothe more or less functional forms, achieving a somewhat redundant impressiveness that has been much sought in simpler form by later German architects of the New Tradition. However, on the Leipzigerstrasse façade his work was closer to that of Jourdain and Chédanne in Paris of the same period; for the stone work was no more than a light skeleton covering the steel frame. In the interior architectural and engineering effects were freely and splendidly fused. At other times like Ludwig Hoffmann, Messel used more or less Baroque formulas but with an almost Romanesque brusqueness and heaviness. After his death Hoffmann added Messel's more Mediæval manner to his own general repertory.

Somewhat parallel work was done by Bruno Schmitz in his Haus Rheingold of 1905 in the Bellevuestrasse. He also and certain others attempted a more extravagant continuation of the German Baroque with much use of curved forms. All this semi-eclecticism was given a certain homogeneity by ponderous tiled mansard roofs, a grandiose and brutal scale, and much mannerism in the treatment of reminiscent detail. Hence the general influence of these architects upon their contemporaries was all in the same direction of what is called néo-monumentality.

Behrens profited from this influence when the time came for him to give more solidity and balance to his personal style. But most important for his later development and for the New Tradition in Germany was the fact that in 1907 he had become the architect of the A. E. G. (The German General Electric Company). Since then his major work has consisted of power plants and factories built for them. This more than anything else settled the general trend of his style and served definitely to separate him from the Austrians who had not been called on to turn their attention to industrial building. For Behrens, more than any one else, established the formula for German industrial architecture, perhaps the finest mass of production within the New Tradition to be found anywhere.

From the beginning in his A. E. G. buildings Behrens attained a monumental impressiveness in terms of modern construction. In the vigorous silhouette and the piling of masses, he rivalled at the same time that he suggested the great monuments of the past. The execution was of the highest quality and the brickwork was adapted to the necessities of rapid and inexpensive building. In work of such utilitarian character there was little use of ornament. These factories were thus set apart from the elaborate constructions of Fischer and Messel, which had nevertheless their influence in larger matters and in other types of edifices. In his office buildings notably, such as the German Embassy at Leningrad built in 1912, he was more constrained by the past. But his Classical treatment was very brutal and large in scale, recalling his factories much more than either the similar work of Otto Wagner or Ludwig Hoffmann.

The industrial architecture of Behrens has been his greatest achievement even though Poelzig and others of his own generation as well as many younger men who have followed his lead have had in the same field in Germany almost equal success. He has, however, applied the same principles of design in large scale domestic building with nearly equal success. While his houses and apartments lack the grace and delicacy of Austrians and the fantasy and humour of the Dutch, they have a sobriety which represents the honesty and the grandeur of conception of the New Tradition at its best. Of this sort of work the Abbey of Saint Peter at Salzburg, built before the War, and the workers' apartment houses in Vienna, built after the War, are excellent examples. In this field indeed his manner was already before the War as simplified as Josef Hoffmann was forced to be in his own post-War apartment houses. But the factories of Behrens and the villas of Josef Hoffmann were at the poles of the New Tradition although both equally representative in their own way. Behrens also applied extreme simplification to his office buildings after the War, abjuring reminiscent detail almost entirely and working more as in his factories with emphasis on the arrangement of the masses, the lines of the construction, and the fine execution of stone, brick or even concrete surfaces. Such monuments lack, however, the strictly industrial features, gas tanks, water towers and turbine halls to which in his factories he gave with such splendid dignity an eminently architectural expression.

After the War Behrens was also touched by the wave of Expressionism which carried away certain other industrial architects of Germany, such as Poelzig and the brothers Taut. But this affected little beyond his interiors. Except for a few designs of 1922-23 in which there was exaggerated emphasis on external buttresses and an abuse of sharp angles in the outline of featured doors and windows, his manner of industrial building hardly changed. Even in these works his sense of scale and the care and sobriety with which the general silhouette was studied, saved them from the utter futility of the designs of the more thoroughgoing Expressionists.
In the last year or two Behrens has attempted designs in the manner of the New Pioneers. But this leaves so little opportunity for the monumentality and for the surface effects of mass which he has always sought that it seems

unlikely that he will achieve great success at it. Like Wright, like Berlage, like Josef Hoffmann, his great period of activity has been the first quarter of the twentieth century. So completely is he associated with the New Tradition that he cannot hope to become a part of a later movement, nor should he desire to. To have produced the magnificent buildings that he has, is enough.

The special manner of architecture based on industrial building is perhaps primarily of Behrens' creation. But to this manner also belong not only Poelzig but also many others such as Fahrenkamp, Albinmuller, Salvisberg and Kreis. Bonatz, whose Stuttgart station is finer than any single work of Behrens (Figure 26), merits particular mention. The Expressionists in general, and such a younger man as Erich Mendelsohn who hardly conforms entirely to the æsthetic of the New Pioneers, have also been much influenced by Behrens, especially in their best work.

But after 1910 the New Tradition was so well established in Germany that there were few architects who did not show its influence even in designs nominally most reminiscent of the past. In restricting the present chapter largely to the development of Josef Hoffmann and Behrens much injustice is done to other men of equal value as architects. But, if not always the most influential, these two have been the most typical; and toward the formulas they established other men, often quite differently formed, have tended to come. The already mentioned work of Tessemow is more or less isolated and independent, but it has followed much the same line as that of Josef Hoffmann. The work of such men as Bruno Paul or of Paul Mebes has evolved from the modified eclecticism of taste of Ludwig Hoffmann until it is hardly to be distinguished from that of Behrens and his direct followers. The Hamburg School, including Schumacher, Hoeger, Gerson and Herman Frank, has in its dark coloured brickwork a certain original character but follows the general tendencies. (Figures 34, 35.) Bonatz and Elsaesser, in Stuttgart, have been specifically products of Fischer's training as well as many others.

The quantity of the architecture of the New Tradition in Germany is so vast, the possibilities of style analysis so unlimited owing to the extreme impressionability of the German architects, that a brief and schematic account may be much more clear than one that goes into detail. Literature in which the study of the architecture of Germany in the first quarter of the twentieth century, is moreover far from lacking. But in addition to the national versions of the New Tradition that have thus far been discussed others of importance exist in France and particularly in the Scandinavian countries. Not only have there been major individual creators but as well a more or less general acceptance of the manner. To some degree the latter is also true for other regions although the work produced is seldom either of high quality or particularly characteristic.

CHAPTER TWELVE

THE NEW TRADITION IN FRANCE, SCANDINAVIA AND ELSEWHERE

DURING the years that Austria and Germany were recreating not only monumental architecture, but domestic architecture and industrial architecture as well, there was extraordinarily little good building in France. The last interesting works in steel skeleton construction of the period of transition coincided in date with the first that marked the appearance of néo-monumentality in Germany. Henry Van der Velde, after influencing the inception of the unfortunate Art Nouveau movement in decoration, went to Germany in 1897 feeling rightly that there he would find better support. The Paris Exposition of 1900 already indicated on the whole a turning back of French architecture into the futilities of the Néo-Baroque, except in the field of decoration, and this general relapse lasted generally until after the War.

Plumet attempted throughout the years down to the War a continuation of the Art Nouveau in architecture, applying increasingly banal linear or naturalistic ornament to late Gothic forms. Other architects used the same ornament on heavy semi-Classical Beaux Arts façades of cut-stone. The culmination of this movement was the Hôtel Lutétia on the boulevard Raspail by Boileau, but it was of hardly greater intrinsic interest than the rest. Sauvage, who began to work in the manner of Plumet, broke away rather boldly in the terraced apartment house of 1912 in the rue Vavin. This was technically more experimental than most German work of the time, but it was hardly fused into architecture, and the covering of white glazed bricks with occasional green spots was merely absurd. Sauvage's originality, however, did not continue. His only other important building, a similar but larger apartment house in the rue des Amiraux built in 1926, was only slightly more successful. His other work with simplified geometrical ornament belongs distinctly to that ubiquitous second boulevard Raspail style which succeeded after the War the first, that strange mésalliance of academic Louis XVI and Art Nouveau.

Those many architects who between 1908 and the War laudably set out to provide more rational solutions of modern problems have been of little individual importance. Unlike the rationalists of the nineteenth century they have generally been unable to raise their buildings to the level of architecture. Their concessions to their Beaux Arts training or to the prevailing mode—curvilinear, naturalistic or geometrical—in ornament are quite without relation to their technical advances, which, compared to those of other countries even in work most intentionally traditional in design, are anything but extraordinary. A few churches, in which some considerable use was made of new methods of construction, were more successful, but even the best of these are pitifully thin and marked by a lack of adequate execution in their vaguely Mediævalistic details quite impossible in more Northern countries where the Mediæval Revivals of the nineteenth century had finally developed a comprehension of the virtues of craftsmanship.

Against this gloomy background of twentieth century French architecture only one man really stands out, but he is of very considerable importance. Auguste Perret indeed has had in France somewhat the position of Wright in America. Only in the last few years has his work come to be generally appreciated. However, even at his best he has not quite succeeded in obtaining the coherence and integrity of the best North European work of the New Tradition. Nor is he quite without the awkwardness in the use of detail and the harsh, undigested rationalism which has marked even the best of the other French architects of his generation. Yet all the same he stands not only against the background of the Art Nouveau and the triumphant Ecole des Beaux Arts, but internationally beside Wright, Berlage and Wagner, as one of the most significant focal points of the New Tradition.

Auguste Perret was born in 1874 and studied in the Ecole des Beaux Arts in the atelier of Guadet who was, after the death of Labrouste, probably the best French master in official circles. However, without completing the Ecole, he began to construct, continuing the contracting business of his father in partnership with his brothers. In an office building of 1898 in the Faubourg Poissonière in Paris he introduced into France the American type of office planning. From the point of view of the formation of a personal manner the Municipal Casino of St. Malo constructed immediately afterwards was considerably more important. Among the innumerable rationalistic rustic works, which have been produced in France since the Second Empire, this almost alone has a certain architectural distinction. Nevertheless, in this casino the ferro-concrete, by means of which Perret was to seek consciously a renewal of architecture, had still only an inconspicuous and subsidiary place.

In the apartment house which he and his brothers built for themselves in the rue Franklin in Paris in 1902-3 the construction was entirely supported by a visible ferro-concrete skeleton. With this and the original plan opening on a half court let into the façade he achieved an eminently simple and logical composition. It even lacked, except in the unrelated mansard roof treatment, the awkwardness of the other work of the period in France. The panels between the concrete beams were filled with tiles covered with a naturalistic leaf pattern. This alone connected the design with the contemporary Art Nouveau. Indeed already here, and more even than in his monumental later works, Perret seems almost to have passed beyond the New Tradition and to have tried with a certain success the equivalent of the principles of the New Pioneers a score of years before they were definitely formulated. He abstained from reminiscence of the past and very nearly achieved an æsthetically conscious engineering. But the leaf patterns were characteristic of his continuing tendency to seek architectural beauty by unrelated decorative adjuncts to his engineering.

The technical importance of this construction was very considerable. It constituted the first attempt to use ferro-concrete as an independent material and not as a mere incidental substitute for masonry in city building of this type. Although the æsthetic expression of Perret was here as in later works debatable, his construction was already at once highly original and perfectly sound.

The garage in the rue de Ponthieu, built in 1905, represented a more definite attempt at the creation of a new manner of architecture on the basis of ferro-concrete construction. There were no longer any traces of the Art Nouveau, such as disfigured the steel skeleton department stores built in Paris in this year. But there was a certain heaviness and traditionalism in the proportions of the open façade as well as in the profiling of the cornice and the door frame and a related dependence on the dubitable ornamental value of the elaborate geometrical glass work. This indicates that Perret, in his crystallization of engineering into architecture, finally had recourse, not to really new principles, but to principles that represent the common denominator of those of the styles of the past. This is even more true of the remodelling of a country house at Biévres. Perret's formula—which has since become more or less the accepted French national formula—of simplified and eclectic Classicism is here fully established. It has seldom been better used.

It was not until 1911 that Perret was called on to build a public monument, the Théâtre des Champs Elysées. With regard to the construction of this building there can be no question that it was due to Perret. It must, however, appear equally clear from published projects that the façade and, in large part, the plan and the treatment of the main auditorium were the conception of Henry Van de Velde. He had been called from Germany to provide a design, and had moreover suggested the use of ferro-concrete with Perret as the constructor.

The exterior was indeed very fine, dependent for its effect on the marble facing and the reliefs of Bourdelle. (Figure 37.) It was moreover somewhat simpler in execution than in Van de Velde's original designs. In its monumentality and its lack of awkwardness it recalls contemporary German rather than French work, and the main auditorium also has an elegance like that of the theatres of Oskar Kaufmann lacking in other work by Perret. The foyer alone with its strong Classical feeling and prominently displayed skeleton construction is fully Perret's in character.

It is not surprising or unfortunate that this monument, in so many ways one of the finest and the freest in the New Tradition, should be due to a collaboration between the two men who were among the greatest experimenters of their generation, the one in abstract form, the other in construction. What is regrettable is that the murals of the large auditorium, ordered of Maurice Denis even before the building was designed, have neither the intrinsic quality nor the appropriateness of the sculpture and the frescos of Bourdelle. In the small auditorium there is far less sumptuousness in the decoration, and the paintings of K. X. Roussel and Vuilliard are most effectively used.

In concluding the account of this theatre it is worth recalling that it was here, just after the opening, that the Ballets Russes, with the music of Strawinski, the choreography of Nijinski and the decorations of Bakst, introduced to Paris that cult of primitive exoticism, bright colour and free pattern which in the minor arts eventually replaced the Art Nouveau with a more eclectic and vigorous manner. But the route from the *Sacre du Printemps* via Poiret to the rue de la Paix, which French decorative art has since followed, has little direct connection with architecture. Although its influence since the War has been quite as great as that of Hoffmann's Wiener Werkstätte, particularly in America, it is most unfortunate that it has so largely obscured in France the more solid, if less versatile, work of Perret.

Just before the War Perret undertook in collaboration with Maurice Denis a monument in the Montparnasse cemetery in Paris, which was not finished until 1921. In this delicate object, all of marble, he was entirely an architect and not at all an engineer. The coldness and exquisiteness with which reduced Classical forms are utilized has more than a suggestion of similar German or Scandinavian work.

In 1922-23 Perret, with his brothers, undertook the construction of Notre Dame at Le Raincy, a suburb of Paris. This is his best known if not his finest building. In spite of the inadequate funds he had to use it illustrated his increasing dependence on eclectic reminiscence. It is a contemporary engineer's version of a Mediæval church, with mounting spire, glass walls, and pillar supported vault. Although it is all built of exposed concrete, the pillars have the fluting of the Classical past and the arrangement of the vaults, longitudinal in the nave and transverse in the aisles, recalls certain early Mediæval schemes. Even the profile of the vaults, although actually determined by forms re-used from previous purely engineering work, suggested the segmental Roman types from which Soane had drawn inspiration. Even the concrete window tracery had an Early Christian character. The glass by Maurice Denis moreover had thirteenth century colouring and was in the figured sections no addition to the whole. The unpleasant texture and colour of the untreated concrete surfaces, the false scale and incoherence of the spire built up of a bundle of fluted pillars apparently supporting nothing, the sharp visual contrast between the lightness of the interior pillars and the solid vaults, all made it evident that Perret was still unable to fuse his brilliant engineering conception in his eclectic architectural expression.

The church of Sainte Thérèse, built at Montmagny in 1925, is simpler but less fine and significant than that at Le Raincy. It displays no further innovations and is definitely inferior in the study of proportions. The immense project for a national church of Sainte Jeanne d'Arc, designed in 1926, is remarkable for its great size and complexity. Yet except for its more effective centralized composition, it is very like that of Le Raincy. His other ecclesiastical work, restorations of the church at Saint-Vaury in the Creuse and of the Chapelle du Prieuré at Saint-Germain-en-Laye, were interesting chiefly as excellent examples of that tact and sense which the Romantic Mediævalists so completely lacked in such work.

In purely engineering work, such as the warehouses built at Casablanca in 1915, or the large studio built in Paris in 1922, Perret came closer than in his architecture to the ideals of the New Pioneers. The department store work-rooms built in 1919 also continued in ferro-concrete and without any decoration the line of steel constructions of the transition in France.

In his Paris banks he remained more Classical. The Société Marseillaise de Crédit, built in 1923, and the Crédit National Hotelier of 1925 were unsuccessful however compared to the foyer of the théatre des Champs Elysées, which they so much resembled. The marble columns without capitals and the thin geometrical ironwork were poorly related to the rational ferro-concrete structure.

In his houses, such as that for M. Emile Gant, built in 1924, in the rue Deutsch de la Meurthe, he was rather heavy-handed and exaggeratedly symmetrical. He retained moreover the traditional cornice above his bare concrete walls. Later houses, such as that of Chana Orloff, built in 1926, or that of Braque, built in 1927, both nearby, show also a lack of sensibility in the use of raked brickwork to fill the ill-proportioned panels of the exposed concrete structure. Among all his domestic work only the villa of M. Mourron, built in 1926 at Versailles, is comparable in quality to the similar work Hoffmann, Behrens and other Austrians and Germans were doing even twenty years earlier.

The Palais de Bois, built in 1924 at the Porte Maillot for the Salon des Tuileries, was much more interesting. Here he achieved a brilliant and elementary expression of ordinary wooden construction.

Among his major works should doubtless be considered the theatre he constructed at the Paris Exposition of 1925. But it was hardly an altogether worthy contribution from France's greatest architect within the New Tradition to that international manifestation of the manner. On the exterior the independent skeleton of projecting cornice and block capped fluted ferro-concrete pillars was excessively awkward, as also the meagre use of marble in the foyer. Yet the staircases were especially well designed and the auditorium, despite the blocky cellular treatment of the ceiling, was admirably planned for the presentation of plays or concerts. In the Tour d'Orientation, built at Grenoble in the same year, both his construction and his eclectic tendencies received more harmonious expression.

Perret's work has been from the first somewhat ambiguous. For all his constructive virtuosity he has been architecturally timid and failed finally, like the other French architects of his generation, to achieve a fusion between his construction and his reduced Classical eclecticism. The same difficulty marks Le Coeur's Paris Telephone Building of 1912, which, despite its harshness and lack of finish, is a fine monument. And Tony Garnier, whose vision of a Cité Industrielle and whose buildings for the city of Lyons have been of considerable interest, is a true son of the Ecole des Beaux Arts, sacrificing everything to brilliant planning, remaining *redardataire* in his construction, and basing his simplified Classical expression usually on Pompeii. In his latest work, which completes the Lyons market begun in 1907, he has been influenced by German industrial architecture, but has hardly succeeded in achieving results that may be compared with the Stuttgart, the Frankfurt or the Leipzig market. His Lyons stadium is more individual and, despite its extreme baldness, perhaps his best executed work.

Among the architects in France who have sought since the War the decorative renewment of architecture none are of great individual importance and the majority have concerned themselves rather with interiors and furniture than with building. Suë et Mare developed a manner in which eclecticism of style was focussed about a sort of Néo-Romanticism, heavy and gloomy, but highly finished. Ruhlmann, working almost entirely in interiors, has achieved occasionally an almost German néo-monumentality, as on the *Isle-de-France*.

The most typical manifestation of the movement is in the Paris shop fronts, whose sumptuous decoration and rich materials, now beginning to be more simplified than at first, have particularly appealed to English and American seekers after the new. Despite the lack of any commanding or initiating figure this manner has spread very widely and hardly any building is done to-day in Paris whose ornament is not more or less renewed. However, the construction and the general composition is usually little affected and follows like the buildings of the Art Nouveau the same late nineteenth century Beaux Arts formulas. This version of the New Tradition in France was given undue prominence by the Exposition of 1925. It is but a late and minor phase, however. It is unfortunate that it should have in England and America such general influence. As mode-modernity it has a greater appeal than that sounder work which is truly architectural. It is easy to apply, amusing at first sight even if it be devoid of almost all other virtues, and makes no excessive demands on either machine or handcraftsmanship.

In the Scandinavian countries the New Tradition established itself earlier and more normally than in France, developing particularly out of the transitional architecture of craftsmanship. Even where Danish and Swedish architects have availed themselves of engineering they have sought even more than the Germans to clothe new forms elegantly with subtle eclectic reminiscence of the past. A rather early monument, such as the Copenhagen City Hall by Nyrop of about 1905 (Figure 25), shows how this eclecticism was arrived at, as in Cuijpers' later work done a quarter of a century earlier, from reminiscence of the transitional architecture of the sixteenth century in Northern Europe. But there was a distinctly higher quality of execution and a greater restraint in detail, both related to contemporary English domestic work.

Since the War this architecture has developed particularly in Sweden. Lallerstedt's Technical High School, Tengbom's Högalids Church, and above all Østberg's City Hall finished in 1923 (Figure 8), all in Stockholm, display a wide dependence on the architecture of the past and magnificent traditional execution integrated into a definite national style. As in Holland, brick has proved itself a material especially suited to the New Tradition.

Domestic building has remained closer to the English work of the transition depending chiefly on proportion and craftsmanship for its effects with a certain use of stylized ornament reminiscent particularly of the Late Gothic or the Baroque. This is nearly equally true of Danish domestic building,

(Figure 36.) But in more monumental work there has developed a cold and barely eclectic Néo-Classicism, mannered in expression but almost devoid of ornament. This is typically represented in the work of Kay Fisker. There has been also some more experimental work chiefly in Exposition buildings of Austrian delicacy and restraint.

From Finland, which has a more robust and Germanic New Tradition, Saarinen has come to America introducing a sounder influence than that of Paris. The versatility in composition and the finely executed, freshly designed craftsmanship of both the work and the projects which he has done in America represent, however, less completely the possibilities of his manner than the more vigorous and brutal railroad station he built at Helsingfors before the War. In that he made brilliant use of engineering and very largely avoided ornament. That, rather than his design for the Chicago Tribune Tower, was the masterpiece which ranks him among the first group of architects of the New Tradition.

Beyond the countries thus far discussed the penetration of the New Tradition has been late and ephemeral. In Russia there exist a few monuments of largely German inspiration, such as the Tomb of Lenin and the Central Post Office in Moscow. Similarly unimportant works are to be found in other East European countries.

The Italians have contented themselves with modifying their general twentieth century Baroque Revival under Northern influence. Such excellent buildings as Piacentini's Cinema Corso and Banca d'Italia, both in Rome, might easily be respectively Austrian and Swedish.

In England also the influence of Sweden has been strong. Easton and Robertson's Royal Horticultural Society Hall is astonishingly close to work at the Göteborg Exposition of a few years ago. Sir John Burnet and Partners have attempted in their City buildings a simplification of the redundant Edwardian Classicism that was so sadly continued in the reconstruction of Regent Street. They have hardly fully assimilated either American or German influences. Adelaide House, their most striking production, is of Egyptian ponderousness and as awkward and clumsy in detail as any French pre-War work. Westwood and Emberton had more success in Summit House with well studied terra cotta covered masses and simple geometrical detail. Other architects, such as de Soissons, Atkinson, and Bushnell, have made more or less overt use of Swedish or Dutch effects. German factories and French shop fronts have also had their rather unintelligent imitations. Those who have in domestic and ecclesiastical work remained more true to the manner of the transition with very slight dependence on reminiscent architectural features, have better if less consciously served the New Tradition. The housing work of the District Councils is often of very great excellence.

The New Tradition in Europe is summed up to-day as before the War in the work of the Dutch, the Germans, the French and the Scandinavians. All else is provincial and imitative, parallel and subsidiary, or merely a continuation of the transitional architecture of craftsmanship. In the same way, it will be seen that the original creators of the manner of the New Pioneers, which is succeeding that of the New Tradition, are to be found in France, Holland and Germany, even though that also is already after only a decade of development in existence in all the countries of the world.

Nevertheless, there are many excellent architects of the New Tradition whom there has not been space to mention, and many individual monuments have been omitted, not because of their inferior quality, but because others served better to illustrate general tendencies. In dealing with the history of early twentieth century architecture it has been necessary to reduce the bulk of the material often somewhat arbitrarily, and in analysis to balance general praise with specific criticisms. But the great monuments of the creative masters rise superior to detailed objections. The latter are indeed intended less to evaluate than to underline the variety of interweaving trends.

The first reintegration of modern architecture in the New Tradition has been a magnificent achievement. The development of the later manner of the New Pioneers should not negative its importance or its value however much it may threaten its continuance. Yet the New Tradition has already in all probability done its best work. Its later monuments often appear distinctly less fine than those which marked its first complete establishment. It is rather to-day the early works of the New Pioneers which are informed with that fire of faith and of promise that the early works of the New Tradition had a generation ago.

PART THREE

THE NEW PIONEERS

CHAPTER THIRTEEN

TOWARDS A NEW ARCHITECTURE

AMONG the nine designs premiated equally in the competition for the Palace of the League of Nations in 1927 there was only one which would be considered in America to be wholly traditional. All the others were marked by the manner of the New Tradition or by that later manner of the New Pioneers which is even less connected with the revivalism of the nineteenth century.

Of the seven designs that belonged more or less definitely to the New Tradition the French and Italian examples whose designers are apparently to build the Palace are still in a general way Classical. But their Classicism is modified by a more or less original study of the massing, a certain eclecticism in the choice of architectural features and a simplification and stylization of the reminiscent detail. They are significant in the present connection only because they indicate that by 1927 even the more official and reactionary architects of the Latin countries were no longer able to design even palaces without being influenced more or less strongly by the New Tradition. The architecture of revivalism according to the principles of the eclecticism of taste as established in the middle of the nineteenth century had already at the beginning of the second quarter of the twentieth century all but universally given place to the architecture of the New Tradition.

But it was not among these more reactionary designs that the finest and most typical manifestations of the New Tradition were to be found in this competition. On the one hand the Swedish design of Ericsson in its chaste and subtle reflection of reduced eclecticism; on the other the more monumental design of zu Putlitz, Klophaus and Schoch in its forceful and reiterative emphasis on mass, as in the later work of Behrens, represented the two chief possibilities of expression of the developed New Tradition.

The design of Fahrenkamp, more typical perhaps than that of zu Putlitz of contemporary German production, was highly significant for itself and as a sign. It illustrated a more extreme simplification of the New Tradition than those just mentioned. This was carried to the point of reducing beyond possibility of identification that eclecticism of style which gave the New Tradition architectural form. Moreover it was clearly marked by the newer positive influences of the New Pioneers quite unrelated to the New Tradition. The manner of the New Pioneers was epitomized in the ninth project, the design of Le Corbusier and Pierre Jeanneret, which for some time was expected to be accepted.

The hundreds of designs submitted in this competition not among the nine to receive equal first prizes might be similarly sorted not by quality but historically—if the term thus used of work of two years ago may be pardoned. Among them there were many more of the general type of Fahrenkamp's and Le Corbusier's as also of the purely revivalist order. As statistics such a listing would have little significance; but the existence in numbers of designs in which the New Tradition is definitely modified by the later manner of the New Pioneers and of designs wholly created in accordance with that manner make it clear that this competition did not truly mark, as it may well have for many Americans, the appearance of the post-eclectic phase of Modern architecture. Indeed along the line of engineering experimentation of the nineteenth century on the one hand and along the line of formal experimentation, as distinct from the revival of more and more exotic forms of the past, in the work of the masters of the New Tradition and their precursors, the roots of this current phase might be carried back at least a century. Its spirit was not wholly unknown in the earlier pseudo-styles of Modern Architecture, the Late Gothic, the Renaissance and the Baroque, but it cannot hardly be isolated until after the Age of Romanticism was well over.

Forgetting their Art Nouveau decoration we admire to-day certain values in the French monuments in steel of the end of the nineteenth century. The existence of these values indicates that during the period of transition to the New Tradition two ways of reintegration existed. The way which was taken was that of recombining the methods of engineering and the revived craft of building with an architecture which summarized the æsthetic effects of the past. The other way of developing from engineering alone its specific and unprecedented æsthetic effects lay dormant during the development of the New Tradition. This second possibility can be clearly seen in retrospect in many of the monuments which mark the inception of the New Tradition. But after the last and finest of the Paris department stores and the decline of the Art Nouveau the eclectic crystallization of twentieth century architecture became more definite and the development of an architecture from engineering was not then carried further.

The reasons for this are not easy to fix at the present time and discussion of them is not very profitable. In a sense the New Tradition exists as its own justification. To have passed beyond it without passing through it would have been to lose the monuments of a brilliant summary phase of the Modern style.

But well within the period of the New Tradition there is a landmark much more definitely connected with the manner of the New Pioneers than even the department stores of 1900 whose importance historically was perhaps somewhat less than it appears to-day. As in the case of the work of Soane just after 1800 the latter seem to have pointed the way on, but they did not certainly do so to those who came immediately after. In the Werkbund Exposition of Cologne in 1914 there were however three buildings which marked in different ways the definite initiation of a new point of view and from which lines of descent may be much more clearly traced.

In the least startling but probably the finest of these, Van de Velde's theatre, there was an æsthetically conscious formal expression of the function and of the concrete material almost wholly without precedent in the architecture of the past. This was not altogether unanticipated in the earlier work of this somewhat ambiguous master. But previously, except perhaps in the Weimar Art School of 1906, his exteriors, whether in traditional materials or not, had been at least unconsciously influenced by the eclectic néo-monumentality of the Germans with whom he was associated so that his creative energies has gone primarily into his interiors and their furnishing. Since it exists no longer for our study it is difficult to say how fully successful this theatre was, how far it was a summary of Van de Velde's earlier work, and how far it marked consciously a new direction as it could so profitably be accepted as doing.

More significant probably was the model factory and office building erected at the Exposition for the Deutz Gas Motor Company by Walter Gropius, destined to become after the War the most important New Pioneer of Germany. This constituted a very definite attempt in the field of industrial architecture to give æsthetic expression to engineering without thought of the architectural effects of the past. It is true of course that in the play of masses there was still a certain predilection for monumentality. In the treatment of the front wall and the entrance moreover architectural features in the simplest manner of the New Tradition and not directly derived from the engineering were distinctly prominent. All this is a reflection of Gropius' training with Peter Behrens. But the glass stair towers studied purely as volume, the long side windows and the open façade of the machine hall are clearer and more unarchitectural in the sense of the time than anything hitherto produced by an architect.

The Glashaus of Bruno Taut was somewhat more experimental in the use of materials and thus more clearly indicative of a desire to derive artistic forms from the intrinsic possibilities of novel methods of construction. It was, however, very much less successful than the buildings of Van de Velde and Gropius. For its general design was based on current German exposition architecture of the New Tradition and only in detail was there further innovation in the æsthetic expression.

Gropius gave a more complete demonstration of the possibilities of his new ideas in the Faguswerk factory in Alfeld-an-der-Lahn completed in the same year as his Deutz pavilion at the Cologne Exposition. Here the entire main building was treated as volume rather than mass, and the ornamental and architectural features are reduced to the clock bay of the entrance which was nevertheless exceedingly simple. Moreover in this elaborate complex of buildings the lyricism of the grouping, especially of the chimneys and other purely industrial features, was not as with Behrens vaguely Mediæval but wholly dependent on a free study of the natural proportions and relations between the parts. (Figure 38.) Although it was the problem of the factory which offered most clearly the possibilities of creation to the New Pioneers and set the terms from which their æsthetic was to derive, no architect achieved a greater success than this Faguswerk until the van Nelle factory outside Rotterdam built in 1928 by Van der Vlugt and Brinkman probably with the collaboration in design of Mart Stam. (Figure 49.)

After 1914 architectural production all over Europe and particularly in France and Germany ceased almost entirely for even longer than the period of the War. It is impossible to find any buildings truly reflecting a new æsthetic until 1922 when they appeared contemporaneously in France and in Holland; and immediately afterward in Germany. Indeed it is not until 1925 that Le Corbusier's Pavillon de l'Esprit Nouveau at the Paris Exposition of Decorative Arts formally presented the manner to the general public and gave illustration to his book *Towards a New Architecture*.

The effect of the War on the incubation of the new manner is difficult to analyze. Forced inaction in architecture undoubtedly encouraged generally the development of tendencies away from the New Tradition. The immense amount of engineering with which a whole generation was brought in contact may even have led some men to seek æsthetic possibilities there who would not have done so otherwise. Moreover the increasing development of the machinery of transportation was beginning to arrive at a sort of purely technical beauty that was quite unrelated to the beauties of the past. This was achieved by refinement of structural necessities, direct non-symbolic expression of function, and intimate relation of forms to materials. When the idea of the technical beauty of boats and aeroplanes was exposed by Le Corbusier and others after the War it is certain that it found a somewhat prepared audience.

Nevertheless this idea as an idea was not altogether new. The writing of men such as Frank Lloyd Wright, Henry Van de Velde, and particularly Adolf Loos before the War made them more or less definitely precursors in principle. They and others had begun to see and to say that handcraftsmanship had become more and more anarchronistic except as a final luxury, and they had urged the possibilities of the machine as an art-tool. Loos notably in his curious article on *Crime and Ornament* published in 1913 in the *Cahiers d'aujourd'hui* had gone further and stated that all ornament was anachronistic. However in his buildings in Vienna, where he stood isolated amid a general revival of decorative art under Hoffmann's leadership, he hardly went beyond an extreme simplification of the New Tradition. His æsthetic expression was largely negative and in retrospect it appears distinctly inferior to the more positive if less "pure" achievements of Wright in certain of his houses, of Van de Velde in his Cologne theatre or of Perret in the strictly engineering warehouses of Casablanca.

More important probably, certainly more definite, was the influence of the abstract painting which began to appear from about 1910 and which suggested strongly the architectural values in the elemental volumes and planes of machinery and engineering. The possibilities of achieving on another scale and in three real dimensions the effects then found in painting to be of æsthetic significance occurred thus to many men about the same time during the period of the War. These effects were not particularly present in the architecture of the New Tradition. Pictorially it still lent itself to evaluation according to the Romantic principles of the "picturesque."

Nevertheless the manner of the New Pioneers did not come into being as directly and simply as what has just been said would tend to indicate any more than had the New Tradition. In Germany for example it was the painting of Expressionism which particularly influenced the architects in their experimental sketching during the War. That influence achieved its most notable realization in Poelzig's Grosses Schauspielhaus of 1919 in Berlin. This was a weird but still New Tradition building as crude in detail as the sketch engendered architecture of the *romantisme de la lettre.* It was moreover eclectically reminiscent of Islamic art and the primitive styles of Asia, Africa and Polynesia, blended by distortion into a nightmare entity. Mendelsohn showed in his War sketches the influence of machines but his imagination was equally Expressionistic. Reduced in scale and modified by the materials used, this order of conception reached execution in his Einstein Tower, built at Neubabelsberg in 1921. With regard to this Einstein made the cryptic and paradoxical comment: "Organic."

Except for the straight engineering projects of Freyssinet, of Limousin & Cie, such as the magnificent hangar at Orly, the War developed no new important building in France. Indeed the rebuilding of the devastated areas has been done in the rationalistic rustic manner of the pre-War period where it does not represent even more out-moded tendencies, which might still be described as provincial Second Empire. In Belgium the rebuilding has been somewhat more intelligently done in fairly successful imitation of the old work. But it is quite as devoid of any new character which might have been developed during the War as Whitney Warren's Flemish Baroque library at Louvain.

The two reviews that particularly championed a newer manner of architecture, *de Stijl* and *L'Esprit Nouveau*, were both in intention international and the former was primarily the organ of a Dutch group. The two architects of *de Stijl* and *L'Esprit Nouveau* who showed in 1922 an integrated post-eclectic manner were the Dutch Oud and the Swiss Le Corbusier, neither of whom had had any connection with the War. Both had been in close relation with extreme abstract painting and related abstract sculpture, Oud with Mondriaan and van Doesburg; Le Corbusier was himself at one time a painter and in *L'Esprit Nouveau* he was associated with Ozenfant. Gropius came out of the War an Expressionist and although he had adopted the new manner by 1922 he did not until 1926 achieve again work comparable to his factory of 1914. His painting associates have been all along the more abstract Expressionists.

As in the opening period of the Age of Romanticism in architecture it was a point of view developed first with regard to painting that crystallized the new manner. But whereas the painting, Baroque or Romantic, which influenced architecture in the late eighteenth and early nineteenth centuries was poetically interpreted, and vague and effective in expression; the painting, Cubist or Néo-Plasticist or otherwise abstract, which influenced architecture during the War and immediately after was intellectually, even cerebrally, interpreted, and exact and specific in its expression. In neither case was architecture necessarily related to the line of development in painting in the appreciation of which the particular point of view that affected it had appeared. It is certain that Romantic architecture went its way independently long after the sort of painting which first helped to set it going had become altogether subsidiary to later and more important developments. It is probable that the influence of abstract painting on architecture will prove also to have been but temporary. Indeed it may already appear that its point of view is better satisfied by architecture than by painting, and that it will be continued in architecture alone; just as the "picturesque" point of view, although it arose in the appreciation of painting, was eventually better satisfied by landscape gardening and has been longest continued in that art.

The architecture of Romanticism adopted archæology as a means of giving solidity to the values of pictorial order that it sought. The architecture of post-Eclecticism found in new developments of engineering a solid basis of structure with which to achieve its more purely æsthetic ends. Moreover the theories of Loos, Van de Velde and Wright provided a body of doctrine which could in large part be taken over; just as the Romantic architects took over certain largely unrelated archæological doctrines. The very archæology on which the Romantics leaned came during the course of the nineteenth century indeed rather to lend its support of theory to the central idea of the New Pioneers: that a style of architecture depends on a method of construction. In their interpretation of Gothic some of the archæologists of the mid-century carried the technical point of view to as great extremes as certain writers of to-day. The monuments in both cases serve to prove the falsity of theoretical exaggeration of rationalism and functionalism.

Within the New Tradition, leaving aside the overt influences of the later manner such as appear in Fahrenkamp's competition design for the Palace of the League of Nations, there has already been remarked the general tendency toward extreme simplicity which has developed particularly since the War, parallel with this manner of the New Pioneers. This has been to some extent due to the economic conditions which have followed the War as well as to those considerations here earlier derived from the theory of the inflation of ornament which have caused the newest architecture to avoid it entirely.

But the newer manner is fundamentally distinct from this version of the New Tradition in that it is based on principles of design not inherited from the art of the past. Instead of composing in three dimensions in values of mass, the New Pioneers compose in values of volume; instead of complexity as a means of interest they seek a strenuous unification; instead of diversity and richness of surface texture, they strive for monotony and even poverty, in order that the idea of the surface as the geometrical boundary of the volume may most clearly be stressed. Their avoidance of ornament is not entirely due to the fact that all ornament is seen to become to-day rapidly worthless from mechanical repetition. Rather it is felt that if the study of volumes and planes is carried far enough ornament as it has been known in the past does not embellish but makes the fullest unification impossible by breaking the surfaces. At the same time there is a certain faith that the possibility of something equivalent to the ornament of the past is not gone forever. Not as in the Art Nouveau on *a priori* grounds, but naturally and from the constructive necessities of the style as in the developing architectures of the far past, a new detail might eventually come into being. It would have to be intimately derived from the design of the whole and utterly subordinate to it, so that it should not interfere, in the way of even the simplest geometrical ornament now used as such, with the fundamental values which the New Pioneers have discovered, or more accurately uncovered. This is very definitely a matter that belongs to the future.

It is worth stressing, since it is a point frequently denied by its theorists, that the new manner constitutes essentially an æsthetic and not necessarily particular methods of construction. Such a new æsthetic could hardly have taken form of course if completely new methods of construction had not called for suitable expression and served to lend it validity. The ferro-concrete structure of Perret is for example probably sounder than that of Le Corbusier; but it is only the latter's which belongs to the new manner since the æsthetic of Perret remains in general that of the New Tradition. The fact that the idea of a new architecture finds support particularly in the engineering of the past hundred years and that its most fundamental principle is to make of engineering an æsthetic activity has not put architects completely at the mercy of engineers. Engineering may change completely from year to year, but the æsthetic of the New Pioneers has already shown a definite continuity of values separate from, and even on occasion in opposition to, those derived purely from the practical and the structural.

In the chief engineering architecture of the past, the High Gothic of France, exactly the same situation existed. The engineers, or rather the builders functioning as engineers, developed their construction to a point which solved their technical and practical problems and made possible a quite new æsthetic expression. After that functioning as architects they were free of engineering. They even mocked it, as for example by placing buttresses where the eyes demanded them instead of at the exact point at which they were most completely effective in counterbalancing vault thrusts. Moreover they indulged as at Beauvais in extreme technical virtuosity for its æsthetic effect, going well beyond their engineering capacity in pursuit of a magnificent vision.

Were the newer manner characterized merely by a determination to make the fullest possible use of the advances of engineering as certain German critics claim, it might well be but a branch of the New Tradition continuing in extremely reduced forms its eclectic æsthetic. But it represents primarily a new feeling for form and the search for certain specific effects. These may hardly be more fully defined in general terms. Specific examples and illustrations which nearly a decade of activity on the part of its leaders provide fortunately make it possible to do so in detail.

But finally as with any manner of architecture it is worth remarking that no name may be more than denotative for the work of the New Pioneers. Yet, for all their vagueness of overstatement Oud's claim that the new manner is a "pure" architecture, or Lönberg-Holm's that it is a "time-space" architecture, even van Doesburg's that it is "elementarist," have some slight meaning. To add another similar term profits little, but perhaps "technical" might be suggested. For the architecture of the New Pioneers in its establishment represented to a large extent—although not quite completely—the triumph of the technical point of view in the same way as the architecture of Romanticism represented in general the triumph of the anti-technical point of view. Although on a plane that admits of a fully developed æsthetic, the buildings of the New Pioneers appeal in the same way as machinery with its generally recognized technical beauty.

When the work is known, however, it is enough to call the architecture of the New Pioneers the international style of Le Corbusier, Oud and Gropius, of Lurçat, Rietveld and Miës van der Rohe, which is enrolling more and more the younger architects in Europe and many as well in America about to begin their building career.

CHAPTER FOURTEEN

THE NEW PIONEERS: FRANCE

"It may be accepted that the great epochs of architecture depend on a *pure system of structure*. This pure system of structure satisfying the extreme exigencies of the reason brings to the spirit a marvellous joy that incites the wholly intellectual expression of a *pure system of architectural æsthetic*."

Le Corbusier, 1927.

It is the vigorous and enthusiastic theoretical writing of Le Corbusier even more than his work which has made him known throughout the world as the type of the new architect. Rather more than the theoreticians of the nineteenth century he has been able to make of his writing and of his work an integrated whole. The problems of the New Pioneers in general are very clearly centred about his ideas and his productions. It is the privilege of the critic to discuss primarily the latter, drawing upon the statements of the artist where they have direct historical significance or where they elucidate his building, and disregarding them where they appear merely to invite polemic.

Le Corbusier, whose real name is Charles-Edouard Jeanneret, was born in La-Chaux-de-Fonds, Switzerland, in 1887. He works in partnership with his cousin, the engineer, Pierre Jeanneret.

At the age of twenty-one Le Corbusier went to work in the atelier of Perret to whom in matters of construction he undoubtedly owes much. Before the War he had worked as well for somewhat brief periods with Behrens and Hoffmann. His first houses built in those early years are wholly works of the New Tradition even to their decoration; yet there was already some rather incidental experimentation with the arrangement of windows, for example, and with plain metal railways. The truly significant event of that period was the voyage to Greece and the Orient which gave him the faith to look beyond the New Tradition in which he had been educated *vers une architecture*. The quotations from his travel diary published in the *Almanach de l'esprit nouveau* are of the highest interest.

But the first projects made in 1915 in which he attempted at once a technical and an æsthetic renewment of the art of building, those for the "Domino" system of ferro-concrete construction for houses in series, did not by any means establish him as a New Pioneer. Despite the extreme simplification, probably in part suggested by the work of Adolf Loos with which Le Corbusier was already familiar, these designs remained still broadly speaking within the New Tradition. The new structure received an expression in terms of traditional proportions; and the balconies, projecting slab cornices and horizontal window arrangement, were not stressed sufficiently to give particular character to the whole. In the scheme for a city on pillars, also of 1915, the technical questions seem alone to have been studied. The architectural expression was neglected, at least as far as can be judged from the published drawings.

The villa built the next year in La-Chaux-de-Fonds had distinct architectural pretentions. Its more elaborate expression was in the manner of Perret with certain Austrian modifications. It displayed however, in the open plan, the large windows and the terraced roof, the embryonic form of characteristic features of his mature work quite as much as the "Domino" houses.

In the designs of 1919 for houses and apartments there was negatively a greater simplification than in any previous projects, and at the same time a very elementary attempt to develop positively the æsthetic effect of horizontally placed windows grouped in rows on the flat façades. They resemble strikingly much German work done nearly a decade later by architects in transition from the New Tradition to the manner Le Corbusier was so shortly to inaugurate in actual building.

In 1920, after some years spent chiefly in business, Le Corbusier began to devote his time wholly to architecture. In his review *L'Esprit nouveau* he gave repeated expression to his ideas, often supporting them with illustrations of the machinery of transportation. The projects of 1920 were not, however, very interesting. It was in the "Citrohan" designs of the next year that he for the first time succeeded in fully establishing his new æsthetic based on his new methods of construction. The models for these houses showed a definite emphasis on the surface as the boundary of the volume rather than on mass. In the general composition and the placing of the windows there was no longer merely the negative simplification previously achieved by reducing the elements of the New Tradition, but a positive simplification analogous to that of stream-lined automobile and aeroplane bodies. Moreover, to obtain his effects, he made fuller and more daring use of his ferro-concrete construction, raising the house from the ground sufficiently to stress the fact that it was an object having six sides.

Another model of 1921 for a seaside villa depended even more upon skilful construction. The strong emphasis on horizontality for its own sake also proved, strangely enough, to be a principle of composition as strikingly new as that of raising buildings somewhat from the ground. But here, more than in the "Citrohan" model, the last influences of the eclectic æsthetic lingered beside the developing machine æsthetic. This may be noted in such Viennese features as the small panes of the immense studio window and in the large round windows toward the sea.

In the next years his projects for houses were technically less original, but they illustrated a significant development of the horizontal ribbon window as a prime motif of the new architecture. In the scheme for an apartment house built as a stack of independent villas like a columbarium he continued his study of the possibilities of large scale production and standardization, coming on this occasion dangerously close to a dull monotony.

Besides the development of exterior expression there had been in these years a parallel development of interior expression. Indeed from Le Corbusier's own point of view, it was doubtless more important. Technically and æsthetically he came early to a treatment of the interior as a single space which in the absence of clients to restrain his imagination was easily exaggerated. How far this might have been justified by the effectiveness of the results it is harder to tell from sketches than in the case of the exteriors. Certainly for *machines à habiter*—which was then Le Corbusier's striking phrase for his housing programme—considerable sacrifices were demanded of the inhabitant of the machine in order that the purely abstract formal development of the interior might be carried as far as possible, as in those sport cars in which no doors are permitted to break the beauty of the stream line.   To this objection Le Corbusier is to-day inclined to answer, not as an architect but as a sociologist, that "modern" men *ought* to find his houses habitable.

The year 1922 also saw the beginning of the first building executed in the new manner, a villa at Vaucresson finished in 1923.   As so frequently happens in such cases, this was distinctly less advanced than his projects.   The street façade is distinctly over-complicated and the side toward the garden in its symmetrical arrangement and uninteresting proportions shows less freedom than his designs of several years earlier.   The elements of which he was more or less the inventor, the terrace roof, and the ribbon window, are not fully or conspicuously developed, and there is a struggle between vertical and horizontal elements not at all resolved into repose.

His earliest and least daring manner achieved far greater success in the small house built in 1923 for his parents outside Vevey on Lake Geneva. Here the fundamental and logical symmetry was skilfully broken at the ends; and the ribbon window toward the magnificent panorama of the Savoy Alps was brilliantly used as the central and practically the sole feature of design.   (Figure 41.)   Already, however, in this same year he had gone further in a house built for Ozenfant on the avenue Reille in Paris.   He made a skilful use of a small and irregular site.   The necessity for providing a large studio lighted from the top explains the somewhat peculiar arrangement of the rooms and the saw-tooth glass roof which sometimes appears a stroke of genius and again as an undesirable complication of the cubic silhouette.   The ribbon window was effectively used on two contiguous façades, thus emphasizing the fact that an architecture of surfaces could have plasticity of volume.   The circular staircase at the entrance not only economized space but provided a technical motif of great decorative value.

This was his first true manifesto in executed building.   Its construction coincided with the appearance of his book *Vers une architecture*, in which his articles in *L'Esprit nouveau* were gathered together.   This book remains probably the most discussed document produced by the New Pioneers and surely the best known.*

* Translated into English and published under the title *Towards a New Architecture.*

In the next year in the midst of that great international manifestation of the decorative arts of the New Tradition, the Paris Exposition of 1925, appeared Le Corbusier's Pavillon de L'Esprit nouveau, the execution of a unit of the project of three years earlier for an apartment house made up of a stack of individual villas. This made much less stir than the "Voisin" plan for a city of skyscrapers intended to replace the present business centre of Paris. These immense cross-shaped towers with corrugated walls were set above the traffic amid ample gardens and surrounded by residential quarters laid out on the principle of the earlier housing projects. They were of course wholly fantastic, particularly considering the chosen site; and in their æsthetic expression they were no more interesting than the schemes of the same period for a worker's city and a university city of separated students' cells.

Fortunately the sociological visionary in Le Corbusier was forced to give place again to the architect. In the two studio houses for the sculptors Miestchaninoff and Lipchitz built at Boulogne-sur-Seine in 1925 his real work continued. In the first of these there is as in the Vaucresson street façade too great a variety as well as too great a dependence on naval architecture. But in the contiguous Lipchitz villa he worked successfully on a larger scale than hitherto and made of the fenestration and the expression of the well-studied plan the particular interest. These two houses together, with their blue and ochre walls, now unfortunately in need of repainting, provided a brilliant demonstration of the wide possibilities of his manner. Independently they were less satisfactory than those that immediately preceded and followed. Yet the Miestchaninoff house despite its obvious faults was, and remains, a splendid *tour de force*.

In 1926 Le Corbusier built several more houses. One of them, another studio house very near those just mentioned, was quite small but very interesting for its dark red-brown colouring and the skilful placing in relation to the garden on an awkward triangular site. Technically it marked a point of rest in which the gains of the previous years were summed up. (Figure 40.) Two more, designed as one unit and built at Auteuil, were more forward-looking. In them the ribbon window theme was further developed than hitherto and the planning was elaborate and even luxurious. From then on indeed Le Corbusier worked chiefly for the rich who could afford his technical extravagance and the heating-expense in houses of glass and concrete.

In this same year he also built in Antwerp a small isolated studio house which recalled in its simplicity some of the units of his earlier projects. Although there was both in the exteriors and in the interiors less indulgence in æsthetic research, it must be admitted that it was also less interesting than the Auteuil houses. The comparison of these two constructions suggests that Le Corbusier's vices and virtues as an architect are so linked that the artist in him succeeds best when least restricted financially.

The first house completed in 1927, that for the American painter Cook, again in Boulogne-sur-Seine, gave him the opportunity for one of his finest designs. The house at least appears to be more completely raised above the ground than even in the "Citrohan" project, and the entirely cantilevered façade received a magnificent and extreme horizontal expression. The posts which broke the line of the windows in the Auteuil houses were no longer needed and bands of glass alternated with bands of cement plaster of exquisite egg-shell colour and texture beneath the open railings and concrete shelter of the roof terraces.

Technically and æsthetically this was a triumph as regards the exterior. But it interfered practically with the arrangement of the interior. Although it does actually contain independent rooms it seems to exist merely as a single rather complicated space. As in the rooms in the Auteuil houses this space was treated as an immense abstract composition with different colours on different walls. Interesting as this is, it is hardly reposeful and lacks particularly when furnished that fusion and clarification which gives such a real integrity to his exteriors.

In 1927 also was completed the first executed housing development, that at Pessac outside Bordeaux which had been studied for the financier Henri Frugés during the two previous years. This was a serious disappointment to all who had taken Le Corbusier seriously as a sociologist. Effective it admittedly was, but practical not at all, even in very elementary matters. He avoided monotony in the grouping and related the buildings pleasantly to the gardens in which they stood. He also applied to exteriors the principle hitherto used only in interiors, of painting different walls different colours.

But Le Corbusier had done too much work for millionaires and artists ready and able to afford the expenses of æsthetic research to be able to carry out in actuality the practical principles of his earlier housing-schemes. Considering the fact that so large a part of the site was given over to gardens it was senseless extravagance to devote nearly half the cubic content of the houses to the luxury of open entrances and terraces. The extraordinary planning which was forgivable in a large villa, made the interiors of these houses particularly uncomfortable for the small-salaried employés for whom they were designed. There was, however, a technical interest in the use of standardized parts in the construction and a not undesirable protest against the extremes of practical expression to which German admirers of the *machine à habiter* were going. But as the first executed housing-scheme of the New Pioneers in France it certainly has done much more harm than good to the development of modern housing there.

Both the single and the double house erected by Le Corbusier in the summer of 1927 at the Dwelling House Exposition of the Weissenhofsiedlung in Stuttgart appeared even more paradoxical to the architects and others who visited them. Here again were houses intended for small-salaried employés devoid of many of the simpler comforts of contemporary life and yet provided with all the expensive technicalities that Le Corbusier had developed in his villas. Unlike the houses at Pessac, however, the expression particularly of the double house was as fine as Le Corbusier had ever achieved and the use of colour far more subtle and effective than at Pessac.

By contrast it was somewhat extraordinary that Le Corbusier again appeared primarily as a practical genius in his designs submitted for the competition for the Palace of the League of Nations, also of this year. Among all the designs, even among those that followed rather completely his own principles, it has been almost universally admitted that his offered the most successful solution of the many and complicated problems of the elaborate programme. The Ecole des Beaux Arts itself admired the plan. His facade expression was simple and eminently rational; and the lack of startling effects was justified by the small amount of money available and the natural beauty of the site of which he availed himself very completely.

Although he had hitherto used always a flat plaster or cement wall treatment which gave most satisfactorily, at least until it began to crack, the continuity and impression of tension that he sought, in this his first monumental project he intended to use a granite veneer. In several ways this magnificent design, rigidly bound by a conscientiously followed programme, and although of necessity very largely devoid of that megalomania which characterized his wholly ideal projects, may mark the beginning of a new and more balanced phase of his work. It is too soon to say, however. The design of 1928 for the Mundaneum, an international intellectual centre in Geneva, is hardly more than a plan. Its central feature, the world museum, is open not only to the technical criticism of hardly adequately providing for its difficult functions, but also to the æsthetic criticism of offering an impression of solid mass altogether inadequately supported for the eye by the pillars on which it rests. The designs for a large building to be built in Moscow are it may be hoped more definitely indicative of the direction in which he is tending.

The last executed work, the villa at Garches finished in 1928, represents in a way the culmination of the line begun with the Ozenfant studio. (Figures 43, 44.) Technically Le Corbusier has never been more extravagant in his use of cantilevered façades, screen walls and terraces. From the last there is a fine view of Paris in the distance. Æsthetically it is a magnificent expansion of the Cook house, and indeed even more. For it is very rich in fine independent effects.

On the basis of his failure as a sociological architect at Pessac and at Stuttgart and of his extreme æsthetic research at Garches the German and Dutch architects have been able to turn his earlier published theories against him. Yet they came strongly to the support of the Geneva design which has quite as much of lyricism as any of the works they condemn. Le Corbusier remains an international leader even for those who are inclined to distrust him. For in his executed work he has certainly achieved a more advanced demonstration of the possibilities of a new æsthetic than any other architect. "Towards a New Architecture" he has moved far and rapidly. Yet many of the tricks which have in his hands the value of *tours de force* appear clearly as in direct opposition to his general principles when they are imitated by others lacking his creative originality.

Nevertheless the international influence of his books, his projects, and his buildings has been without equal since the War. It is he, not the practical Germans converted wholesale to his earlier theories, who has succeeded best in destroying the validity of the New Tradition by offering, however prematurely, rhapsodic expression of ferro-concrete construction. But his lyricism surpasses a rigid machine æsthetic. As early as 1925 he was being unintelligently imitated; and to-day a stern younger generation of architects is turning away from architecture as an art toward architecture as a branch of sociology because of him. Paradoxically the effect of his earlier writing and projects is being continued by the reaction from the extreme æsthetic research of his executed building.

Despite the intoxicating quality of his writing and of his work Le Corbusier is by no means necessarily the greatest of those who have introduced a new architecture. Fortunately even in France he is not the only New Pioneer. Compared to Le Corbusier his chief French colleague, André Lurçat, may at first appear somewhat slow and plodding. Nevertheless his work has increased in excellence regularly from year to year and his influence for being the less has been altogether to the good.

Lurçat was born in Lorraine in 1894 and received his architectural education at the Ecole des Beaux Arts. In his first independent projects of 1917 he already showed a greater negative simplification of the New Tradition than Le Corbusier in his villa of the previous year. There appeared also the characteristic corner windows made possible by ferro-concrete construction, which assist so definitely three-dimensional expression in terms of volume and not of mass. Le Corbusier's designs hardly showed such originality before the "Citrohan" house of 1921.

Lurçat's first house built in 1924, the year after Le Corbusier's Vaucresson villa, was a mere box. It was influenced, it would appear, by the pre-War work of Adolf Loos and the *Cité industrielle* of Tony Garnier. In his own words, everything in architecture was *a priori* to be rejected, and then to be revised or created anew. This represented the first step. However in a model for a seaside villa made a year or two earlier there were already definite indications of the direction revision and new creation were to take. The innovations were less startling than those of Le Corbusier in the "Citrohan" house but they were assuredly more sound.

The eight houses built in the cité Seurat from 1924 to 1926 marked a distinct advance. Being conceived in relation to one another the lack of great interest in the individual units is very much an advantage. They rested completely on the ground and the planning did not demand of the inhabitants that they change their entire manner of living. In the two larger houses here, one that of his brother the painter Jean Lurçat, with a large corner studio at the top, and the other that of Mme. Bertrand, he introduced more features than in the others. Particularly in the latter he made very effective use of asymmetrical balance and the corner window. (Figure 46.)

The two villas built at Versailles in 1925 were even more elaborate in their expression. But they were less successful except perhaps the very mannered garden façade of one with its narrow ribbon windows. All this work had, however, a solid reality, a plausibility which contrasts strongly with the ethereal and fantastic quality of Le Corbusier's visions.

The housing projects of Lurçat are also very different from those of Le Corbusier. In them he has eventually achieved a real superiority. A design of 1926 represented little more than a large scale standardized development of the houses of the cité Seurat. Another of the same year for workmen's houses at Villeneuve-Saint-Georges, although excellent technically, was somewhat monotonous and uninteresting in expression. In his later projects of this order, however, of which one is shortly to be executed, he has succeeded in retaining the practical virtues of the earlier ones and at the same time providing more than adequate æsthetic expression without depending on any *tours de force*. For these he has by no means the proper temperament.

In his important villa, the Guggenbuhl house, built in the rue Deutsch de la Meurthe, Paris, in 1927, the attempts at virtuosity were far from completely successful. The blank side wall with one window, the bay-window of the studio, the strange pierced roof suspended above it, the contrast of white and yellow surfaces are not quite acceptable æsthetically in the way of the audacities of Le Corbusier. It represented nevertheless a broadening of his manner and the interior is much more practical and livable than those of Le Corbusier. The several terraces particularly are more than justified by the way in which they seem to attach to the house the entire Parc Montsouris.

The small villa built in 1928 at Boulogne-sur-Seine attempts much less, but it is extraordinarily successful. (Figure 45.) Unfortunately the same cannot quite be said of the apartment house of the same date. The mouldings underneath the windows and balconies recall a little the simplified Expressionism of Mendelsohn and other Germans, and the whole is somewhat heavy and graceless. The entrance pavilion in the garden was however very excellent. The later designs for rows of small standardized villas, for a large Riviera hotel and for a sanatorium are at once highly characteristic in the matter of fact treatment, and most successful in scale and proportion. Indeed, when the last is erected, it should be the most considerable new work in France.

In his two installations of Paris art galleries the sumptuousness and elegance he attempted was as foreign as virtuosity to his temperament and distinctly outside the range of his talents. His full capacity will only be revealed when his large projects are executed. For on a small scale his lack of perfect intuitive assurance and finesse causes him to fail just where Le Corbusier succeeds.

Lurçat indicates in many ways far better than Le Corbusier the possibilities of the wide development of the new architecture. He is not at all the genius, but he has a real grasp of the problems of contemporary architecture and a willingness to attack them slowly and solve them one by one. Lacking the Messianism and the passion for theory of Le Corbusier, his work is not contradictory. Yet he shows a very desirable capacity for dealing with separate difficulties in separate ways without confusion of genres. Furthermore, while Le Corbusier has proved a difficult master, at once dogmatic and changeable, Lurçat has had a very healthy direct influence on many young architects for the very reason that they are more able to keep pace with him in his advance.

Beside these two men the other architects in France who work in the new manner are of far less importance. Robert Mallet-Stevens, on account of the quantity and the importance of his commissions, has achieved considerable prominence. His essentially publicist talent has thus had the chance to produce the two most interesting façades in the centre of Paris: the General Motors garage, just off the Champs Elysées, and the Bally Shoestore, on the Boulevard de la Madeleine, entirely covered with lacquered metal plaques. As the interiors reveal, neither of these are altogether sound specimens of the new architecture.

The promise of his extensive Riviera villa built for the vicomte de Noailles in 1924, so admirably in place against the meridional landscape, has not been fulfilled in the group of houses of 1926-27, which fill the rue Mallet-Stevens in Auteuil. These must appear mere meaningless piles of blocks to the critic most sympathetic to the new manner exactly as to the most naïf and traditional observer. The extraordinary general bareness of these exteriors is in strange contrast to the luxurious touches of elaborate geometrical decoration, recalling the worst of the Exposition of 1925. Where at Boulogne-sur-Seine a villa of Mallet-Stevens stands beside the Cook house of Le Corbusier, the inferiority of the former is startlingly revealed to the most casual observer. His yellow casino at Juan-les-Pins has at least no such disconcerting rival.

Fischer is an architect even less serious than Mallet-Stevens. His very unsuccessful houses in the new manner are significant only in that they were thus designed by the wish of the clients. Much more interesting is the small quantity of executed work of Guevrekian and of Moreux, which compares favourably with that of Lurçat. A further architect working creditably in France in the new manner is the Pole, Elkouken. Among several decorator-architects Djo Bourgeois is also worth mention.

But the æsthetic of the New Pioneers is very far from dominant in France. It has nevertheless distinctly influenced many who still work in the New Tradition, such as Pierre Patou and Michel Roux-Spitz, without causing them entirely to abjure the ornament of the Exposition of 1925. Indeed, even the engineering works of Freyssinet, where they are architectural in intent like the new Reims market, are still marked by the now declining influence of the Ecole des Beaux Arts as well as by the æsthetic of Perret. Fortunately this is not true of such a magnificent monument as the hangars at Orly.

It is a curious and general error to consider the movement of the New Pioneers as particularly French. Only the accident of Le Corbusier's working in Paris—and even so often for foreigners—has made it possible to suppose that the work of the new manner is largely to be found there.

Beside the inspiration of Le Corbusier, the sober accomplishment of Lurçat, and the other less important manifestations in France, the parallel later developments in Holland, although obscured by the continuing dominance of a particularly successful form of the New Tradition, are quite as significant and distinctly more varied.

CHAPTER FIFTEEN

THE NEW PIONEERS: HOLLAND

"WITHOUT succumbing to an arid rationalism the new architecture will be essentially utilitarian; but utilitarian without excluding aspirations of a superior order. In radical opposition to the too familiar sort of production resulting from the inspiration of a moment and devoid of technique, of form and of colour; a new architecture will create technically, even quasi-impersonally, works perfectly adapted to the assigned end, clear in form and pure in proportions. In place of the natural charm of walls and roofs of rough materials, unstable in their plasticity and uncertainly patined; in place of windows cut into small panes, nebulously glazed and irregularly coloured; a new architecture will offer us the definite values of artificial materials, surfaces polished and finished, the scintillation of steel and the brilliance of paint, the transparent openness of large windows of plate glass, . . . Architectural evolution thus will lead us toward a style that will appear liberated from matter, although it is joined with it more completely than ever. Disengaged from all impressionistic sentimentality; dependent on clear proportions, frank colours, plainly organic forms; divested of all that is superfluous; the new architecture will be able to outvie even Classical limpidity."

J. J. P. Oud, 1921.

The literary activity of Oud has been less extensive than that of Le Corbusier but of the most valid sort. Less intoxicating than the aphorisms of *Vers une architecture* such a passage as that just quoted is more intelligible, more clearly thought out, and more specific. It is unfortunate that up to the present neither the writing nor the work of Oud has been so universally noticed as that of Le Corbusier.

Oud is unquestionably the most important architect of Holland. Neither the work of the men more closely affiliated than he with the group *de Stijl* nor the building of men such as Van der Vlugt or Bijvoet, who have moved somewhat later than he along the road towards a new architecture, is comparable in quality or significance. On the one hand the men of *de Stijl* have devoted themselves chiefly to æsthetic experiment little controlled by practical experience. On the other, those who have shown particularly excellent and original command of new structural possibilities have seldom achieved altogether adequate architectural expression.

Internationally it is less easy to determine the comparative importance of Oud. But beside Le Corbusier, the lyrical visionary, whether as a sociologist in his writing, or as a technician and an æsthetician in his building; beside Gropius, above all the organizer, Oud stands as primarily and completely the architect. If his influence and his fame have thus far been less, it is because his work has kept him more out of the public eye and its character has been much less superficially startling. After the healthy discipline of his position as architect of the City of Rotterdam the future holds more possibilities for Oud than for Le Corbusier or Gropius who have spent more extravagantly their creative energies.

The story of Oud's development is peculiarly central to the establishment of that new architecture he so early and well defined. It is the more significant because he was hampered by an already academicized "modernism," that of the New Tradition, in many ways at the poles from his own, and yet as nowhere else vigorously national, independently developed, and universally accepted. The very greatness of Berlage made it the harder to develop beyond him. Oud was born at Purmerend in 1894. After studying in the Amsterdam School of Arts and Crafts, he went to work in the office of Stuijt and Cuijpers, the latter the son of the architect of the Rijksmuseum. At this time he built two houses in whose design he was much influenced by Muthesius' *Das Englische Haus,* which had just appeared. He next continued his studies at Delft in the University and the Technical Normal School. From there he went to Munich where he worked for a few months in the office of Theodor Fischer, then certainly the best master in South Germany.

When he returned to his native town and went into practice the influence of Berlage replaced that of the English country house and the related Mediævalism of Cuijpers and of Fischer. Through the writing and the lectures of Berlage he was soon led also to an interest in Frank Lloyd Wright. But his work of these years in Purmerend, Aalsmeer, and Leiden was pre-eminently Berlagian, whether done alone or in collaboration with Kamerlingh Onnes, van den Steur, or Dudok. The same is true of the more elaborate projects done at the same time, of which a bath establishment based on the Amsterdam Beurs is typical.

But soon after this in the early years of the War, Oud, whose relations with painters had previously been among men such as der Kinderen and Roland Holst, followers in fresco of Puvis de Chavannes, came into contact with Cubism and Futurism. At first he found in this new painting only an incomprehensible fascination. Later the meaning of it for architecture became clearer to him and it had eventually an influence on his designs even more important than that of Berlage and Wright. In 1917 Oud together with van Doesburg and Mondriaan, who was the chief force among the Dutch Cubists, founded the review *de Stijl* as a vehicle for their ideas and to present their work.

The dull project for a double workmen's house in concrete designed in this year still shows in its heavy simplified forms the mark of Oud's dependence on Wright. It was indeed from any point of view much less satisfactory than the somewhat similar houses actually being erected at the same time by Robert van 'tHoff, another early member of *de Stijl*.

However, the project for a row of seaside cottages in concrete, published in the first number of *de Stijl*, was much more interesting. Moreover it was more significant as pointing the way to a new æsthetic of architecture better than anything done thus far by Le Corbusier. But the expression was of the most elementary order and in the executed work of this year Oud still followed a very simplified form of the New Tradition. In the house built at Katwijk Kamerlingh Onnes was however responsible for the "impressionistic sentimentality" of the exterior which suggested the Sahara. In another house at Noordwijkerhout it was the study of colour by van Doesburg and particularly his arrangement of the interior floor tiling which was new and effective. So also in the designs for housing blocks published the next year in *de Stijl* Oud's manner remains excessively monumental and clearly related to that of Berlage and Wright.

In 1918 Oud became architect of the city of Rotterdam and undertook in his official housing work a burden of large scale production such as the

French New Pioneers have never known. In this year and the next he executed his first extensive projects in the Spangen blocks at Rotterdam.

In 1919 also appeared in *de Stijl* the most significant of his free designs. The bonded warehouse shows him still a follower of Wright. But the factory design, although not without heaviness, illustrated a determined effort to achieve in architecture the effects of Néo-Plasticism—the specific name for the Cubist painting of Mondriaan and van Doesburg. In the intricate play of rather meaningless horizontal and vertical masses one part of this design might well be the abstract construction of a sculptor. This experiment in incompletely digested Cubist architecture had a considerable influence in Holland, particularly in Dudok, and even further afield in Germany and Russia. To Oud it was hardly more than an exercise in free creation; but it was accepted too seriously and much imitated by the borrowers of tricks who have taken so much from the architecture of Le Corbusier.

The development of the years of the War and the association with the painters of *de Stijl* had tended to carry Oud dangerously far in the direction of free æsthetic experimentation. It was in some sense a break with his friends the theoreticians when he began to work for the city of Rotterdam and was forced to devote himself primarily to technical matters. The Spangen blocks, particularly, continued to compromise with the manner of Berlage; and even in the Tuschendijken blocks of the next year in which he freed himself from the visible roofs, the broken pavilions and the dormers of the Spangen blocks, the clarification of expression was largely negative. Although the windows were completely standardized, their forms were not new; and the raised panels above the entrances, the coloured brick banks at the base of the walls continued from the work of the year before a last echo of the decoration of the New Tradition. The corner treatment was indeed novel and technically interesting; but its lightness was somewhat out of keeping with the solidity and monotony of the whole. It was in the courts that he advanced furthest, omitting completely all that was merely ornamental. But no more than in the corner treatment toward the street was there any great success in the positive creation of a new manner.

Thus directly influenced by the work of the New Tradition about him, even to the retention of something corresponding to its decoration as well as its brick construction, and reacting against it hardly more than in the avoidance of its specific effects, these buildings were typically transitional, of more historical than intrinsic value in the architectural expression. The new manner triumphed so barely that it had little chance to display its possibilities. But the difficulties of large scale execution, the intellectual study of a complicated technical problem, restored the balance which had tipped so far toward abstract research of form in the factory project of the previous year. Moreover, in the compact planning and in the way in which the apartments opened on the large garden in the centre of the courts, he achieved a very real utilitarian success which was continued in later building along the same lines at Rotterdam. Architecture as a branch of sociology was at least admirably served.

In 1921 in a competitive design for a country house outside Berlin he reached a more perfect synthesis of the technical and æsthetic tendencies of the new manner than any one had thus far achieved, except possibly Gropius in his factory of 1914. All traces of the influence of Berlage and of Wright had disappeared as well as the specifically Cubistic features of the factory projects. Cubistic significance was given not to one or another part but to the whole, without adding to or subtracting from its technical integrity. The material was to have been concrete, as in all the free designs since 1917. But no special advantage was as yet taken in the window arrangement or in balconies of the possibility of long spans in that material. The house might equally well have been built with masonry lintels. But if Oud was very far from the technical virtuosity which Le Corbusier displayed this same year in his "Citrohan" model, he was able nevertheless much more soundly and with less overt demonstration to indicate what a new architecture might be.

In the next year he was able to introduce in his executed housing work the completely integrated æsthetic of the Berlin project. The village built all at once at Oud Mathenesse outside Rotterdam showed a fine variety in its group planning in combination with a very complete standardization of the elements of construction. As this was only built for twenty-five years on land which was intended to become a park, the construction was only semipermanent and was chiefly of wood and other traditional materials. Thus the terraced roofs of the Tuschendijken blocks and the Berlin house were not used; and the tile covered gables and heavy wooden window frames, although technically justified in the occasion, recalled in some degree the picturesque traditionalism of the previous Dutch manner of contemporary architecture.

However, the geometrical design carried out brilliantly the new principles of composition. Oud's wider experience made it possible for him to avoid the uncertainty which is still manifest in Le Corbusier's Vaucresson villa built in the same year. The fine proportions reduce the technical complexity of the scheme to a rich simplicity, and in the rhythm of the standardized units there is a positive quality that integrates the whole. (Figure 33.)

In two or three years Oud had travelled from the position of a mere insurgent against the dominant New Tradition, involved with painters in æsthetic research, to that of the creator of a new architecture according to the principles that have been quoted from his writing of 1921 in *de Stijl*. The ease with which he was able to do this even while retaining traditional construction was particularly noteworthy. At the same time this constituted a model village of great sociological interest in which practical organic arrangement made a more perfect whole than had been possible in similar work which followed more picturesque principles. Oud was already well repaid by this accomplishment for his subjection to the discipline of building for the city on a large scale.

In the next year Oud built outside Rotterdam a little temporary building, a superintendent's office, of complicated shape and painted in primary colours. In a sense it was a retrogression toward the first Cubistic phase. Yet it represented not the decorative Cubism of the factory but, although in exaggerated form, the integral Cubism of the Berlin house. Its shapes were determined by the rooms within; its purpose demanded that it be conspicuous. The surface patterns were formed by the planks of which it was built and its expression was wholly his own and not dependent upon the Néo-Plasticist painters of *de Stijl* of which Oud had ceased to be a member in 1920.

The Café de Unie in Rotterdam built in 1925 was of much the same order. Its brilliant colour and prominent lettering were justified as advertising. Less constrained by technical necessities it lacked nevertheless the simple clear forms and proportions of the Oud Mathenesse houses. This temporary return to æsthetic experiment, however, this playful indulgence in extreme freedom had its advantages. It widened his grasp of architecture and loosened a manner whose expression had been almost too subordinated to practical necessities.

The street of houses in the Hoek van Holland which followed is indeed probably the finest monument of the new architecture. It was designed in 1924 and executed in 1926-27. Here the new manner is entirely devoid of inherited elements and the use of colour is delicate and discreet. The yellow brick basement, the dark grey band beside the blue door, the black iron work with only a touch of red on the lighting fixtures, provide against the reduced white of the plaster exactly the proper amount of contrast and variety. The ribbon windows and the balconies are used to emphasize the horizontality of the magnificently serene proportions. And in the circular corner stores the necessary elements of construction are given an expression as lyrical as anything to be found in the work of Le Corbusier. (Figures 47, 48.)

The later housing projects, in which the particular problem was to provide the smallest possible accommodations for whole families, are still in construction. They are technically very excellent; but perhaps not so rich in expression as those at the Hoek van Holland. The row of houses built at the Stuttgart Exposition of 1927 are also less interesting in design. But he followed literally, as almost no others did, the programme of the Exposition and produced the cheapest possible good workmen's houses. No others were as fine in technicalities of planning, and hardly any others were more advanced in expression, except those of his friend Mart Stam and Le Corbusier, in the case of the latter by disregarding the programme.

Finally, there remain to be mentioned several projects of the last three years in which he has turned his attention to other functional problems than that of housing. The design for the Rotterdam Beurs was unfortunately not accepted. In this immense monument with its aluminum window-frames between bands of concrete he gave splendid expression to a plan which has influenced Staal in the designs which are now to be executed. The project for a hotel in Brno, Czechoslovakia, submitted in a competition, is less successful. He handled height with less ability than he had breadth, and the complexities of luxurious planning interfere with the clarity of expression. A church, the first project of similar monumental importance to be erected, is now, spring 1929, in process of construction. The designs for this indicate that he is ready as perhaps no architect of his generation to develop fully and without exaggeration the new manner in a simple and yet striking individual building.

Oud's career has been thus far assuredly less conspicuously brilliant than that of Le Corbusier. In his finest work, however, he has already truly fulfilled the programme of a new architecture which he set in 1921. That the renewment of architecture is to be centred in technique is his prime contention. He has had his training in its most difficult problems. That architecture must advance equally in its expression has been quite as clear to him. Along his own lines he has on occasion gone as far as any in æsthetic experimentation. But particularly he has felt the necessity of the complete and balanced fusion of technique and expression. This he has sought and attained. Of his constructions of the last decade it may be said in the terms of Valéry's *Eupalinos* that they were mute until they could talk sense; that next they spoke clearly and intelligibly; and that finally they were able to sing as melodiously as those of Le Corbusier who had essayed lyricism from the beginning in his executed buildings.

More than that of Le Corbusier, therefore, the story of Oud as a New Pioneer indicates a sure route forward. When his influence comes generally to surpass that of the other, the new architecture will be more completely and soundly established. Le Corbusier's villa at Garches is like a photograph brought back from an aeroplane flight over new territories. Toward these new territories Oud has mapped the roads along which advance may be made. Even if his church will be perhaps but a frontier post, it should have a solidity and a reality lacking in the designs of Le Corbusier which remain still dreamlike even when they are executed.

Oud's projects of 1917-1919 were not the only contributions of *de Stijl* to the new manner; nor even the most direct and important. The houses of van 'tHoff, who unfortunately ceased to build immediately afterward, have already been mentioned. Van Doesburg himself has made many projects, usually in collaboration with other architects, Rietveld, van Eesteren and van Leusden. Not the first design, that for a fountain in Leeuwarden of 1918, nor the house executed at Alblasserdam by van Eesteren in 1924, of which van Doesburg was only responsible for the study of colour, were the most significant of these. It was the models of 1922 for an artist's house and two other houses, one very large, which were the most interesting and also the most widely remarked. The large country house model had even greater influence than the factory design of Oud in Germany and Eastern Europe. Indeed, in the case of Gropius it would appear from the projects he made just after its publication to have been particularly formative, freeing him from the monumental and Expressionistic tendencies about him.

The executed work of van Doesburg and other men of *de Stijl,* such as Huszar, Vantongerloo and Ravestijn, has been almost entirely in interiors. The most notable of these was the reconstruction of the cafés and so forth of L'Aubette at Strasbourg done in 1927 by van Doesburg in collaboration with Hans Arp and the latter's wife Here Elementarist painting so dominates the designs that they have little architectural existence. There remains practically none of the three dimensional study of volume which made the models of 1922 of such great interest. Despite ideas and valuable experimentation *de Stijl* has however produced almost no actual buildings. A few of its members have become true architects only by breaking with its theoretical stringencies.

After Oud, Rietveld is unquestionably the best of the group, even though he has only executed a few houses and shop installations. The first house built in 1922 at Utrecht remains one of the most original achievements of the New Pioneers as well as one of the earliest. It was related to Oud's Cubist detail of 1919 and to the *de Stijl* models of 1922. But it was already an extreme development in which exterior and interior were interwoven in one composition of open spaces and planes of different colours. (Figure 42.) Ingenious moving partitions made it possible to utilize the upper storey as one room or four, and the furniture, of which Rietveld had previously been particularly a maker, completed the extraordinary effect of a piece of abstract sculpture enlarged to architectural size. The house he built at Wassenaar in 1924 was both less extreme and less interesting. But although it was sounder architecture it had nothing like the influence of that at Utrecht which was much imitated, at least on paper, by many East European Constructivists.

Another small house above a garage, built in 1928, marked as extreme a point in technical research as the first in æsthetic research. The visible steel skeleton filled with windows or black and white enamelled cement plaques is primarily an experiment in construction. Like his first house it cannot be considered in the sense of the work of Oud an altogether definite contribution to the new architecture. Lately however Rietveld has produced a project for inexpensive housing in Utrecht which is more practical and more sober. It suggests, like the League of Nations project of Le Corbusier, that even those who have been primarily visionaries are now at last ready to profit by accepting restraints to which Oud submitted a decade ago.

But the cerebral quality which has thus far marked the houses of Rietveld as much as the designs of van Doesburg and his associates has been rivalled in Holland by the practical achievement of certain other men. Although they are undoubtedly less gifted they have been able in a considerable quantity of executed work to display effectively the potentialities of those new methods of construction to which the manner of the New Pioneers owes so much.

In the competition for the Chicago Tribune Tower of 1922, which coincided with the first buildings of Oud and Rietveld in the new manner, Holland was represented by a project of Bijvoet and Duiker intended to be constructed of ferro-concrete. Still influenced by Wright to some extent, it was interesting for the virtuosity of its expression of structure among the few projects which already represented in this competition a reaction from the New Tradition. In the next years in their executed housing work at Kijkduin and elsewhere Bijvoet and Duiker continued to follow Frank Lloyd Wright, achieving like Jan Wils, a less extreme member of *de Stijl*, van Loghem and others, a considerable simplification of the Dutch New Tradition. Its least excusable crudities were however too frequently retained. The continued use of brick as in the house by van Eesteren already mentioned was fatal to really new æsthetic expression. This was associated in Holland, as in France and Germany, with smooth cement surfaces applied to ferro-concrete construction.

Later Bijvoet and Duiker succeeded in their factories in providing a clear and logical expression of the new methods of construction and broke quite away from the "picturesqueness" which had controlled their individual country houses quite as much as those of any of their Dutch contemporaries. It is however the sanatorium Zonnestraal outside Hilversum, finished in 1928, which best represents their work. Its technical extravagances in the use of glass and balconies are wholly justified by the specific problem. Although in perfection of proportions and the study of plan and composition it leaves much to be desired, it is none the less at once one of the most considerable and one of the most valid in the new manner.

The work of Van der Vlugt and Brinkman is of much the same order. It is always of great constructive interest. Since as early as 1922 this Rotterdam firm has shown an increasingly sure comprehension of the technical problems of the New Pioneers. In the van Nelle factory outside Rotterdam, of which the first section was completed in 1928, they achieved for the first time a magnificent if somewhat forced æsthetic expression. (Figure 49.) This may possibly have been due in part to the collaboration of Mart Stam. Stam is one of the youngest and most capable Dutch architects. In his first houses which were executed at the Stuttgart Exposition of 1927 he already showed great promise. His published designs for buildings now in course of construction at Frankfurt suggest that his development may be, despite his very different temperament, as well balanced as that of Oud.

The new manner has furthermore made at least many partial converts in Holland even among these who have been definitely the members of the Amsterdam school. Among those already mentioned in considering the New Tradition in Holland, Staal and Dudok are the most important. Wijdeveld, the editor of *Wendingen,* an important Dutch magazine devoted in large part to architecture, has gone even further in his executed work than they; but like them he is nevertheless somewhat unrepentant as regards "picturesqueness."

Yet even setting aside the work of those in Holland who still thus compromise, the building by Oud, Rietveld and Stam, the experiments of *de Stijl* and the later constructions of Bijvoet and Duiker and Van der Vlugt and Brinkman constitute a mass of work by New Pioneers greater in quantity and more varied than that of France. The new architecture needs not only men like Oud, who can combine æsthetic experimentation and technical development satisfying the elaborate functional needs of contemporary life; but also those who can forget the integrity of architecture in the analytical pursuit of one line of research or another. The New Pioneers are moreover not alone those who are altogether original, wholly sincere and rigidly conscientious. The establishment of a manner of architecture requires a much more general support. Otherwise it can be no more than a wing of a wider movement as was for example Gothic Revival in the Age of Romanticism.   Architects willing to take over the new manner when barely formed and to apply it on a large scale, even imitatively and without full comprehension, have been very few in France and in Holland.   But in Germany, as in the case of the New Tradition a score of years earlier, almost the entire younger generation has set out on the new road.

CHAPTER SIXTEEN

THE NEW PIONEERS: GERMANY

WALTER GROPIUS was the first architect in Germany to build in a fully developed post-eclectic style. His work is also most typical of what is best in German architecture to-day. He was born in 1883 and received his training by working under Behrens. Since 1910 he has practised independently.

His pre-War buildings at the Cologne Exposition and in Alfeld have already been mentioned. (Figure 38.) In them he was already some distance from the particular monumentality of Behrens and was seeking, at least in industrial building, the direct æsthetic expression of engineering. After the War he took over the Weimar School of Art of which Van de Velde had been the director and reorganized it as the Bauhaus Institut. In this work he called to assist him the painters who were carrying German Expressionism to its extremes, the Russian Kandinsky, the Swiss Klee and the German Willy Baumeister. Another painter at the Bauhaus was the American Lyonel Feininger whose less abstract manner had nevertheless more connection with the possibilities of a new architecture than that of the others. Gropius' first post-War construction, a monument in Weimar built in 1920, was a large piece of abstract Expressionistic sculpture in concrete. Unlike van Doesburg's Leeuwarden fountain, it was quite devoid of architectural significance.

His first real post-War building, a theatre built in 1922 in Jena, marked a reaction from the Expressionist influence. Aside from this it represented little more than excellent technical organization in terms of concrete. In its expression it recalled the earliest designs of Lurçat and Le Corbusier in its reduction of the forms of the New Tradition to the simplest geometrical terms. The project of the same year for the Chicago Tribune Tower was the result of more advanced technical and æsthetic research. Nevertheless, the Constructivistic expression applied to the visible ferro-concrete construction was highly arbitrary. As in the projects of *de Stijl*, the expression was more or less independent of the technique. The houses actually executed in this year and the next displayed even more uncertainty. In one, the concrete forms were used for angular Expressionistic effects. In the other, the construction was entirely of heavy wooden logs and the traditional features of the blockhouse gave the exterior its architectural character, while in the interior there was much abstract carved detail by a collaborating sculptor.

It is only in the unexecuted projects of 1923 that Gropius appeared truly as a New Pioneer with an integrated programme. A factory design presented a use of ferro-concrete as clear and effective as his use of brick and steel in those before the War. In a design for an international academy of philosophy he applied similar principles to a larger and more complicated scheme. In this as well as in the many models for houses to be built of standardized elements, his expression seems to have been crystallized by the models van Doesburg and his associates had made the preceding year. But Gropius' æsthetic research was definitely controlled by technical possibilities and related to the means of organizing a new achitecture on a large scale.

The house built in Jena at the end of this year although already very different from the blockhouse was much less excellent than his projects. But with all its heaviness and awkwardness it was completely freed from the New Tradition and from Expressionism. It was also less directly marked than the models by Constructivism and Néo-Plasticism.

The chief activity of the Bauhaus at this time was in connection with the organization of the contemporary interior. In this Gropius and his associates, of whom Breuer was the most important, had a considerable success. They achieved a valid balance of new technical and æsthetic values. More practical than Le Corbusier or the men of *de Stijl*, their expression was equally highly developed. They established as well the large scale production of the movable furniture, lighting fixtures and small household objects of which they had need. Thus to-day these adjuncts of contemporary living are more obtainable in Germany than in France or Holland.

Gropius' large architectural project of 1924 appeared to show some slight influence from the later work of Mendelsohn. But this incipient phase had no continuance and it may well have served merely to broaden his manner.

The next year the Bauhaus moved from Weimar to Dessau. Here Gropius developed the instruction of the school on a wider scale and published the first of the *Bauhausbücher*, that devoted to *Internationale Architektur*. Although this is without explanatory text, the principles of selection were anything but rigid. The illustrated examples of contemporary building show that Gropius' chief interest was in the possibilities of large scale architectural development in answer to contemporary sociological needs.

In 1926 Gropius had his great opportunity and rose magnificently to meet it. He was able to provide a complete new installation for the Bauhaus at Dessau. One immense building contained workrooms, classrooms, a whole wing of apartments and another wing for the local technical school. It is still assuredly the most successful demonstration in execution of the technical and æsthetic possibilities of the manner of the New Pioneers in dealing with a large and complicated functional problem. It lacks entirely the tentativeness and the reflection of others which had marred Gropius' previous post-War work. (Figure 50.) No less successful was the row of houses erected for the professors of the Bauhaus in a grove of pines not far from the main building. In these there was an interesting variety in the use of standard elements, sound if not revolutionary planning, and exterior and interior expression of original character.

More than the villas of Le Corbusier and the housing schemes of Oud, the Bauhaus constructions make clear how the new manner may be widely applied. They also indicate that even a man whose talents are perhaps not specifically architectural can add to the fine monuments of the new architecture by conscientious effort and by organization of production.

The workers' houses which Gropius built in Törten near Dessau in that year and the next were less excellent in quality. They are technically interesting; but there is an unresolved conflict between their design as surfaces and the visible ferro-concrete skeleton. The Stuttgart houses of

1927 are also more particularly a technical experiment. Although his proportions were better than at Törten the use of steel plates on a steel skeleton was more ingenious than admirable. In his desire to develop a new architecture further he was anxious to extend the acceptable building methods beyond ferro-concrete. Whether this is yet necessary technically it is not easy to say. Certainly, however, it produces a difficulty. Either a quite new expression must be found or the expression developed in connection with ferro-concrete construction must be, as in these houses, somewhat illogically continued.

Gropius left the Bauhaus in 1928 in order to practise independently in Berlin. His successor as director is the architect Hannes Meyer to whom was due the most interesting German project in the new manner for the Palace of the League of Nations. Whether Gropius' achievement will be able to continue under different conditions it is impossible to say. But his example has made an impression all over Germany. In many cities there is a concerted attempt to follow in all classes of construction the principles of the New Pioneers of which Gropius offered the first and the best national demonstration.

Technical experimentation has been developed most successfully by the other chief architect of the new manner in Germany, Ludwig Miës van der Rohe, who had general charge of the Stuttgart Exposition of 1927. He was born in 1886, and was first remarked internationally on the publication of his project for a glass skyscraper in 1921. In the technical development of this he displayed extraordinary imaginative power. The steel skeleton was reduced to a minimum and all the surfaces were of transparent or at least translucent glass. The forms, however, were influenced by a monumentality of the New Tradition and the crystalline planning of the Expressionists.

In a similar project of the next year the organization of the construction about interior supports was even more interesting. But the pseudo-organic shape and the scalloped plan related it even more closely to such extreme points of Expressionism as Mendelsohn's Einstein Tower built the previous year. In his next project, which followed immediately after, Miës van der Rohe developed his idea of the glass skyscraper with less technical extravagance. In this exceedingly influential design he made use of ferro-concrete which supported cantilevered bands of wall between the continuous bands of windows. The æsthetic expression was simple and elemental in sharp reaction to the earlier weirdness and the plan, covering an ordinary square city block, was broken only by the necessary regularly placed supports. The restraint of this design has been continued in his later work.

In 1923 he made projects in which he sought an advanced treatment of the country house depending extensively on ferro-concrete construction. There is a certain parallel to the contemporary studies of the men of *de Stijl* in the way the plan is opened up so that exterior and interior flow together. But the whole was far better related to structure and function, and far more clearly and more architecturally expressed. The country house he actually built outside Berlin in 1926 was of excellent quality although much less free and less highly articulated both technically and æsthetically than his projects. The use of brick, the rather small and somewhat accidentally grouped windows, suggested a certain relation with the New Tradition which the purity and originality of the proportions and the mechanical perfection of the technique denied. (Figure 39.) The relation to the landscape was also interestingly studied.

The apartment-houses built in 1926 outside Berlin were likewise somewhat disappointing. But even more than in the country house the expression was clear and simple. They illustrated a very individual approach little affected by the work of others. This was particularly unusual in Germany.

The apartment-house, which dominated the Stuttgart Exposition and which compared better than most of the other work there with the houses of Oud and those of Stam, developed very clearly from the Berlin work of the year before. Steel skeleton construction was effectively used in places of ferro-concrete, but it was not exposed. The plans and the technical details were excellent although the æsthetic expression was somewhat heavy. In the interiors Miës van der Rohe had his greatest success. He used large wooden panels running from floor to ceiling set in metal chassis. The clarity and the originality of the treatment was extraordinary; and the almost Japanese lightness contrasted curiously with the still somewhat monumental exterior. In other Exposition interiors at Stuttgart he made similar use of transparent, translucent and opaque glass panels. The continuation of this idea in the German pavilion at the Barcelona Exposition is of the greatest importance, particularly as regards the exterior plating of immense polished marble slabs.

Miës van der Rohe is at present constructing in Berlin an office building based on his glass skyscraper projects. The details of this will be modified surely by his experience at Barcelona. He remains still primarily a man of promise. The line of his works suggests that that promise will in time—for he does not build much nor move rapidly—be amply fulfilled.

In general German architecture has tried to move very rapidly and many men all over the country have organized even more than Gropius for extensive production. The quantity of construction is enormous, but the quality leaves generally much to be desired. On the one hand there is the official city building, of which the most interesting is that directed by Ernst May at Frankfurt. On the other hand, there is the building often comparable in amount by individual architects of whom Karl Schneider is typical. There are many other architects besides May and Schneider doubtless quite as important, but in such a mass of production all so nearly mediocre in expression it is necessary to restrict the account to these two examples, omitting work of at least equal technical interest such as that of Otto Haessler at Celle, or of Luckhardt and Anker in Berlin.

May is to be considered primarily as a regisseur, a sort of baron Haussmann, and not as an architect. He was invited in 1925 by the city of Frankfurt to establish a ten years' building programme and was given all those positions in the city administration which were connected with the problem. The extent of the work already accomplished is extraordinary. In the year 1926 not 1200 houses as projected but 2000 were built, and in 1927, 3000 instead of 1400. The number for 1928 was set at 2500.

The financing methods which make this possible are beyond the scope of the present study. But the way in which advantage has been taken of the lovely landscape of the Nidda valley, with extensive developments on either slope and the centre left open as a park, is a brilliant demonstration of what can be accomplished by means of concentration of powers and large scale planning. The special forms of the standardized elements, doors, windows, and so forth, with which this work is carried out, are incidental to the general effect. However standardization in 1925 was regrettable: four years later the architects find themselves tied to forms still considerably dependent on the æsthetic of the New Tradition. Thus it is that despite the admirable planning and the advanced technical equipment none of this work bears examination in much detail. Like the constructions of the early

Romantics, it is best seen from a distance and particularly against the splendid background of the Taunus mountains.

May has many collaborators of whom those who have thus far been most active are Rutloff and Kaufmann. Forming part of an immense technical organism, working with the elements decided in advance and with the study of colour by which the blocks are tied together or contrasted entirely in the hands of the painter Leistikow, the individual architects have had little chance for personal expression. The results have indeed been rather monotonous. Nevertheless these new Frankfurt housing colonies are far from being entirely without æsthetic interest and are often superior to the parallel work elsewhere, such as that of Riphahn and Grod at Cologne or Gutkind at Berlin. They display primarily the technical advantages for large scale production of centralized control, but they also indicate that this is not enough to assure production of really high quality. Compared to Le Corbusier's Pessac this building is more practical and sounder even if less exciting. Compared to the work of Oud it illustrates clearly that no organization, however perfect, can replace the artistic conscientiousness of an individual architect.

Production certainly is inflated in German civic building projects. Very few of the architects engaged in it have time even to think out completely what they are doing. They borrow from others; they vary somewhat at random their compositions; they improve their technique; all within an arbitrarily imposed rigidity of manner that has been established perhaps as much for economic as for æsthetic reasons. There has naturally been thus far little creative development such as marks the work of the French and the Dutch or in Germany of Gropius and Miës van der Rohe. At Frankfurt, however, an Austrian, Anton Brenner, and Mart Stam, already mentioned in discussing Holland, are attempting to carry to execution in this immense work of production their better articulated and more subtle ideas. Aside from this, the general conversion to the *Neue Sachlichkeit*, as it is called, has developed thus far little original talent. It has, like any general expedition, however, fully opened new territory and among the horde of camp followers there are no doubt some men who will later establish themselves as significant creators.

German organization has not merely taken the form of immense building enterprises. Recurring expositions, such as that at Stuttgart, have displayed the results of technical research. There have also been quantities of books in which the accomplishment in different methods of construction or in the treatment of special modern problems are summed up. There have been still other books in which the possibilities of endless new and old materials are imaginatively explored with all the feverish technical enthusiasm of Miës van der Rohe's glass skyscraper project. Thus far all this activity has divided the energy of architects, offering so many alternative suggestions that the positive results have been negligible. The general German passion for research, for organization and for production will doubtless, however, have its value in saving from many mistakes those less inclined to rush headlong into the new. Out of innumerable bad examples moreover occasionally something of real significance and worth will surely be turned up as in the case of Miës van der Rohe's interiors. The use of new materials in the remodelling of store fronts and city buildings generally has moreover been very successful in Germany. Particularly at night the Potsdamer Platz and the Kurfürstendamm in Berlin are extraordinarily effective and not surpassed by any similar arrangements elsewhere, so fine is the artificial lighting and so well studied its effect on architecture.

The work of Karl Schneider in Hamburg represents admirably the effect of the current situation in Germany on an individual architect not without talent. Born in 1892, he had already worked with both Behrens and Gropius before the War. The Michaelsen house, built at Falkenstein in 1922, remains his most original and successful production. It was, however, characteristically marked by the imitation of the features of ferro-concrete construction in more traditional materials and by the picturesque grouping and monumental disposition of the New Tradition. The expert utilization of a magnificent site and the personal expression of a transitional phase of style gave it, nevertheless, a real excellence. The large house built near Hamburg in the next year was much less important. Although more honest in its expression of construction, it was heavily massive, exaggeratedly symmetrical and somewhat influenced in its individual features by Expressionism.

A house in Blankenese, built in 1925, and his own first house displayed a very original experimentation in the use of exposed terra cotta block walling. It was hardly a success, and since then he has used entirely the smooth cement walls of the New Pioneers varied occasionally with the dark brick of the Hamburg New Tradition. (Figure 51.)

What is really significant about Schneider and typical of German conditions is that he alone since 1925 has executed quite as much building as the total production of the new manner in France and Holland in those years. It is not surprising, therefore, that in the mass, although it is generally perhaps of higher quality than most parallel German work, there is little originality and hardly a single design of which the expression has been really thoroughly studied. Yet this mass would constitute an entire city, with apartments, suburban houses, stores, cinemas, hospitals, amusement parks and even subway entrances, of at least arbitrary coherence of style. Even the close relation of his earlier large-scale housing developments with the Hamburg work of the New Tradition is definitely disguised, as far as the use of a construction already standardized by others permits, by the use of applied features borrowed from similar buildings by other New Pioneers, and by an admirable attempt at clearer and less "picturesque" massing.

With equally immense opportunities for building presented nearly everywhere there is naturally more construction in Germany comparable to that at Frankfurt and to that of Schneider than to that of Gropius and Miës van der Rohe. But a whole younger generation of architects, and even many older men as well, has been enlisted. It is difficult to estimate the significance of this contemporary German phenomenon, particularly as the æsthetic based on the forms of ferro-concrete taken over by the organizers of production and used so uncritically is being more and more undermined by the organizers of technical research.

The Stuttgart Exposition of 1927 was in many ways symbolical. It was arranged by Germans, but among them only Gropius and Miës van der Rohe were able to offer work at all comparable to that of Oud, Stam and Le Corbusier. Visitors already familiar with the ideals of the New Pioneers could not but be astounded by the simplified New Tradition apartment house of Behrens and the modified Expressionistic constructions of Scharoun and the Tauts, at the same time they were bored with the purely conventional *Neue Sachlichkeit* of Hilberseimer and Döcker, and bewildered by the technical curiosities in the way of new building materials that were displayed. But there was no country besides Germany which could have organized such a demonstration in 1927, and none besides France and Holland which could offer single works to compare with those of Gropius and Miës van der Rohe. The publications which the constructions at the Stuttgart Weissenhofsiedling engendered—cement hardly drying in Germany before buildings there are published in illustrations and text—presented to the world more completely than any previous books both the accomplishments and the dangers of the manner of the New Pioneers. The innumerable other works in which the Germans have provided a full documentation of the new manner already have their influence, particularly in Eastern Europe. Doubtless they will in time replace even in America the documents of the Paris Exposition of 1925, as those have replaced the handbooks of the styles of the past. But this is a matter of the future. The results may, however, already be surmised by examining such work as essentially or nominally subscribes to the æsthetic of the New Pioneers in other countries than France, Holland and Germany, where its earliest and finest expressions have appeared.

CHAPTER SEVENTEEN

THE NEW PIONEERS ELSEWHERE

ALTHOUGH the influence of Le Corbusier has been everywhere strong, it is from Germany that the manner of the New Pioneers has more directly spread, particularly into those countries that habitually turn to her for technical and cultural leadership. Even as far as Constantinople there are isolated examples of the new manner; but it is in Poland and Czechoslovakia that there is the most considerable activity along German lines. Russia and Austria both show a rather more independent development.

The later work of Josef Hoffmann has been mentioned, as also that of Josef Frank. (Figure 31.) Frank in his new projects has shown a very delicate and individual post-eclectic touch which sets him apart from Anton Brenner. The latter, now as has been said among those working at Frankfurt, is more primarily a technician. But none of these Austrians are as interesting as Adolf Loos who began a few years ago to fulfil the promise of his activities as a precursor before the War. The house he built at Montmartre in Paris in 1927 is most original and successful, worthy to rank with the work of Le Corbusier and Lurçat. Some of the interiors such as the plain oak panelled living-room are very fine. (Figure 57.) In occasional details there is, however, a hint still of the later works of William Morris and his imitators on the Continent. In a house located on the heights of Montmartre terraces are magnificently justified by the views on one side toward the city, on the other toward the country.

In Russia there was a long period of frenzied Constructivism. This produced many projects on paper, unbuilt and unbuildable. They were of exaggerated factory character considerably affected in expression by the experiments of the Néo-Plasticists. This subsided a few years ago and real building began of a much milder order. The brothers Vesnine have attempted to give a definitely proletarian character to their work with some success. Barkhine has built much more heavily under the influence of contemporary German work in the simplified New Tradition. Ginsburg has been particularly an organizer with far less talent than the young Buroff who built the model dairy used in the film *October*. (Figure 52.) Several others have built interesting factories. But for the most important constructions foreigners such as Mendelsohn and Le Corbusier have been called in.

The Czechoslovakian New Pioneers may be divided into three groups. There are those who are allied particularly with the Germans and still marked by the continuing influence of Expressionism; those who are content to copy Le Corbusier; and finally those such as Gočar in Prague and Fuchs in Brno who have distinct originality. The Czechs have even had their Weissenhofsiedlung, Novy Dum, and an international exposition at Brno. The former was chiefly marked by the imitation of Le Corbusier; but at the latter the pavilion built by Fuchs for the city of Brno was of interesting form, well emphasized by a novel surface covering of small dark coloured tiles. (Figure 56.) This was much more successful than the similar German experiments have usually been. Gočar's pavilion was also interesting particularly in the very effective use of suspended sculpture in front of the façade.

Conditions are similar in Poland but there is somewhat less activity among the younger architects. The mass of work still follows the German New Tradition. Syrkus and the review *Praesens* representing the New Pioneers are closely associated with the more abstract painters.

In Switzerland also there is a very close connection with Germany. Moser departed in intention from the New Tradition in his immense church of Saint Anthony in Basel and achieved an impressive if somewhat transitional monument. Younger architects have also tended either to compromise somewhat or to copy foreign work. The most independent are perhaps Schmidt and Artaria. Favarget in Lausanne is doing effective work on a large scale with city buildings. Switzerland has also two excellent critics in Giedion and Meyer. This perhaps bodes better for the immediate future than all the activity in Slavic lands so lacking balance and restraint.

There is hardly more than one Scandinavian New Pioneer of individual importance, Lönberg-Holm in Denmark. His excellent design for the Chicago Tribune Tower of 1922 has been mentioned. Ragnar Östberg has in his writing shown some comprehension of the new manner. It may be that it is already developing, quietly and imperceptibly, as the New Tradition did a generation ago, without much relation to foreign work. Already certainly there have been several very excellent factories and powerhouses.

Sant' Elia in Turin even before the War had made designs that foreshadowed the New Pioneers. He died in 1916, without building anything of importance. Italy has few architects beyond the somewhat mediocre Sartoris who work in the new manner to-day. It has however strongly influenced considerable numbers of architectural students. In Spain Mercadal stands also much alone. His Goya Memorial in Saragossa is, however, much more successful than Sartoris' buildings.

England also has little activity in architecture that is related to the work of the New Pioneers. The houses at Silverend by Tait have little originality and the subway entrances of Adams Holden and Pearson are rather in a simplified Germanic form of the New Tradition. But there is a suggestion of something more independent in certain work of Clough Williams-Ellis. Compared to Latin countries and to England, Belgium has much to offer. The work of Bourgeois, Eggerickx and others is, however, somewhat heavy and half-hearted. Henry Van de Velde at the head of the Institut Supérieur des Arts Décoratifs at Bruxelles is very probably developing a well trained younger generation. His own new work is as always of interest, particularly in the study of volume, but it is technically less significant.

As regards America it might easily appear as if the architecture of the New Pioneers belonged only to the future. The situation is peculiar and its full meaning has been little understood either at home and abroad. There has of course been very little conscious adoption of the new manner by established architects. This is hardly surprising, considering how slowly America is coming generally to accept even the New Tradition. But during the years in which the New Pioneers have been developing their way of building and their æsthetic America has been less cut off from contemporary European architecture than during the years of the establishment of the New Tradition in the early twentieth century. As early as 1922 several New Pioneers offered designs in the international competition for the Chicago

Tribune Tower. But there were certainly few then to distinguish them essentially from the simplified work of the New Traditional. Except in the case of Lönberg-Holm's project, indeed, they were hardly worthy to be so distinguished. As has earlier been said Bijvoet and Duiker's was still much influenced by Wright in its expression, and that of Gropius was an arbitrary Constructivist arrangement of an elementary structural scheme.

It is indeed doubtful whether either Oud or Le Corbusier could in that year, and particularly in dealing with a problem so unfamiliar to European architects, have had much greater success. If both were then constructing for the first time definitely in the new manner, it was after a series of studies which hardly led to the design of the single skyscraper. Le Corbusier's skyscrapers were sociological rather than æsthetic in intention and distinctly visionary. Miës van der Rohe's were at least equally visionary. He was moreover just freeing himself from Expressionism in 1922. Ferro-concrete also is technically unsuited for buildings as tall and as circumscribed as the Tribune Tower had to be. But it was almost solely in connection with ferro-concrete that the new manner was being practically developed.

One foreigner, of course, in this competition made a very great impression although his design only received second prize. But Saarinen's project was generally liked and has had ever since a very considerable effect on the surface expression of the skyscraper. It was indeed a brilliant design, brilliantly presented. But even within the New Tradition it did not represent a very advanced version. For it showed not at all the tendencies toward extreme simplification which were general by 1922.

The Tribune competition particularly opened American eyes to the contemporary architecture of Europe. Yet the net result of it for years was little more than that a foreigner had shown a new way of decorating skyscrapers. Public opinion even among architects still held that there was nothing in the new architecture of Europe of equal significance to the skyscraper. It was then felt and boldly announced that while its decoration might be further studied, while its cornices, for example, were better omitted, the skyscraper represented an architecture comparable to the greatest the Classical or the Mediæval past had created.

In a sense, indeed, this might be true as regards the potentialities of the skyscraper, but in the sense it was proclaimed it was more nearly nonsense.

The engineering of the skyscraper provides certainly a magnificent raw material for architecture. But to take that raw material and give to it qualities of mass based on the towers of the past, or on building groups of the past, stylized in the direction of height in order to fill out the necessary proportions, is no more to create an authentic architecture than had been done by applying to it Flamboyant or Renaissance detail; if only because the vital questions of scale and the standpoint of the observer are totally neglected.

As has already been said, there is in the handling of the skyscraper since 1922 quite as before no achievement to compare with the consciously "modern" work of Wright. This is particularly true where it exists in unrelated clusters rather than as a single tower. There is indeed little to compare with the unconsciously "modern" work of those architects who continued the English tradition. To have treated the skyscraper in their manner was of course impossible. Unlike the house it had no ancestors upon which it might be modelled and it could only use traditional materials as a surface skin. This is still however being attempted to all intents and purposes in immense "Tudor" apartment houses.

The method of Wright was not so impossible. Yet even his own projects showed no great success. He was as unable in the architectural expression to grasp the scale at which the raw material of the skyscraper pre-existed as those who took a more conventional route. All the same the "modernist" skyscrapers such as Walker's Telephone Building or Kahn's Park Avenue Building or Rogers' Medical Centre have been the most successful. (Figure 22.) Yet they have not considered its specific construction and have sought eclectic effects of mass and detail more or less in imitation of European work of the New Tradition. Unlike the European work which was not called on to fuse into architecture any such immense technical advances, even such skyscrapers lack full reality. Having no relation with the past at all they cannot, in the way of the New Tradition in general, sum up the past except superficially and incidentally.

The skyscraper therefore awaits the first American New Pioneer who will be able to take the engineering as a basis and create directly from it a form of architecture. He will have no real support from Europe. The executed skyscrapers of Europe are hardly skyscrapers in the American sense at all. The nearer they approach being such, the more open they are to such objections as have just been advanced. Moreover, although the use of steel skeleton construction in Europe is increasing and is being characteristically studied with great enthusiasm in Germany, it has so far received adequate expression only on a very small scale.

The nearest approach to a more satisfactory treatment of the present day American skyscraper lay probably in the first skyscrapers built, the Tacoma and the Home Life Insurance Buildings of the eighties in Chicago. The architect who with a real appreciation of their quality and with full knowledge and understanding of the way in which the New Pioneers have developed a new architecture from other new problems of function and construction will stand beside them as great a creator as any in Europe. Thus at last might become true all that has been written of the skyscraper and the remains of the Romantic point of view that still control our vision of its æsthetic problems give way to a new point of view analogous to our comprehension of its technical problems.

It might as a warning be set down in this connection that the later more geometrical dreams of Mr. Hugh Ferris are no nearer to this than his earlier traditional or Saarinenized designs. For they ignore if not always the question of scale at least the equally important questions of the observer's standpoint and of the necessary related development of city planning. This alone, as in Le Corbusier's "Voisin" plan, would make a further development of the skyscraper sociologically as well as æsthetically acceptable.

In other fields of construction than the skyscraper, city buildings, factories and so forth in which ferro-concrete is used rather than the steel skeleton, there is a similar American problem of raising engineering to the level of architecture. For this the work of the New Pioneers in Europe offers much assistance as also many of the features of the work of Wright if his ornament and his emphasis on mass rather than volume be forgotten. The road to the future lies open, but there are endless dangers along the way of which the chief is indicated by the fashion in which the new manner has spread in Eastern Europe. It will prove as easy to apply the tricks of Le Corbusier or some other European to American engineering as it has been to apply the ornament of the Paris Exposition of 1925.

The work in which Parisian, or Austrian, or Dutch ornament has been imitated lies all around us to-day. Its lesson is clear and has been once stated. Thus has hardly been produced a single good monument of the New Tradition. Had the Americans who visited the Exposition of 1925 and returned so affected by it studied as well the Pavillon de l'Esprit Nouveau of Le Corbusier, or *a fortiori* the Information Office of Mallet-Stevens, they would have succeeded no better, it may be feared, in creating fine works in the manner of the New Pioneers. Now that all American architectural students, and particularly those who go to Europe to travel or to study, are open to the influence of the later manner, however little they may frequently distinguish it from the New Tradition, the situation is changed; but it is not necessarily more immediately auspicious.

Four years ago when the manner of the New Pioneers was only just taking form it was perhaps easier to understand it thoroughly than it is to-day. In Le Corbusier's pavilion, which was the only really adequate presentation of the new architecture at the Exposition of 1925, there were no more motifs that might be imitated, or surface marks of style, than in the visionary "Voisin" project for a Paris of the future. There was only an *esprit nouveau,* capable of firing the imagination of those fully prepared for it. In them in a sense it moreover already lay latent. To-day the houses of Le Corbusier, Lurçat and Mallet-Stevens and the larger mass of work in Holland and Germany already provide a considerable repertory of specific effects which may be borrowed in accordance with the *vieil esprit* of imitation.

Against the not very bright prospect of a real American group of New Pioneers as an immediate possibility must be set the fact that unconsciously the building of American engineers has already achieved results that appear at first sight, and by reaction to the building of American architects decorated in accordance with mode-modernity, to vie with the best new constructions in Europe. The anti-æsthetic point of view which controls to-day in the study of nineteenth century engineering has been amply rewarded in the Garment Centre in New York, the grain elevators of the Lake Cities and even in the factories of Detroit. Yet æsthetically all these constructions fail to fully exist as architecture because they were not built as architecture and because the only spirit that informs them is economic.

They may not thus be wholly dismissed by any means. So unusual is the perfect expression of technique, so often do æsthetic considerations defeat their own ends that the crude magnificence of this sort of building has artificially and symbolically the significance that the "sublimity" of the Alps or the Ocean had for the early Romantics. But the poetization of industry, the idealizations of a proletariat world has less than the vision of Romantic travellers to do with architecture. When these contemporary cults lead to creation, that creation is even more controlled than the most "picturesque" architecture by the deadliest of æsthetic *snobismes,* that of making art give the impressions that are received from what is not art. We are, however, in America a long way from this danger which has received expressions as diverse as the war projects of Mendelsohn and the park buildings of Gaudì at Barcelona. Nevertheless, this point of view has already been critically presented in modified form by Gilbert Seldes in the *Saturday Evening Post.* The central significance of all this engineering, and even of the cult for it, is that it educates the technical sense. It leads also by reaction to the general demand that engineering be raised to the level of architecture. That demand will perhaps in time be satisfied.

This is not the whole story of the New Pioneers in America. There are in the first place several foreign architects working in the manner in different parts of the country. The most important is surely the Austrian R. J. Neutra in Los Angeles. His book *Wie Baut Amerika?* described American steel construction for the benefit of European architects, as well as illustrating in its text and projects that the author was an urbanist and an architect of very real value. His skyscraper design, for example, came nearer to accomplishing the feat of making its engineering a new way of architecture than any other. (Figure 58.) His railway stations and his houses displayed a sort of technical research infrequent in America and an integrity of æsthetic expression only found in the best work of Wright within the New Tradition. Neutra had indeed worked on the Imperial Hotel in Tokio and may be considered the latter's most significant pupil.

The apartment house he built in 1927 in Los Angeles and other executed constructions are not, it must be admitted, of the quality of his projects. But Neutra's work, although not specifically American, illustrates that the new manner can cope individually and effectively with American conditions. He is also conducting architectural courses in the Los Angeles Academy of Modern Art.

Another Austrian in California, Schindler, has remained closer to the New Tradition. Yet at the same time he has paralleled with mediocre success the more extreme æsthetic researches of Le Corbusier and the men of *de Stijl*. The Dane, Lönberg-Holm, was for a time in Detroit. The work of the Swiss Lescaze in New York has been chiefly restricted to interiors in which he has shown perhaps more virtuosity than integrity. But the difficulty of receiving effective co-operation in a city whose "modernism" consists in copying the poorest French models of the New Tradition excuses much, as does also the inherent difficulty of installing completely coherent New Pioneer rooms in old buildings. This is equally true in the somewhat parallel case of Kiessler, an Austrian member of *de Stijl* working in New York. His store window backgrounds were immensely effective, but more than a little arbitrary. A school now approaching completion by Lescaze and a cinema by Kiessler indicate that both are capable of more solid works when conditions are more satisfactory. (Figure 54.)

Among the architectural students who follow the New Pioneers it is difficult to distinguish. They exist in all the schools of the country and even in some numbers in the Ecole des Beaux Arts in Paris. The new manner has attracted their attention and it offers a new form of that popular intransigeance which could be achieved five years ago merely by preferring Rococo to Louis XVI detail. But how fully these students comprehend the new architecture in the general absence of knowledge of actual buildings and with the American tendency to keep æsthetic theories vigorously apart from questions of construction, it is not safe to say.

Peter van der Meulen Smith, perhaps the most gifted of these younger men, died in the autumn of 1928 in Berlin. His designs, done in the office of Lurçat, were marked intelligently by a certain influence of Le Corbusier. But in his theories he was closer to Oud. (Title page and Figure 53.) Paul Nelson, a disciple of Perret, makes in his projects an attempt not yet altogether successful to give to the construction of the latter an æsthetic expression in the new manner. Yet in an apartment installation done in Chicago under difficult conditions he produced probably the finest contemporary interiors in America.

Another who has made a fine design in the new manner is the associate editor of the *Architectural Record*, A. Lawrence Kocher, who has also brought to American attention so much contemporary foreign building. His treatment of the problem of the New York apartment house was clear and original, if perhaps somewhat hampered by the pyramidal grouping imposed by the zoning laws. But to deal with projects generally unpublished is to be necessarily arbitrary in one's choice. Those mentioned are surely rivalled by others which have not come to notice.

Moreover to deal with projects of the past year is, in a sense, to deal with the future; and the question of the future is far more general than those matters concerning America alone which have been set down here. But the existence of vast masses of raw engineering, the general interest of students, many projects, a few interiors, one or two executed buildings: all this illustrates that already the manner of the New Pioneers exists in America at least as effectively as in Europe before 1922. Indeed it exists probably more soundly than in those Eastern European countries which have taken the new manner over bodily and uncritically, giving it little form of their own. Besides France, Holland, and Germany it is already America which appears to have the greatest significance for the development of a new architecture. There very possibly in the future it will take the most individual and characteristic form.

CHAPTER EIGHTEEN

THE ARCHITECTURE OF THE FUTURE: 1929

THE competition for the Place Louis XV in 1748, the London Exposition of 1851, the Cologne Exposition of 1914, the Chicago Tribune competition of 1922, the Paris Exposition of 1925, the League of Nations competition of 1927: all these and many other expositions and competitions have been milestones in the history of Modern architecture, not so much because they necessarily produced exceptionally fine work as because they focussed the architectural tendencies of certain years. By studying the later of them it is moreover possible to approach a statistical statement of the comparative dominance of different manners which have existed side by side for considerable periods of time although they appear to be rather consecutive in reality.

The competition for the Columbus Memorial Lighthouse at Santo Domingo, for which the designs are being received and judged this Spring of 1929, will have doubtless less significance than that still perhaps not entirely settled for the Palace of the League of Nations. An immense lighthouse is so much a monument of engineering that projects related at least to the manner of the New Pioneers will doubtless be offered in the greatest numbers. Yet a jury of three, composed of one European architect, one North American, and one South American, will probably be rather conservative in its judgments, and schemes of a New Tradition type will presumably be premiated.

The Chicago Exposition of 1930, now being planned, will provide also a sign of the times. Without knowing anything of the plans it is safe to prophesy that it will represent primarily the complete, although somewhat superficial, acceptance of the New Tradition in America. It will in a sense annul finally the effect of the Chicago Exposition of 1893, which re-established eclectic revivalism. Definitely revivalistic buildings will be as few comparatively as in the League of Nations competition. Yet it is almost certain that several foreign countries and even certain American organizations will display work within the manner of the New Pioneers or at least strongly influenced by it. This was certainly the case even with the greater number of the pavilions at the Brno Exposition of 1928. The Exposition of 1930 will have for America the significance that the Paris Exposition of 1925 had for Europe, winding up the New Tradition and opening the way positively and negatively for the conscious development of a later manner.

Beyond the first milestones it is impossible to analyze specific events in the future. More profitable than prophecy is the discussion of certain of the general questions which the New Pioneers present and of which the definitive solution remains uncertain. It may be accepted of course that even revivalism will continue yet a decade or two and the New Tradition, at least in simplified form, perhaps another whole generation. Their problems are in a sense already settled. The real problems of the future, therefore, are only the problems which now confront the New Pioneers.

That is of course a limited future. For Scott in 1857, although he certainly saw the problems in general of the New Tradition, hardly saw beyond them. The future as far as it may be conceived at all cannot profitably be made to extend beyond that period of which the majority of constituent factors are not only in existence but even conspicuous. Reinforced concrete was invented in 1849; but Scott, even if he knew of it, gave it no particular attention. It is not impossible that similar matters destined in fifty years to begin to come into their own already thus exist to-day. Yet even if searched for they are not to be found. Or if they were to be found they would come into their own much sooner.

Moreover, although much of the political and industrial development since 1857 which has had its effect on architecture could hardly have been dreamed of by Scott, nothing surely before the War, by which time the New Tradition was already flourishing, occurred to change fundamentally the place of the building arts in Western civilization which they already held in the latter part of the Age of Romanticism. Discounting cataclysms, one may therefore assume that the place of the building arts in contemporary civilization, either judged in the most advanced American, Italian or Russian forms on the one hand, or in the at least superficially less advanced French or German forms on the other, will not fundamentally change within the present century. As there is nothing in contemporary democracy and capitalism, or in Fascism, or in Sovietism which is essentially inconsistent with the architecture of the New Pioneers, it is unnecessary to assume that there will appear prominently within the next two generations anything more disruptive than any of these would have appeared to the men of 1750.

A new religion alone, or a new relation of some existing religion to civilization, might relatively soon make wholly new demands upon architecture that are now inconceivable. Although Spengler prophesies the appearance of such a new religious development, it would hardly appear to be in existence even in the embryonic form in which reinforced concrete existed in 1857, eight years after its discovery. Néo-Thomism is as well satisfied by the architecture of the New Pioneers as atheistic Liberal Protestantism. If Humanism be not, so much the worse for it.

Furthermore it is an illusion that we move to-day more rapidly than in the past, except as regards technics. Technics only form a part of architecture; and as has been stated the architecture of the New Pioneers reposes more centrally upon an æsthetic, or at least a point of view as to the relation of æsthetic and technical matters, than upon technics. Considering the phases of architecture since 1750 as forming one unit and comparing that with a preceding unit of architectural history doubtless as arbitrary, the architecture of the Baroque period, the rapidity of evolution would hardly appear to have increased, any more than that evolution would appear to represent æsthetically anything that could be considered absolute progress.

The difference, for example, between the buildings of Palladio at Vicenza in the mid-sixteenth century, still at least as much High Renaissance as Baroque, and the Landhaus von Kamecke erected by Andreas Schlüter in the early eighteenth century is surely as great as that between Gabriel's constructions in the Place de la Concorde, designed in 1748, still at least as much in the Baroque tradition as according to the new programmes of Romanticism, and Le Corbusier's project for the Palace of the League of Nations in 1927. That is: the difference is as great if the monuments are considered ideologically as existing in the stream of history and not in timeless space. In the latter case the close relation is obviously between Palladio and Gabriel on the one hand and Schlüter and Le Corbusier on the other. But such a way of looking at works of art, although often necessary to the critic, has little absolute meaning. It does, however, seem to indicate that however much there may be progress technically, æsthetically there is only more or less sequential change.

The most central question that lies open to-day in architecture is that of the relation between technics and æsthetic expression. Much has indeed already been said with regard to it. It already appears that the more extreme technical point of view often professed by the New Pioneers is primarily a battle cry and a subject for manifestos. It had its use in the establishment of a new æsthetic, but it has probably no continuing validity. There is no assurance in view of the development of engineering that the ferroconcrete construction upon which the present æsthetic of the New Pioneers largely reposes will continue to be technically the most satisfactory. Certainly it is already not so for many types of buildings; and the Germans particularly have begun a definite move away from it. The rigid principles of the New Pioneers would demand a repeated revision of expression based on each new technical change. But there is much reason to believe that the creative power of the human race is limited in æsthetic matters. Without a considerable lapse of time the forces of originality are at a low ebb after an important creative effort. They cannot indefinitely provide new means of expression for every new means of construction when it appears.

Thus there is already a clear division into two parties. On the one side are the technicians who, with optimism undiminished, are as ready to-day to throw over the accomplishments of the last decade as they were once to throw over all earlier traditions. On the other are the architects who, having found, as had been done only a very few times before in the past, what appears to be a really new style based on a still comparatively new means of construction, would continue the development of that style as long as it is fruitful. This might well be for far more than a century. As in the case of any pioneers who settle in the territory they have opened and do not keep moving on, the latter course would entail a certain conservatism. The continuation of the use of ferro-concrete wherever possible would be encouraged since it served best the already formed æsthetic of the style. Furthermore there would be, as has already been pointed out in the work of Gropius and Miës van der Rohe, a tendency to base the expression of other types of construction when they were used on the expression of ferro-concrete, in clear contradiction to the way in which that expression was itself established.

It is dangerous to make catagorical general statements with regard to the art of the past, particularly without the support of examples. Yet it is generally accepted that it was in the latter fashion that the styles of the past, even those most completely dependent on certain methods of construction, were continued and developed after their first inception. The point has indeed once been made with regard to the Gothic. Of course technical progress in the past was apparently less rapid than to-day, but the principle nevertheless remains the same. Thus the future of a perhaps more completely radical style than even the Gothic might show a considerable period as lacking in significant change as were the late thirteenth and early fourteenth centuries in France.

Furthermore this may certainly be psychologically supported in general terms. The need for the new is recurrent but not continuous except as a matter of mode. A part, at least, of the satisfaction of accepting the new is the idea that it shall be as permanent as what preceded. There is an illusion closely connected with each innovation that because that innovation appears temporarily more valid than whatever it is replacing its validity is actually more absolute. The present treatment of the evolution of architecture since 1750 is very clearly marked, as any history coming down into the present must be, by such an illusion. This does not, however, negative the value of recognizing it as an illusion. The significance of the present paragraph is indeed rather thus reinforced.

In architecture the new, when solidly based on new methods of construction, can at first only be appreciated by those who understand that construction either discursively or intuitively. Ferro-concrete building cannot be appreciated by the naïve who analyze it consciously or unconsciously in terms of masonry or wood. Comprehension must for the majority of people become automatic, since few take architecture seriously enough to give much effort to its appreciation. It establishes itself slowly as the result apparently of what amounts to an act of faith. The peasant entering Laon cathedral or even seeing it from a distance would have been terrified but for the knowledge that the Church, perhaps indeed the Holy Virgin, had inspired and directed it. On the other hand the builders there had not yet given up the use of round arches except in functional positions. The American countryman of to-day is not terrified by Wall Street because of his belief in science and money power. The slightly less ignorant moreover see the cornices and columns whose meaning they are prepared, however falsely, to grasp. To extend the matter again beyond architecture, it may be remarked that even chickens have learned the danger of the automobile.

The faith in a new method of construction once established becomes so inherent in observers that it is not easily or rapidly changed. Indeed, to change it too frequently would have the very opposite effect to that desired by those who urge it. For appreciation of architecture as the æsthetic expression of structure would generally cease if newer methods were perpetually substituted for those in use before the belief in those in use became inherent and unconscious. A symbolism in fact is eventually necessary and may not be successfully changed very often, any more than religious symbolism.

There is as regards the architecture of the New Pioneers another question of related order. They have as far as possible excluded the use of traditional materials in order to emphasize the importance of their innovations and because the interpretation of traditional materials was too completely dependent on the æsthetic of the New Tradition. This also may be in part a gesture of manifesto. Once the new æsthetic was sufficiently established there would be no possibility of ambiguity in the interpretation of traditional materials or traditional methods of construction, provided they were selected and used completely in accordance with the new æsthetic. There are obvious reasons against the structural use of wood on a large scale. But there are no real reasons why the expression of the new manner could not be given to buildings in wood. For it permits many, if not all, the technical feats of ferro-concrete. Indeed, Perret's Palais de Bois was his nearest approach to working according to the æsthetic of the new manner, while in his ferro-concrete architecture he still remains faithful to the New Tradition.

Neither Miës van der Rohe's use of brick in his villa (Figure 39) nor Le Corbusier's granite veneer on his League of Nations project were quite as successful as the less durable cement surfaces in which the new manner was conceived. They are nevertheless in this connection more significant than the mode-modernity of Mallet-Stevens' metal shop front. The Art Nouveau had little luck with faïence facings because they permitted extreme indulgence in ornament and were seldom good in colour. Fuchs' pavilion at the Brno Exposition of 1928 (Figure 56) and certain façades on the Kurfürstendamm in Berlin-Charlottenburg display that contemporary architecture may yet without at all imitating it rival the Islamic use of this ancient material.

Yet certain materials as Oud suggested in 1921 are definitely unsuited to the symbolism of the new manner by their irregularity and natural character, that is in a sense, their "picturesqueness." For the same order of reasons few people can accept Mediæval brick churches as really Gothic. Thatch and tapestry brick are, for example, quite impossible. In the present period of transition, however, not merely such extreme examples but traditional materials in general imply the past rather than the present and must be avoided for psychological, not technical, reasons. This is clearly seen in certain Belgian houses in brick, and particularly in Schindler's premature attempt to place a wooden superstructure on a concrete base in 1928, although the result was, all the same, the best house he has so far built. Thus also the use of rubble party walls, required by French law, gives to the sides of some of Le Corbusier's and Lurçat's villas a totally inharmonious character which they are powerless to control.

Yet there is no assurance that in certain fields of architecture, such as domestic building, plaster surfaced ferro-concrete is superior to construction largely of some sort of masonry. Once the traditional interpretation of brick and stone is forgotten there may well be a considerable return to their use where they are technically and economically satisfactory. This general principle was even from the beginning made perfectly clear by Oud's success with semi-permanent construction at Oud Mathenesse in 1922. For he emphasized the new symbolism and minimized the old as he had not in his Spangen and Tuschendijken blocks really been able to do.

The argument of permanence itself may be introduced here. The pyramids offer the assurance of at least relative durability for the most solid form of masonry construction; the Roman monuments of engineering testify nearly as effectively for their sort of reinforced concrete. As regards the lasting power of our own sort, however, we have not so much real faith as a very considerable hope based on the conclusions of science and the experience of a few decades. Whoever desired to erect a monument to-day with as good reasons for ensuring its permanence as the pyramid makers had would still be well advised technically to use their methods of construction. For

Behrens' traditionally built convent at Salzburg it is far safer to prophesy several centuries of life than for his factories, actually as well as functionally. For of course the needs of the A.E.G. will change more rapidly than those of the Benedictine order, if that continue at all to exist.

At least for surfaces, also, there is much to be said for traditional materials. The experience of a decade has not shown that modern cement treatments are even relatively permanent. The question of surfaces might appear to be subsidiary to what has already been said. But it is peculiarly central since the new æsthetic is concerned primarily with the surfaces of volumes. The entire use of glass has been proposed and is being illustrated by Miës van der Rohe. Surface treatment remains certainly that which more than anything else requires the attention of technical experimenters, and in which the use of traditional materials is most obviously precarious psychologically as the earlier examples have pointed out.

Of equal importance to the relation of the now established æsthetic of the New Pioneers to materials and methods of construction is the possibility of the eventual reappearance of ornament already once mentioned. The success of the attempt to deflate ornament by the New Tradition was already open to question by 1922, or more exactly the continuing validity of the methods of creation of ornament which had achieved notable accomplishment before the War was being widely questioned. The New Pioneers set out therefore without ornament and they have consciously remained without it. They do not necessarily subscribe, however, to all the implications of the association of crime and ornament which Adolf Loos announced even before the War. Many of them would like some sort of ornament. But when some man such as Mallet-Stevens attempts it, the relation to the last feeble geometrical wanderings of the New Tradition is perfectly apparent. The more intelligent therefore avoid it. For they are justly convinced that the period of sterilization, which can only cure the maladies to which ornament has been subject at least since the Rococo, is far from being over. It is better that ornament should definitely die than that it should continue to introduce into architecture focal points of decay.

However, if the manner of the New Pioneers really constitutes a new style and not merely a final post-Romantic style-phase, it is highly probable that in time a new ornament will develop, as in the past from the symbolic use of features originally constructive, once the new structural symbolism becomes unconsciously and universally accepted. The Indian stupa and the related Chinese pagoda, whose elaborate forms were arrived at by reduplication and compression of a simple constructive unit, illustrate an extreme example of this. It is of course highly unlikely that a new occidental development would take any form at all parallel to such oriental manifestations. At the present time the specific line a "pure" ornament would take cannot be conceived beyond the central idea. For it remains not by any means clear whether the architecture of the New Pioneers represents truly a first phase or a final phase. The fact that it does not as treated here seem to conclude what had been going on for five hundred, or even a hundred, years, more definitely than the New Tradition has already done cannot be taken as a sure augury. Judged from other and more Spenglerion points of view it may readily be made to appear a final phase.

Ornamental preoccupations, in so far as they may be distinguished to-day, are concerned with the study of surfaces and of edges and a related use of colour which has, one may again feel as Scott did, vast untouched possibilities. There is, of course, no assurance that another Albert Memorial is not on the way. It could moreover hardly be considered, like the extravagances of a few years ago, a manifestation of Expressionism. For the influence of Expressionism on architecture must surely be over. Even to suggest that certain features of executed buildings of the New Pioneers represent ornament in embryo is still to say that those features are false to avowed principles. To point them out is to criticize and the success of the whole venture would depend on its being free to advance a considerable distance without being remarked and criticized. If a new ornament does develop, the historians of the future will be freer to indicate its incipient forms in work to-day already executed which is in intention devoid of anything approaching ornament.

A further point which the future will clarify is the question of symbolic expression of the functional use of buildings. This was a matter which the eclecticism of taste was forced to take very seriously since it was its only guiding principle of a positive and intellectual order. Otherwise it is of less importance than the symbolical comprehension of materials and structure which has been discussed at some length. It would be very easy to say in the still current terms of the eclecticism of taste that Oud's church design did not look like a church. For churches are very definitely associated with the revival of Mediæval forms. Considering this in archæological terms of style and not in terms of coexistent "styles," which are no longer acceptable except in England, America, and perhaps certain more backward Latin countries, this is somewhat of an absurdity.

In reverse form, it is clear, a Gothic garage, if it were at all plausibly Gothic, would not look like a garage. Indeed a Gothic Museum of Natural History, such as that at Yale, suggests not at all its real uses, even though it is not very good Gothic. Le Corbusier's project for the Palace of the League of Nations did not look like a palace. This indeed seems to have been what caused the committee of diplomats, all very familiar with palaces of one kind or another, to turn it down. We are aware in America, however, that the Classical factories which Ford commissioned of Albert Kahn before the Finnish influence became dominant in Michigan look like factories only at the expense of the Doric order.

Each real style of architecture is able to express certain functions perfectly by a happy combination of direct statement and symbolism. Only by a loss of perfect integrity and coherence can a style succeed in giving the most adequate expression—at least for a generation trained in the eclecticism of taste—to all the functions for which architecture is called on to provide. The Mediævalists' objections to those ballrooms of the Lord, the seven basilicas of Rome, or more specifically C. H. Moore's suggestion that Bramante would better have used Byzantine detail in Saint Peter's, are finally much on the order of that touching simplicity which calls a pointed arch a "church window." They are not, of course, for that reason the less valid sentimentally.

Oud's church project provides complete direct expression of function: it is obviously an important place of gathering and not a house or a hotel or a store. Symbolic expression is lacking because the churches have to-day beyond the Cross no readily usable or generally accepted emblematic symbols. Even the Cross in plan is ill adapted for congregational worship and now little used, even by revivalist architects. The attempt to make extensive architectural use of the Sacred Heart in South America was extraordinarily unsuccessful. The Christian Science churches of America moreover, had they not succeeded in winning from the eclecticism of taste general approval for their Classical forms, could be, and doubtless frequently are, mistaken for banks, libraries, or even cathedrals of the motion picture.

Le Corbusier's palace certainly does not appear to be a palace in the traditional sense of the word. But the Palace of the League of Nations is not a palace in the traditional sense of the word. Le Corbusier's design gives full expression of its real functions. Its industrial symbolism should only be displeasing to those who have a false idea of the League of Nations. Yet it is that false idea which apparently is receiving expression from M. Nenot and his collaborators working within the New Tradition.

For the difficulty of symbolic functionalism arose even less with the New Tradition than the difficulty of structural symbolism. It was always possible in a manner of eclecticism of style, no matter how much reduced, to suggest the "style" favoured by the eclecticism of taste for a building of a certain definite purpose or even in a sense to invent one of even more precise or comprehensive significance. Ostberg's eclecticism of style in the Stockholm City Hall might almost be explained on this ground alone. For almost all his borrowed features had sometime and somewhere been associated with civic grandeur. Perret, as much as the German Expressionists, was careful in his churches to suggest broadly but definitely the religious glory of the Middle Ages even to the ignorant and unobserving.

In houses, moreover, the New Tradition always succeeded in fulfilling that mysterious Anglo-Saxon prescription that they must look like "homes," as the New Pioneers do not. The definition of this word is so intangible and it has been so abused in America that the point can hardly be completely and fairly discussed. The objection thus raised against the villas of Le Corbusier is to some extent intelligible and valid since they are sometimes difficult to live in. It is hardly so against those of Lurçat, particularly in comparison with such French manifestations as the *Bungalow du home du jour* at the Exposition of 1925 consciously intended to imitate Anglo-Saxon models.

It is perhaps not valuable nor general testimony, but against this stupid prejudice it might be set down that Anglo-Saxon visitors could not possibly desire anything in the spiritual sense more homelike than the environment of J. J. P. Oud, and that an American family has been able very fully to make of Le Corbusier's most extravagant villa *Les Terrasses* a home. (Figures 43, 44.) For *Les Terrasses* it might be added that this is true in the symbolically material sense as well as in the spiritual sense. For the house is furnished with fine articles evidently gathered together during a lifetime and not merely with modern pictures and radios. The last moreover, if not the paintings by Picasso and Matisse, seem, despite their contemporaneity, to have been accepted into the Anglo-Saxon home. They are even supposed—and Le Corbusier as a sociologist indeed particularly desires this also—to have given a new integrity to the family home as a social unit, preserving it against the centrifugal forces of modern life. It makes more sense to the French for whom the home is the *foyer*, the hearth, but it is further worth stating that Le Corbusier can also be more surely counted on for fireplaces than many American revivalists.

To examine further the architecture of the future is to embark on ground even more dangerous than the question of the home. Nevertheless the statement may be hazarded that the new manner may well have already produced its greatest masters although not equally probably its greatest works. This statement derives from the far from generally accepted theory that the innovators are the geniuses, the art-creators; and that those who merely follow Saint Thomas' *viæ certæ et determinatæ* of a new analogue of the beautiful which has already been established are less great.

In connection with this it is worth noting that between one style or manner and another, one analogue of the beautiful and its successor, there is little possibility of absolute judgment. The catholicity of the eclecticism of taste finally recognized the truth of this after the fruitless quarrels of the Age of Romanticism. In times of rapid change, as in France in the sixteenth century and in our own day since the War, it is not at all necessarily true that the artist who is young, and without being a creator of it follows the new movement, is superior to the artist who is older and still works in the movement which is passing. Historically the poorest work of the new movement is doubtless more important than the finest still produced by the earlier. But of such advantage is the support of a well established tradition to minor and second rank artists in full possession of even mediocre powers that the critical judgment of value, if it be attempted, will be in opposition to the historical estimation of importance.

Therefore it is that any movement, any manner of art, continues to produce fine work—though usually not the finest—well after it ceases to produce work of any positive historical significance. Hence too rapid and too general a conversion of artists to a new movement is unfortunate; and great artists are ill advised late in life to try to follow their younger contemporaries. This applies of course more definitely to the continuing work of the founders of the New Tradition than to an unknown future with unknown possibilities of new style origination. But except for him who succeeds in at last creating the architecture of the skyscraper it is not likely that architects will for some time have the opportunities for creation that Le Corbusier, Oud, Gropius and certain others have already had.

The work of the oncoming generation now beginning to build will doubtless be of less interest. For theirs will be the hard task of consolidating what has so far been done and theirs the real struggle with those problems which have been outlined in previous paragraphs. It will be too soon for further innovation and they must follow the *viæ certæ et determinatæ* of their elders without descending to imitation. But they will surely be able to add worthily to the quantity of the new architecture and occasionally to give riper, more complete expression to ideas thus far hardly more than brilliantly sketched.

How long the period of development will last, how long it will be before the architecture of the New Pioneers, no longer new, reaches its climax, how long before it will be in its turn superseded, it is absurd to attempt to say. The tempo of the future escapes us more than anything else about it. The general impression of a crescendo is surely illusory and due to the fact that very minor events of the present appear to set a pace equivalent to that of the major events of the past. That is noticeable even in the list of specific events with which this chapter opened. The parallel impression that with the rather immediate future "the Golden Age begins anew" and time becomes immobilized must also be illusory. The limitations of human imagination alone seem to lend it support. Scott's *Architecture of the Future* would seem to be already more or less over. The present less definite prophecies might easily be as soon wound up, even if they prove to be not altogether false.

The fact that the New Tradition worked itself out so rapidly is not a sign to be taken too seriously. For in a sense an architect of genius like Soane was able to anticipate it a century before its day. There are no such early precursors of the New Pioneers among Romantic architects. The New Tradition summed up Romanticism and opened the way for a more definitely new manner. Thus the new manner was prepared for by the architecture of more than a century and might on that score alone be expected to last as long.

Yet cutting the cards another way the three phases with which the present book has dealt may appear perhaps but as parts of a single larger one. The connections between the analysis of architecture affected in the disintegration of Romanticism and the rigid reintegration of the last few years are certainly close, closer perhaps in many ways than they have always here been made to appear. All the New Pioneers, for example, and as will surely have been noted, particularly the French and Germans, are very careful to relate their architecture as fully as possible to the natural surroundings, although without in any sense merging it therewith. But the expression of Le Corbusier's League of Nations project was definitely studied in such a way as to make the most of a magnificent site. May's treatment of the Nidda valley is even more that of a conscientious landscapist. Uvedale Price, the great authority on the picturesque, would have approved both terraces and ribbon windows. In a sense indeed he recommended them more than a century ago when he suggested that houses might be "picturesquely" designed solely with the idea of making the most of the circumambient view. Romanticism is still much nearer to us than it was to the Baroque. The great change has been that while Romanticism made of architecture the least of the visual arts, it is to-day nearer to being the most important.

APPENDIX

APPENDIX

WHILE the Gothic had reached its culmination before the middle of the thirteenth century, its impetus was too great and its hold on the builders of Western Europe too strong for a rapid change of style. But by the fourteenth century there had already begun to appear the features which represent the first development of Modern architecture on its non-reminiscent side. In the Gothic lands north of the Alps the builders discarded little by little the logic of origins until their structure and ornament depended primarily on the logic of materials and decorative value.

After the main structural forms of the Gothic were completely evolved and began to be repeated as a matter of course there thus appeared, with the accumulation of gradual changes away from inherited tradition, a new style-phase. This was in its engineering still Mediæval, of course, but in its expression it was already Modern. Between the High Gothic of Amiens or of Salisbury and the Flamboyant of Notre Dame de Cléry or the Perpendicular of Kings College Chapel, Cambridge, lies the break between the old style and the new. Very frequently, as in the examples given in the Introduction, Mont-Saint-Michel (Figure 2) and Westminster Abbey, the two are seen in sharp contrast in a single building.

In thirteenth century ecclesiastical architecture the structural readjustments of the Romanesque elements left a maximum of inherited features hardly at all modified. The Late Gothic builders worked strenuously to reduce the number of these features to a minimum when they in their turn inherited them. They replaced schemes of design which required the memory of the past for their appreciation (like the non-functional design of men's clothes, of which lapels on waistcoats and buttons on coat-cuffs are examples today) with schemes which expressed more accurately the actual and not the theoretical construction.

Formal force was derived from the comprehensiveness, even the monotony of linear pattern. For example the capital, which in the Early Gothic retained much of its Romanesque virtuosity, was gradually reduced to a mere band and finally often quite eliminated to avoid breaking the continuous moulding—at once shaft and vaulting rib—running from the floor to the ridge rib at the top of the vault. Compound windows in the Early Gothic revealed their origin as groups of windows in a wall by their so-called plate tracery. Already in the High Gothic this had given way to a sort of bar tracery which still recalled in its membering at least symbolical structural origins. With the advent of the Flamboyant, to which it gave its name, bar tracery became merely an arabesque screen whose intricately interwoven double curves gave the whole building the air of flickering upwards. (Figures 1 and 2.)

The triforia of the interior, which in the High Gothic retained their character as distinct covered galleries, a third element under the aisle roof between the nave arcade and the clerestory, were first glazed and then joined with the clerestory in a single scheme of tracery. Finally indeed clerestory and triforia were completely merged as the builders were led to extremes by their instinct of unification. Both of these last two related tendencies—and indeed others here to be mentioned as well—unquestionably had their inception early in the thirteenth century. They may indeed be found in a fairly advanced state of development in monuments otherwise definitely High Gothic. Yet as tendencies they are characteristic of the Late Gothic.

In the Perpendicular remodelling of the choir of Gloucester cathedral the mullions of the clerestory were even brought down across the spandrels below the triforium to penetrate the mouldings of the nave arcades. Thus the Late Gothic interior was more and more covered, with little concession to its independent features, by a continuous network of rising mouldings through which the few necessary horizontals passed in penetrations. The whole scheme, however, grew richer when it reached the curving tracery at the top of the windows and the similarly interlacing ribs of the vault whose original structural sense was forgotten now that they were thought of primarily as decoration. In English fan and pendant vaulting the ribs became merely a sort of applied ornament cut in the stones of vaults constructed on Roman and not Gothic principles. Of this development the Tudor royal chapels provide familiar examples; but Spain and Germany can show others somewhat different and equally extravagant.

The same process of gradual change that has been traced in interiors brought in time a similar but perhaps generally less conspicuous change to the exteriors of Late Gothic churches. Façades in the High Gothic had been statically designed by the skilful additive combination of their constituent parts. The Late Gothic treated the parts dynamically so that all flowed upward together as one whole. This was partly done by making the individual features more alike. Windows were introduced in the tympana of portals; towers were opened up into baskets of tracery; and everywhere, even on solid walls, vertical mouldings and flame-like enrichment threw over the surface of the exterior as of the interior a continuous network. Furthermore separate features were frequently made to overlap: pierced gables rose in front of balustrades and windows above, window-patterns in tracery extended beyond the actual boundaries of the openings. The sides of the church and the chevet, however, were more dominated by the inherited features of Mediæval engineering and therefore less free to display new tendencies than facades and towers.

The relation of subordinate plastic decoration to architecture underwent a significant change which was in part necessitated by the separate development of sculpture. On the twelfth century front portal of Chartres the figures were treated first as architectural detail and only secondarily as independent works of art. But figure sculpture already began to free itself from architectural canons with the development in the thirteenth century of Gothic Idealism. No very great break came, however, before the development of Realism with the fifteenth century. From then on not the figures but the niches in which they were to be placed served as architectural features. At the same time sculptured ornament became increasingly reduced in importance until it ended as the mere enrichment of mouldings with a sort of elaborate three-dimensional pattern hardly recognizable as representation.

Even mouldings themselves, once reminiscent of their separate origins and with forms dependent on their diverse functions, tended universally in the fifteenth and sixteenth centuries to approach a single type. More and more they were sharply stylized into angular shapes called prismatic which emphasized very little their constructional function, now so largely lost, and very much the linear skeleton of the design as a whole. Later, in vertical supports angular forms were often replaced by wide undulations into which the other prismatic mouldings penetrated.

In civil architecture more even than in religious the appearance of a new style-phase at the end of the Middle Ages is clear. There was an increasing avoidance of the specifically Mediæval constructional features of vaulting which had always been more associated with religious than civil architecture but had hitherto been freely reflected in civil building. In the later fourteenth and fifteenth centuries, palaces, châteaux and manors began to be studied artistically for themselves and with regard to their specific problems. Particularly in England, where the Renaissance as such practically never appeared and the change was directly from the Late Gothic to the Baroque, it is evident that these tendencies had little to do with the Renaissance.

Although in ecclesiastical architecture the ground plan did not materially change in the Late Gothic period, except in so far as there was a certain tendency to substitute prismatic for curved forms, in domestic architecture, as the necessity for defense grew less, it became possible to develop the plan in relation to the manifold needs of civil life. This brought with it an increasing simplicity in the general scheme of the elevations. There was, however, by way of contrast a related development of a minor and adventitious complexity of detail. Decorative features borrowed from contemporary ecclesiastical architecture provided readily a superficial and sophisticated picturesqueness in place of the essential and unstudied picturesqueness of the High Middle Ages. For example, the standardization of recurrent features such as windows was relieved by the high roofs, dormers and turrets that were freely and ably used to vary the silhouette. As in churches a small module of design was used to fuse entire buildings, and even groups of buildings, into single coherent compositions. Of this the colleges at Oxford and Cambridge provide excellent illustration.

In place of cut-stone, Late Gothic builders were ready in châteaux and manors to experiment with new materials, especially those of local origin, developing from their character such minor structural and major decorative possibilities as were latent in them. As a result of the increasing use of brick and of wood even in luxurious construction, there occurred a considerable modification of inherited Mediæval features in stone. Flattened arches certainly, probably also the ubiquitous oblong panelling, even it may be moulding penetrations, are thus to be explained. Furthermore, the use of permanent polychromy of brick and flint and stones permitted a variety of wall treatment, encouraging that emphasis on the surface as an entity that surrounds the mass, rather than as merely the boundary of the mass, which distinguishes Modern from Mediæval architecture. Incidentally this tendency led as well to the paper architecture which we have so often had since the Renaissance. Modern vices as much as Modern virtues were already inherent in the Late Gothic. Castles and palaces such as Hurstmonceux or Hampton Court, complex mansions such as Layer Marney Towers or Oxburgh Hall, even irregular manors such as Compton Winyates, illustrate admirably the new coherence of scale and formality of plan that so easily approaches monotony, the repetition of detail that frequently becomes trivial, and the virtuosity of surface that is now and again carried to extremes.

The Late Gothic use of wood and varied building materials has been much misunderstood. The handcraftsmanship which was thus so prominently continued into the first phase of Modern architecture is an element that good Modern architecture can well exist without. In its day this sort of craftsmanship was really experimentation in technics and its analogue to-day lies not in the anachronistic continuance of hand technics but in the substitution of our own technics of the machine, even though they are still perhaps in the experimental stage.

The Late Gothic civil monuments already mentioned in England, or such examples as the château du Plessis-Brion (Figure 3), the Louis XII wing at Blois, or the city-hall at Bruges on the Continent, provide excellent examples of how far the hand of the craftsman would be used as a tool by the guiding intelligence of the master of the work. Mechanical coldness of execution is indeed characteristic of the English Perpendicular, particularly of the more important monuments. It is certainly not in itself praiseworthy; but it is indicative of a changed attitude toward execution. No longer was building a co-operative art, and no longer were the craftsmen individual although subordinate artists as in the Romanesque and High Gothic. Once the conception of the design as the work of art—not the design on paper but the design carried to execution by the best technical means available—became dominant, the hand of the craftsman was destined eventually to give way to the machine as a more exact tool. But until well into the twentieth century the Modern technical point of view was always tempered either by conscious reminiscence or by direct inheritance from the past.

In Italy, where the High Gothic had been an imported style, the fourteenth century very easily introduced in decoration tendencies which the Renaissance was soon in some degree to hide—but never to suppress—in the flood of copying of the Roman past. The Loggia dei Lanzi in Florence and the interior of the Cathedral of Orvieto belong as definitely to the Modern style as the Galleria Vittorio Emmanuele in Milan. Michelangelo's feeling for the abstract side of Modern architecture is as well illustrated by his desire to continue the Loggia dei Lanzi about the entire Piazza della Signoria as by his extraordinary architectural drawings.

But the new spirit of the fourteenth and early fifteenth century buildings of Italy is not manifested in quite the same way as in the North. On the one hand certain features, such as permanent polychromy of wall surfaces, which have the significance of free experiment in the North were traditional in Italy. On the other hand there is the Italian tendency to treat all the Gothic they borrowed from the North not as a real Mediæval architecture, such as their Romanesque had been and in the most places continued to be down to 1300, but as an ornamental novelty. Underneath this foreign veiling an increasing interest in geometrical masses and spaces is perhaps easier to discern, but more difficult to illustrate point by point than in the Late Gothic of the North. Nevertheless most of what has been said of the North applies in a general way also to Italy.

The late Gothic forms a transition between the Mediæval and the Modern and it has with much justice usually been classified with the former. Vast quantities of provincial work of course belonged quite definitely to the earlier period. The brief analysis that has been given here is based on the more complete and important monuments. Few even of them, however, carry out to the full the implications that have, for the sake of clearness, perhaps been overstressed.

Modern architecture was finally divorced from the Mediæval past only with the reminiscent style-phase which followed the Late Gothic. But in the Early Renaissance in Italy, before the revival of Classical antiquity became a definite programme, there was an important continuing interest in abstract form and as well a gradual definite disappearance of all Mediæval features. Such monuments as the Badia Fiesolana outside Florence, S. Maria dei Miracoli at Venice, the Palazzo Pitti at Florence (Figure 4), and the Palazzo Venezia at Rome have essential qualities which are neither inherited from the High Middle Ages nor imitated from the still little understood antique. In them interior space and exterior mass are studied for themselves with even greater success than in the preceding period. The rather free and inaccurate Classical detail even was of more interest than the borrowed Gothic detail had been in the fourteenth century, and it was long more particularly elaborated in monuments of sculpture than of architecture. Yet Donatello and other fifteenth century sculptors were on the whole quite as experimental in their ornament as were the architects in larger matters.

The Classical orders were little used except as decorative trophies, and full entablatures and imposts were avoided in favour of simple cornices and continuous mouldings about arches. Colour contrast and simple panelling were preferred to the use of elaborate architectural features in the most typical work. For by their use the interior space or the exterior mass was less broken. Although courts were usually given over to a series of tiers of the Roman arch order or some lighter variant, the palace façades previous to the time of Alberti and even later were as regularly devoid of the orders except sometimes at very reduced scale within the moulding-encircled window arch. The massive exterior cornices were therefore related not to orders but to the building-solid as a whole. Similarly the exterior wall surfaces were treated so as to emphasize their integrity at the expense of the subordinate features, which were simple and rather standardized.

The masters of the High Renaissance also had a sense of space and of mass which was of its own time and not derived from the past. Something of this C. H. Moore felt, although he expressed it badly, when in his account of Renaissance architecture he wrote that Bramante should have made the marvellous interior of St. Peter's in Rome Byzantine and not Renaissance in detail. And such a church as S. Maria della Consolazione outside Todi (Figure 5) illustrates even more clearly how the elaborate central schemes of the High Renaissance were capable of free expression in spite of the Classical members in which they were clad.

The Early Renaissance architecture of the North is hardly to be distinguished from the Late Gothic. The new borrowed detail which appeared on civil architecture—for ecclesiastical architecture was very slow to succumb to the Renaissance—was considered by the builders foreign and Italian rather than ancient and Classical. It was used quite indiscriminately in heterogeneous conjunction with inherited detail that was still Mediæval and with more exotic detail borrowed from the Late Gothic of other foreign countries; in Spain and Portugal, even from America and India.

The High Renaissance was hardly important outside of Italy. So much more difficult was it merely to be scholarly and correct in architecture beyond the Alps that the monuments—such as the Belvedere in Prague—belonging to the High Renaissance were almost never fine since they were primarily academic exercises.

The succeeding style-phase, the Baroque, retained the Classical grammar of the High Renaissance as codified by Palladio, Vignola and others; but even these men of the mid-sixteenth century had been little content with the mere repetition of formulas. Less than the Late Gothic did the Baroque transform the features which it received from the immediate past, but it discarded them freely or used them for ends quite unconnected with their original structural meaning. Even in such monuments as Bernini's Colonnade before Saint Peter's in Rome, where the Classical grammar is so obvious, the real value of the work is not in the parts but in the general effect.

In the architecture of the period from 1550 to 1750 there is a distinct division into two sub-periods. Nearly to the end of the seventeenth century Italy retained the architectural hegemony which was hers in the Renaissance. Later, architectural leadership passed beyond the Alps, particularly to France. In many ways the methods by which the Italian Barocco sought to unify and dynamize the schemes of the High Renaissance were very similar in principle to those of the Late Gothic. The Late Gothic had already related buildings loosely in groups. In Italy with the Renaissance city-planning developed more consciously, but not on any large scale before the Popes of the Counter-Reformation began their embellishment of Rome. One of the earliest instances was Michelangelo's Campidoglio. Of a greater scheme leading up to Saint Peter's only Bernini's magnificent colonnade was executed. The most typical project perhaps was the arrangement of the Piazza del Popolo only entirely completed by Valadier in the early nineteenth century. Only the two small churches which flank the entrance to the Corso are of the Baroque period. Taken alone they are unsymmetrical and unbalanced; together they form one central focussed composition. By means of the two side streets, moreover, a whole quarter was organized from this point.

The most notable individual creations of the Barocco are the church façades. As they were to stand in rows of buildings of much the same height they had in themselves to be given an importance such as earlier churches had more usually had in their entire exposed mass. Therefore they were conceived as having mass of their own. They are so eminently plastic that they are like immense abstract sculptural reliefs although their necessary features are no more than one or more doors with perhaps windows above. The effect of scale was increased by varying the alignment of the applied Classical orders so that their three-dimensional value was enhanced, and by shaping the whole façade regardless of what lay behind into an emphatic outline. The actual doors and windows were slurred over or stressed as the abstract requirements of the entire composition made necessary. Thus a dynamic fusion took from the individual features all independent existence. In the plastic whole sculpture might be used for accent to stir by its tortuosity the somewhat sluggish elements which the Classical grammar imposed.

The masters of the Barocco frequently worked in the theatre, and they had little compunction at providing effects of perspective artificially in actual buildings, as for example in Bernini's Colonnade before Saint Peter's or his Scala Reggia at the Vatican. Once the fundamental unified formula of church interiors was set by Vignola in the Gesù, there was nothing further to do but to vary the theatrical illusions with which the builders played. Of these the most used was that of opening out the vaults by means of painting so that the whole empyrean was annexed by the architect and subordinated to his desired effect as in Sant' Ignazio by Fratel Pozzo or in the great hall of the Palazzo Barberini by Pietro da Cortona. The Classical orders were among the lesser of the many tools with which the architect shaped and ornamented the space he created, and they were even then more often the work of the painter. Gold and colour were used not to underline and separate individual features but to join them; and the human figures of sculpture and painting gave a scale and a focus to these cycloramas, vast in effect no matter what their actual size.

In the palace façades of the period the designs are centred on the elaborate central portals which are echoed in the even rows of windows with which the wall surfaces are studded. The composition is looser, the architectural features fewer, than in the church façades; but the same principles are as well displayed in the Palazzo Doria as in Sant' Agnese in Piazza Navona.

For these church and palace façades the Roman Travertine provided a marvellous medium, large in scale and so rough that delicate detail could not be expected of it. In interiors, the material, usually stucco as the cheapest and easiest to handle, was quite lost sight of beneath paint and gold. Yet at the same time the desire for richness and brilliance led also to the use of highly coloured marbles and even semi-precious stones; as for example the green and white marble brocading and the lapis altar of the Gesuiti in Venice.

In the work of some later masters, the experimentation was carried further than in that of Bernini, Maderna and Fontana, to which the last paragraphs particularly apply. More liberties were taken with the Classical inheritance; plans were tortured in accordance with a desire for more theatrical effects; detail less held in check became not only coarse but redundant and gongoristic. In this form of the Barocco, represented in Borromini and Guarini, the style-phase strained itself beyond the balance between tradition and experimentation which characterized the earlier work. But this sort of building even more than the more central variety of Roman Barocco had its influence on the Baroque of the North: French Rococo detail would perhaps never have been but for Sardi's Santa Maria Maddalena dei Pazzi; and the Rokoko of Bavaria also particularly profited in the eighteenth century from the Italian extravagances of the seventeenth.

In the first century of the Baroque the only work outside Italy of independent character and value is that of France and the Low Countries. In the reigns of Henri IV and Louis XIII we find an important phase of style in which the elements inherited from the Renaissance or Gothic past are reduced to a minimum. There is simple polychromy of brick and stone, and dependence in the articulation of design chiefly on the most elementary features of the Renaissance vocabulary, mouldings and rustication. The typical monuments of the time, such as those of the Place Dauphine or the Place des Vosges in Paris, or the Hôtel de Ville at Doullens, exhibit considerable skill at obtaining brilliant effects with the simplest means. In the more elaborate contemporary châteaux, as also further to the North where the possibilities of the manner were more fully exploited, the complete effect is less fine because of the vast quantity of sculptured ornament originated by the Flemish Late Renaissance or borrowed from the Italian Barocco. But much of the less sumptuous building has more of the Modern virtues and fewer of the Modern vices than the equivalent civil and domestic building of the Late Gothic.

After the third quarter of the seventeenth century the Baroque in the North showed a wider distribution of fine building and a greater variety than the Italian Barocco. There was perhaps generally less virility and force in the experimentation, but there was more subtlety and at times certain architects succeeded in departing even further from tradition than the most daring of the Italians without loss of the interior balance of the manner. In France the *style Louis XIV* began to some extent as an academic reaction against the Northern manner of the early seventeenth century, but it developed early in the eighteenth century into the free Rococo which was carried in the second quarter of the eighteenth century quite widely over Europe. The Barock of the Holy Roman Empire, to which Vienna and Prague in particular owe their splendour, was more directly a continuation of and a mere variation on the Italian manner.

In the more important works of the time of Louis XIV the delight in the mere use of elaborate Classical paraphernalia is very evident. In the palace of Versailles or in the chapel of the Invalides the work of Mansart represented a very much chastened form of the Baroque in which the dependence on the cumulative effect of the Classical orders is as great as upon the unification and coherence of the mass. This is even more noticeable in Perrault's Colonnade at the Louvre. But in other buildings, such as the Ailes des Ministres and the Stables at Versailles, the non-ecclesiastical portions of the Invalides, all by Mansart, and many châteaux and city hôtels by himself or his followers, the manner showed itself clearly as a continuation of the Northern work of the first half of the century relieved of its excessive ornamentation, a new and independent movement in which the experimentation of the Italian Barocco was further developed and in a totally French fashion.

The orders were all but completely eliminated. Little more was retained of the Classical grammar of architecture than the simplest elements, cornices, mouldings, flat pilasters with moulded capitals, rustication and various forms of the arch. Buildings for nearly a century depended chiefly for their effect on the successful proportioning of the necessary elements of standardized uncomplicated structure; primarily mere flat walls stressed as surfaces with penetrations for doors and windows grouped in the most rigid symmetry. In place of the Classical round arch, the segmental arch, more practical for use with limited spans, or the flat arch, technically more ingenious and more consistent with the general rectangularity, were universally preferred. Merely ornamental decoration was very much reduced until finally it hardly appeared at all except for example in the occasional elaboration of the keystone to lend emphasis as a central motif. At the same time there was in civil architecture (for ecclesiastical architecture remained closer to Renaissance and early Baroque canons) a further new development of commodity in planning. As a consequence of this the façade schemes were multiplied in their parts. Despite the simplicity of the expression and the repetition of standard units they often became exceedingly complex in the relation of pavilions and bays of different shapes and sizes to the whole design. Occasionally the polychromy of the previous period was continued and often the solid parts of the walls as well as the doors and windows, were treated as rectangular panels enframed horizontally by cornices, mouldings and balustrades; and vertically by orders occasionally, but usually by plain or rusticated pilasters. Here, as in the Late Gothic, interior wood panelling seems to have had a definite effect on exterior stone-work.

This architecture was very generally a paper architecture, and its buildings may be almost as completely appreciated in the engraved plates of Mariette or Blondel as in actual execution. The high roofs inherited from the Late Gothic did, however, give to the compositions a three-dimensional existence which they would otherwise have lacked; and some monuments such as the Versailles Stables and those at Chantilly have an unexpected force and effect of mass. The French architects of Louis XIV and Louis XV were economical of architectural features, scaling them in importance so that a few round arches became the focal point in a scheme of flat or segmental arches, or so that a pair of coupled columns or a sculptured trophy alone would by skilful placing enrich a whole façade. Even the heavy rustication with which the architects of Henri IV and Louis XII had laid out their design as with a measuring tape was chastened in form and used much less frequently. The Faubourg Saint Germain in Paris still possesses many hôtels which illustrate this splendid economy.

The architecture of the reign of Louis XIV and of the succeeding Rococo in France is one as far as exteriors are concerned. But as regards interiors there is a change. The Rococo showed a considerable experimental development beyond the Baroque of the seventeenth century. Rococo architecture still desired on exteriors the dignified simplicity of the first decade of the eighteenth century, with the analysis of which most particularly the last paragraphs have been concerned, and it attained it with the same means. But from the latter part of the reign of Louis XIV in interiors it was lightness and richness that were sought, and with wood and plaster rather than with the marbles, metals and gilded stucco which the French Baroque took over in rather restrained form from the Italian Barocco. The orders were no more frequently used in interiors than on exteriors; and even where Corinthian capitals appeared on the pilasters, the pilasters themselves were generally treated as narrow vertical panels and the foliage of the capital made light and delicately tortuous regardless of Classical canons.

The structure of these interiors was no more than the casing of a given space—naturally in domestic rooms less vast and impressive than in the churches of Rome or the great public reception rooms of Louis XIV—with wooden panelling. Above a dado there was a succession of broad panels separated by narrow panels or pilasters treated as panels, and the whole was capped with a cornice which had lost in its fragility and intricacy all feeling of Classical exterior stone-work. Upon this, instead of a vault, there rested lightly a coved ceiling of plaster whose fantastic enrichment is quite in keeping with its barely structural character. For the decoration of these interiors the dependence is particularly upon mouldings, hardly constrained by functional purpose, which surround and enrich the panels. These mouldings burst freely into asymmetrical decoration wholly without precedent, scaled in its exquisiteness to the small rooms of the period. The focal points above doors, windows, and fireplaces were ordinarily those chosen for further enrichment with figure painting or sculpture; but always the sense of the delicately plastic surface was kept, and on account of the small scale of the whole there were less frequent attempts to include the heavens by means of illusionistic ceiling painting as had been done earlier. The larger interiors, of course, remained closer to those of Louis XIV and the Barocco, although the detail was universally smaller in scale.

It was this interior architecture of the Rococo especially which spread widely over Europe. In Germany the princes of the Empire ordered, usually of French artists, the finest individual works in this manner. Besides the interiors of the Amalienburg and the Pagodenburg outside Munich there are few French examples of equal quality; and the Neue Palais and Sanssouci at Potsdam are nearly as fine and more extensive.

But in general the problems which confronted Austrian and German architects, churches and city palaces, were more comparable to those of the Italian Barocco. This in its later more intricate form had been brought North at the end of the seventeenth century by travelling Italian architects and stage designers, of whom the best known are the members of the Bibbiena family. Fischer von Erlach and Lukas von Hildebrandt of Vienna, Johann Balthasar Neumann, the Suabian Dienzenhofers and the Bavarian Asams remained close to this tradition. Their exteriors show sometimes, as at Würzburg, a combination of the free later Italian redundance with the more academic magnificence of Versailles. But except in interiors and in smaller houses French influence was not very far-reaching. In examples of the latter sort, such as Andreas Schlüter's Landhaus von Kamecke at Berlin (Figure 6), there was a greater boldness and plasticity, made possible in part by the use of poorer materials, than in the contemporary French work. But even in work generally Barock in conception, such as the exterior of the Neue Palais at Potsdam or the Kaisersaal at Würzburg, the lighter and more irregular detail is definitely at least Rokoko—that is a well Germanized version of the French Rococo.

The German Barock as a whole differed chiefly from the Italian Barocco in the greater tortuosity which lessened its dignity, and in an inappeasable desire for splendour which was sought more frequently in multiplication of features than in scale. The silhouettes of church façades were more complicated and the surfaces more varied. But essential plasticity was lost in the attempt to multiply rather than to magnify. In the palaces the orders were more frequently used but with a greater freedom. Everywhere the

ornament was further removed from Classical canons and crowded un-
necessarily. The extreme point of this tendency is seen in Pöppelmann's
Zwinger at Dresden, which is nevertheless without French influence and not
to be considered Rokoko. But the greatest masters were skilful enough
to control the torrents of Germanic energy and the tendencies of Germanic
craftsman toward extreme virtuosity. Such a group of buildings as Jakob
Prandauer's Benedictine monastery at Melk in Austria or Johann Michael
Fischer's Rokoko Benedictine monastery at Ottobeuren in Bavaria are the
equal in their kind of anything in Italy; while it was perhaps only in the
Würzburg Residenz that Tiepolo had wholly adequate surroundings for his
ceilings.

In England even Vanbrugh, the architect of Blenheim Palace, appears timid
beside his German contemporaries. But in the minor architecture there and
in America, which we know as Georgian, this very timidity produced a
manner that is comparable to the best French work. The orders were little
used, yet even so more frequently than in France. The main emphasis was
on the simple and dignified expression of plain and ordinary masonry structure. The flat arch and the lintel were all but universal and even in the
characteristic brick construction the segmental arch so popular in France
is little used. The round arch was reserved for positions of emphasis and
gained immensely as decoration from its infrequency. The very simplest
elements, which can hardly be considered Classical at all, rustications, flat
pilasters without capitals, balustrades, and panels, were less used in England than in France; but conversely pediments, elaborate cornices, and such
very definitely Classical elements held a more important place. Plans
less elaborately developed led to a façade expression that was less complex.
At the same time there was more general dependence on the polychromy of
brick and stone—or in America usually wood—and a greater ruggedness
at the expense of refinement which made the architecture less a paper architecture and even despite its timidity more akin plastically to the Italian
Barocco than to the French work of Louis XIV and Louis XV.

The Baroque of Spain and her dominions on the other hand was not at all
timid but rather brazen. Its excessive theatricality and lack of balance
negative to a large extent its very real virtues of originality. To enter into
a discussion of individual monuments, such as the gorgeous façade of San-
tiago of Compostella, or of individual men, such as Churriguero and his
relations to the Late Gothic and the Flemish proto-Baroque, would profit no
more than a fuller examination of Germany or England. There has been
no intention in this Appendix of covering at all completely the architecture
of the earlier post-Mediæval style-phases. But the examination of certain
national groups of monuments in some detail, the presentation of a few
better known examples, should have made somewhat clearer the conception
of the Modern style briefly presented in the Introduction.

The Baroque was the last wholly integrated style-phase of the Modern period in which the balance between sentimental reminiscence and intellectual experiment was to a large extent naturally and even unconsciously maintained. Sophisticated it was, but not in any analytical sense. Because moreover it was self-conscious and assured, once well started it continued without at all losing its extraordinary optimism. The Baroque tradition, so firmly ingrained in all Europe, came to no sudden and final conclusion. Down to the end of the eighteenth century and even further it combined readily with newer enthusiasms. So very satisfactorily did it fuse reminiscence and experiment that it has been hard for the nineteenth and even for the twentieth century to believe, as to a less degree of the Late Gothic, that it really worked itself out. The most successful revivals of the nineteenth century were those in which there reappeared or remained the most of Baroque tradition; the most plausible theorists of revival have been those who were most appreciative of the Baroque. Here Geoffrey Scott took most definitely his stand in *The Architecture of Humanism*. Fortunately the value of that book as a partial study of the physiological æsthetic of architecture is not negatived by this fact, and the architecture of the New Pioneers, if not at all an architecture of humanism is nevertheless the more comprehensible critically to those who are familiar with, if not altogether won to, Geoffrey Scott's theories.*

* As this book goes to press I have learned of the death of Geoffrey Scott. It is more than sad to think that there may now be no further work on architecture from a pen that set forth the subject more brilliantly than has been done since Ruskin. But the *Architecture of Humanism* will continue to hold its place, reminding us of a time when Humanism had a brighter meaning than it has to-day.

BIBLIOGRAPHICAL NOTE

BIBLIOGRAPHICAL NOTE

THE literature of contemporary architecture exists in vast quantities as the Introduction suggested. There is no intention of listing it at any length. It is more important to aid the reader in supplementing the highly selective group of illustrations by means of books consisting chiefly of plates. Generally the German series known as the *Propyläen Kunstgeschichte* will be found useful. Since the present study has been primarily concerned with architecture since 1750 there need be no attempt to support bibliographically the sketch in the Appendix of the period from 1250-1750. The appropriate *Propyläen* volumes provide, however, quite as well as any others a corpus of illustrative material for the Late Gothic, the Renaissance and the Baroque.

For Romantic architecture it is unnecessary to add many more to the considerable number of volumes, mostly of the period, that have been given in the text. Of course any general history of architecture in one country has at least something to offer on what has been called the Baroque-Romantic compromise and on the architects of the Classical Revivals. Fiske Kimball's *American Architecture* might be specifically mentioned although it is not well illustrated. Gromort's *Histoire abrégée de l'architecture en France au XIXe siècle*, from which a considerable quotation was made in the text is, I believe, the only work of the sort, but it is far from being wholly satisfactory. Thus aside from accounts in general works such as the appropriate volumes of Michel's *Histoire de L'art* or of Elie Brault's *Les architectes par leurs oeuvres*, the former poorly illustrated and particularly inadequate as regards Germany, the latter only with portraits and quite lacking in proportion, Pauli's *Kunst des Classicisimus und der Romantik* in the *Propyläen* series, of which about a quarter of the plates are devoted to architecture, is almost alone to be recommended. There are of course monographs on single architects in considerable numbers, and even upon single buildings. The illustration of the later chapters of Part One is generally and easily to be found everywhere in actuality. It may safely be said, *"Si monumenta requiris, circumspice,"* with the assurance that the reader will have adequate control of the majority of the statements that have been made.

As regards the New Tradition and even the New Pioneers it is again the *Propyläen* volume, Platz' *Baukunst der Neuesten Zeit,* which is particularly satisfactory. Yerbury's *Modern European Buildings,* unfortunately quite without dates, and the books of plates he has prepared in collaboration with others on *Modern Dutch Architecture, Modern Swedish Architecture* and *Modern French Architecture* are also valuable. So probable has it appeared that the reader would desire to use either Platz or the first mentioned book by Yerbury that duplication of their illustrations has been avoided almost completely. For the masters of the New Tradition there is a rather larger group of monographs than for the Romantic architects. On many of them several works exist. Thus one has the choice of studying Wright in two German books, one Dutch book and one French one; but not in English except for a few articles in the Dutch book and in the general histories of American architecture. Since I prepared the text of the French monograph, I may state that it is very much less complete than the account given here. There are of course many more illustrations, among which are those used here. A certain warning is worth offering with regard to the monographs on many minor German architects of the New Tradition. They are often paid for by the architect with whom they deal and do not therefore constitute a very valuable testimony as to the esteem in which they are held by their contemporaries. For the early days of the New Tradition in America Tallmadge's *Story of American Architecture* has in the text much particularly interesting material to offer on the eighties and nineties in Chicago. For twentieth century American architecture in general Edgell's *American Architecture of To-day* provides a wealth of illustration.

There is no lack of books on the New Pioneers. The writing of the precursors, Wright, Loos, and Van de Velde, is, except for the *Formules d'une esthetique moderne* of the last, to be found chiefly in magazines and frequently has been referred to in the appropriate chapters of the present text. Le Corbusier has written several books since *Vers une architecture* less directly connected with architecture. *Vers une architecture* exists in translation as *Towards a New Architecture* and his *Urbanisme* may also be had in English under the title of *The City of To-morrow.* None of his books are very well illustrated and as they are generally based on lectures the style is somewhat overemphatic and repetitious. The last, *Une maison, un palais,* dealing in considerable part with the Palace of the League of Nations, is however better written than most and has rather more reproductions of his work than any except the first. Lurçat has written a book called *Architecture* that is excellent. Mallet-Stevens' published book of projects was devoted entirely to early work, very little of which had anything to do with New Pioneers.

Several volumes of plates in the series, *L'Art international d'aujourd'hui,* deal with architecture.

Oud's *Holländische Architekture* as well as Gropius' *Internationale Architektur* have been mentioned. It is among the further German works on the New Pioneers that it is particularly difficult to choose. For there are very many of them and the illustrative matter is often repetitious. Certain of them are, however, very worth while. The most useful are perhaps those devoted to the Stuttgart Exposition, particularly *Bau und Wohnung 1927.* Three inexpensive books in the series of *Blaue Bücher, Bauten der Arbeit und des Verkehrs, Bauten der Gemeinschaft* and *Wohnbauten und Siedlungen,* are good although they reproduce quite as much that belongs to the New Tradition. Three books by Ludwig Hilberseimer, *Internationale Neue Baukunst, Groszstadt Architektur,* and *Beton als Gestalter,* are also valuable. Among further books mentioned in the introduction Behne's *Neues Wohnen, neues Bauen* and Behrend's *Sieg des Neuen Baustils* are primarily criticism or at least propaganda. Out of the many books on steel construction Girkon's *Stahlkirche* is doubtless the most interesting to the general reader. The others are distinctly technical and like the yearly *Wie Bauen?* issued by the brothers Rasch and the books on inexpensive housing of value chiefly to those who wish to study practically new construction methods. Giedion's *Bauen in Frankreich* is excellent, particularly historically.

More German titles have been given than French because the German books for their price offer distinctly more illustrations. However, it is worth stating that among the periodicals none has treated the work of the New Pioneers so fully as *L'Architecture vivante.* For contemporary architecture in general the periodicals of different countries offer the most complete information. Mentioning only those which are typical, the *Architectural Record* in America, the *Architectural Review* in England, *Wendingen* in Holland, *Wasmuth's Monatshefte für Baukunst* or *Moderne Bauformen* in Germany, and *Das Werk* in Switzerland, examined with the quarterly *Architecture vivante,* or *L'Architecture* and *La Construction moderne* which appear more frequently, would provide any one interested to pursue the matter thus far with a very complete and perpetually renewed documentation. *L'Architecture* and the *Journal of the Royal Institute of British Architects* have even in the last year published articles on the architecture of Romanticism.

New Dimensions, by P. T. Frankl, with which the Introduction opened, is largely devoted to interiors and beyond its startling title of little interest as regards architecture. Finally Peter Meyer's *Moderne Architektur und Tradition* may be set down, for like the present book it attempts to bridge the gap between the Hameau de Trianon and *Les Terrasses* at Garches.

Chamarande, 26—iii—29.

INDEX

INDEX

ILLUSTRATIONS

1. Choir of Saint Maclou, Rouen. Flamboyant interior with Rococo
decorations (*Photo. Beaux. Arts*)

2. Abbey Church, Mont-Saint-Michel.   Romanesque nave and Flamboyant choir
(Photo. Chevojon)

3. Château of Le-Plessis-Brion (Oise). Late Gothic civil architecture

4. Palazzo Pitti, Florence, by Filippo Brunelleschi (?). Mid-XV century
(Photo. Alinari)

5. Santa Maria della Consolazione, Todi, by Cola di Caprarola (?). Early XVI century (*Photo. Alinari*)

6. Landhaus von Kamecke, Berlin, by Andreas Schlüter. Early XVIII century (*Photo. Staatl. Bildst.*)

7. Maison du Seigneur, Hameau de Trianon, Versailles, by Richard Mique with the advice of Hubert Robert. 1783

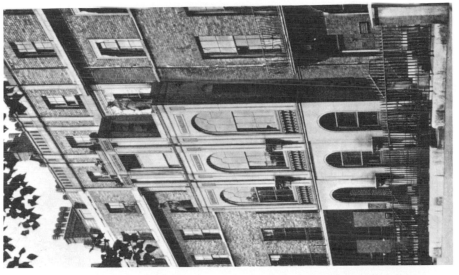

9. Soane Museum, London, by Sir John Soane.
1812 (*Photo. Yerbury*)

8. Detail of Townhall, Stockholm, by Ragnar
Østberg. 1912-1923 (*Photo. Yerbury*)

10. *A Cottage Orné designed for the neighborhood of the Lakes,* from
Papworth's *Rural Residences.* 1818

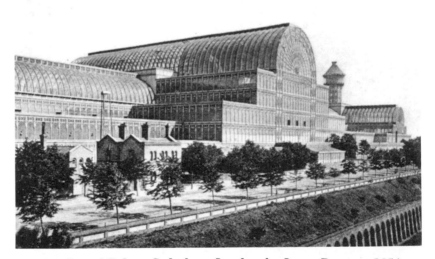

11. Crystal Palace, Sydenham, London, by James Paxton. 1854

12. Viaduct, Morlaix, by Fenoux. 1861

13. Viaduct, Garabit, by Charles Eiffel. 1885

14. Chapelle d'Orleans, Dreux, begun in 1816 and finished by Pierre Lefranc in 1847. *From a somewhat later engraving by J. Sands after T. Allom*

15. Hofgärtnerei, Potsdam, by Ludwig Persius. *Circa* 1840 (*Photo. Staatl. Bildst.*)

16. House in Saint Louis, by H. H. Richardson. 1886

17. House at Concord, Massachusetts, by Thomas Mott Shaw. *Circa* 1912

18. Deanery Gardens, Sonning, by Sir Edwin Lutyens. 1900

19. Bibliothèque Sainte-Geneviève, Paris, by Henri Labrouste. 1843-1850

20. House near Chicago, by Frank Lloyd Wright. 1910

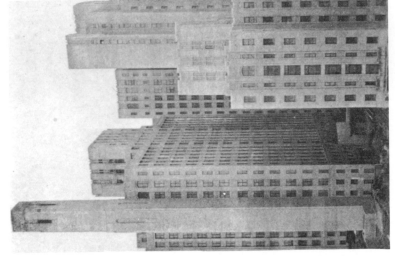

22. Medical Center, New York, by
J. G. Rogers. 1927

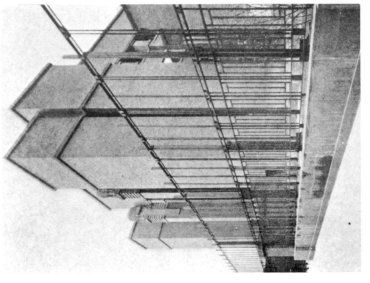

21. Larkin Soap Factory Offices, Buffalo, by
Frank Lloyd Wright. 1903

25.

26.

24.

23.

23. House at Pasadena, by Frank Lloyd Wright. 1923
24. Lansdown Tower, near Bath, by Goodridge. 1827
25. Townhall, Copenhagen, by Professor Nyrop. *Circa* 1905 (*Photo. Yerbury*)
26. Railway Station, Stuttgart, by Paul Bonatz. 1913-1927

28. Holland House, London, by H. P. Berlage. 1914

27. Diamond Workers' Building, Amsterdam, by H. P. Berlage. 1898

29. School, Amsterdam, by the City Office of Public Works. 1926

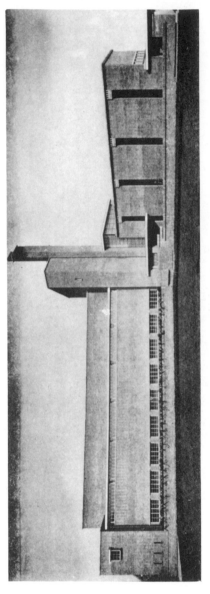

30. School, Hilversum, by W. M. Dudok. 1928 (*Photo. Deul*)

31. Workers' Apartment House, Vienna XVII, by Josef Frank. 1924

32. Street of shops, Oud Mathenesse, Rotterdam, by J. J. P. Oud. 1922

33. (Top.) Austrian Pavillon, International Exposition of Decorative Arts, Paris, by Josef Hoffmann. 1925 (*Photo. Yerbury*)

34. (Bottom.) House at Iserlohn, by Bensel & Kamps. 1925

35. Workers' Apartment House, Hamburg, by Herman Frank. 1927

36. House at Copenhagen-Klampenborg, by G. Tvede. *Circa* 1925
(*Photo. Yerbury*)

37. Théâtre des Champs Elysées, Paris, constructed by Auguste Perret in part following designs by Henry Van de Velde. 1911-1913 (*Photo. Giraudon*)

38. Faguswerk Factory, Alfeld-a.-d.-Lahn, by Walter Gropius. 1914

39. House at Guben, by Ludwig Miës van der Rohe. 1926

40. House at Boulogne-sur-Seine, by Le Corbusier. 1926

41. House at Vevey, by Le Corbusier. 1923

42. House at Utrecht, by G. Rietveld. 1922

43. Garden façade of *Les Terrasses*, Garches (Seine-et-Oise), by Le Corbusier
1927-1928

44. Lodge and entrance façade of *Les Terrasses*, Garches
(Seine-et-Oise), by Le Corbusier.   1927-1928

45. House at Boulogne-sur-Seine by
André Lurçat. 1927

46. Garden façade of house, Cité Seurat, Paris, by André Lurçat.
1925

47. Shops at the Hoek van Holland, by J. J. P. Oud. Designed 1924, executed
1926-1927

48. Shops and houses at the Hoek van Holland, by J. J. P. Oud. Designed 1924,
executed 1926-1927

49. Van Nelle Factory, Rotterdam, by Van der Vlugt and Brinkman. 1928

50. Bauhaus Institut, Dessau, by Walter Gropius. 1926

51. House at Altona-Othmarschen, by Karl Schneider.   1927

52. Dairy near Moscow, by A. Buroff.   1927

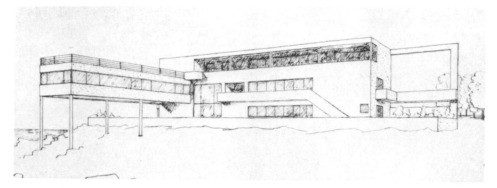

53. Ocean front of a house designed for the Massachusetts North Shore, by
Peter van der Meulen Smith.   1927

54. School, Oak Lane, Philadelphia, by Howe and Lescaze.   1929

55. Orangery, Saint Audries House,
Somerset. *Circa* 1800

56. Pavilion of the City of Brno, International Exposition, Brno, by Bohnslav Fuchs. 1928

57. Living-room of a house at Montmartre, Paris, by Adolf Loos. 1927

58.   Project for a Skyscraper, by R. J. Neutra.   1927